THEOLOGY AND EVANGELISM
IN THE
WESLEYAN HERITAGE

THEOLOGY AND EVANGELISM IN THE WESLEYAN HERITAGE

Edited by

James C. Logan

KINGSWOOD BOOKS
An Imprint of Abingdon Press
Nashville, Tennessee

THEOLOGY AND EVANGELISM IN THE WESLEYAN TRADITION

Copyright © 1994 by Abingdon Press

94 95 96 97 98 99 00 01 02 03 — 10 9 8 7 6 5 4 3 2 1

Library of Congress Cataloging-in-Publication Data

Theology and evangelism in the Wesleyan heritage / edited by James C. Logan.
        p.   cm.
Essays from a symposium held Feb. 5–9, 1992, at Emory University.
Includes bibliographical references.
ISBN 0-687-41395-8 (alk. paper) :
    1. Evangelistic work—Congresses.   2. Wesley, John, 1703–1791
—Congresses.   3. Methodist Church—Doctrines—Congresses.
I. Logan, James C.
BV3755.T44   1993
269' .2' 08827—dc20   93–6428
                                                                  CIP

CONTENTS

PREFACE

A symposium on "Theology and Evangelism in the Wesleyan Heritage," involving Christian scholars and leaders from four continents, was held February 5–9, 1992 at the Mission Resource Center, Emory University, Atlanta, Georgia. This event was conceived, developed, and funded by The Foundation for Evangelism, an affiliate of the General Board of Discipleship, The United Methodist Church. Its detailed preparation and actual program were led by Dr. James C. Logan, the E. Stanley Jones Professor of Evangelism at Wesley Theological Seminary in Washington, D.C. Dr. Logan, who also presented one of the major papers commissioned for the symposium, has edited this volume, which makes available to a wider audience the principal presentations by the array of world Methodist leaders who composed the personnel of the symposium.

This particular effort defines a new and important direction on the part of the Foundation for Evangelism, founded in 1949 by the late Dr. Harry Denman, Methodism's famous lay evangelist. The symposium was not the Foundation's initial venture into the intellectual realm of the Christian faith, since its most ambitious (and expensive) program is the establishment and funding of Professorships of Evangelism in United Methodist seminaries. It was, however, the most sharply focused undertaking in the arena of theological thought and evangelistic mission which has been attempted by the Foundation, and perhaps by any agency of United Methodism.

The rationale for the symposium was bifocal. The long-range purpose was related to the Wesleyan conviction that authentic evangelism must always be based firmly in theology. The struggle within a context of intellectual respectability and integrity remains a precious principle, and can be traced historically to Charles Wesley's statement about uniting knowledge and vital piety. We have believed, often with desperate sincerity, that a marriage must be effected between the study-desk and the altar, the library and the sanctuary, the mind and the soul. The

7

unfortunate aberrations that have characterized some evangelistic efforts across the years, perhaps particularly in more recent times, have been traceable in most instances to the absence of a carefully constructed intellectual and theological foundation. There is no effective way to recover authentic confidence in the evangelistic mission of the church without recapturing this essential base.

The nearer, more immediate purpose of the symposium was to address the effect of certain contemporary theological trends upon the evangelistic impulse within the church. Let me mention two: the resurgence of interest in the old idea of universal salvation, dismissed as heretical by John Wesley in the eighteenth century; and the syncretistic proposal that the time has come to abandon the uniqueness of Jesus Christ, an effort to accommodate the fact of religious pluralism in contemporary culture. Other trends within the modern church which may call for a reinterpretation of evangelism include the church's failure to coordinate the personal and social messages of the Gospel, and its ignoring of the plight of the poor in designing its evangelistic appeal.

As the essays contained in the following pages show, the forty women and men who participated in the symposium grappled seriously and intentionally with both the long-range and the near-at-hand biblical and theological issues related to the recovery of evangelistic urgency in our time. These participants represented the continents of Africa, Asia, Europe, and North America, and included ten bishops, one former bishop, one who would be elected to the episcopacy five months later, one university president, three heads of theological institutions, twelve seminary professors, six pastors, four connectional leaders, one District Superintendent, and the General Secretary of the World Methodist Council. This does not include Foundation personnel and trustees who were present.

The spacious and comfortable facilities of the Turner Conference Center and the hospitable assistance of the Reverend F. Stuart Gulley of Candler School of Theology, the Reverend Susan Henry-Crowe, Chaplain of Emory University, and Dr. Milo Thornberry and Mrs. Judy Montgomery of the Mission Resource Center, provided assurance that a closely scheduled program would operate smoothly and efficiently.

One of the delightful collateral experiences of the five-day period proved to be the informal table fellowship at meals when distinguished leaders who knew each other's work but had never met were privileged to engage in stimulating and often inspiring discussions. While guests from the church and university communities were welcomed at all sessions, the public event to which most outside leaders received special invitations was the Saturday evening banquet featuring a dialogue presentation by Bishop and Mrs. James K. Mathews about the lives and work of Mrs. Mathews' parents, the late Dr. and Mrs. E. Stanley Jones.

Beautifully boxed and labeled sets of the fifteen color videocassettes recording the twelve major presentations and responses were presented as gifts from The Foundation for Evangelism to the thirteen United Methodist seminaries in this country, the Evangelisch-Methodistische Kirche Theologisches Seminar in Reutlingen, Germany, selected ecumenical theological institutions, the General Board of Discipleship, and the World Methodist Council.

◆   ◆   ◆

Very special appreciation needs to be expressed to Dr. Logan, editor of this volume, whose broad theological knowledge and dedicated churchmanship enabled him to design the symposium program, preside over it with grace, and coordinate its results in a way which helped the church media convey its meaning and importance to the wider community of faith. His sensitive understanding is reflected in his introduction to the volume.

The Foundation for Evangelism is profoundly grateful to three of its trustees, Dr. William B. Barnhart, Mr. Phillip F. Connolly, and Mr. Robert E. Miller, for providing the seed-money for this project. To express adequate gratitude to the many who contributed ideas, leadership, and labors to this symposium would be quite beyond the realm of possibility. Staff and trustees performed splendidly in spite of the fact that this particular project was totally new to everyone. Dr. William L. Apetz, Foundation trustee, and Dr. Rex D. Matthews of Abingdon Press deserve special mention.

Underlying this symposium was the desire of the Board of Trustees of The Foundation to stimulate a better understanding of Wesleyan evangelism in contemporary life, and to motivate the church toward more effective action in leading people to accept the Savior. Many years ago the late Dr. Lynn Harold Hough crafted an unforgettable sentence: "True evangelism is intelligence on fire." Few statements could capture more vividly the mood which prevailed during this historic gathering.

Earl G. Hunt, Jr., President
The Foundation for Evangelism

INTRODUCTION

In recent years evangelism has emerged as one of the top priorities on the agenda of mainline Protestantism. The very fact that evangelism is now singled out with such passionate zeal is but one indication that something is seriously amiss. The church has a confused sense of identity. Mission and evangelism have become compartmentalized rather than functioning as the central core of the church's identity.

We are victimized by amnesia. Our memory fails us. Where is the awareness of the biblical story of the God of grace who redemptively seeks and finds, and then in turn calls us to join in the divine venture of seeking and finding a world which in Jesus Christ God has so loved? Where is the awareness of our traditions which have transmitted that story of God's saving grace? In short, where is the theological vision which can animate and direct us as pilgrims in a new time?

The Council of Bishops of The United Methodist Church sought to recover or re-discover that which is so essential to the church when they penned their *Pastoral Letter* of 1990:

> We . . . yearn for a vital congregation in every place. We yearn because so many people of our societies, including many in our church, have no vital relationship to God, and are lost: lost to drug addiction, lost to self-centered materialism, and self-righteousness, lost to the demonic forces of racism and every form of human oppression—lost to sin. We are concerned that as our world becomes more secularized, new generations increasingly are bewildered by every form of temptation and desperately need the saving grace of Christ.

So spoke the Bishops and so speak many contemporary Christians who long to see a genuinely apostolic or "sent" church.

Certainly one glaring illustration of forgotten or fragmented vision is the separation of evangelism from hard theological reflection. Even to conjoin the two, as in the title of this book, with the conjunction "and" indicates a fundamental problem which we face as the church. Are the two so discreetly distinct as to make it necessary to interface them with a conjunction?

To put the matter bluntly, evangelism is an essential theological task of the church—yet a "great divorce" has in effect been enacted in our church. Only recently, as William Abraham has cogently argued, "One of the undeniable features of modern theology is the scant attention it has given to the topic of evangelism."[1] Abraham goes further to observe that without rigorous theological reflection concerning evangelism, we find ourselves lacking "even a sense of what the questions are, where we should turn in order to assemble the evidence, what criteria are appropriate in evaluating the possible answers to our queries, and how we might begin to make steady progress to the problems that confront us." The *modus operandi* of the church rarely provides for the integration of theology and evangelism, when truthfully the livelihood of both depends upon their integral unity.

The essays in this volume constitute one attempt to unite the two with a focus upon our Wesleyan roots. Such an effort is indeed appropriate. The two were one in the Wesleyan revival of the eighteenth century. John theologized from the saddle, and Charles evangelized as the people sang. A symposium sponsored by the Foundation for Evangelism was the occasion for more than forty church people from various branches of world Methodism to share in dialogue with the insights of these essays. The effort was not to be exhaustive in dealing with all issues of evangelism. The focus was upon the theological task. Even here the effort is to deal with theological issues suggestively rather than systematically. Coming from diverse sectors of the church, the unifying conviction was that neither theology nor evangelism can faithfully exist apart from one another.

We need each other! In recent decades the discipline of systematic theology has in many quarters suffered a loss of confidence in identity. Some theologians have become so methodologically preoccupied as to bury themselves deeper and deeper in their methodological reflections. The result has been a loss of concrete reference to the faith community known as church. Others have turned to specific topics, and we have a plethora of "adjectival theologies" bordering on faddism. Rare is the theologian today who cares to attempt to articulate a vision of the wholeness of Christian faith and practice as did an Augustine in the fourth century, a Calvin in the sixteenth century, or a Barth earlier in this century. Consequently, theology as a discipline has increasingly distanced itself from the actual life of the Christian community, seeking to find its home more and more in the academy rather than in the church. Perhaps when the crucial theological questions are raised from the standpoint of the evangelical theological imperative to name the name of Jesus Christ in and for the life of the world, theological reflection can receive a new impetus in terms of function, message, and direction.

We need each other! Evangelism has in our century become increasingly concerned with methods and programs to the extent that a practical pragmatism ("what's right is what works") threatens to become the criterion. This occurs from a loss of theological "conscience." In fact, we experience difficulty even in defining the term. David Barrett lists at least seventy-odd definitions.[2] Perhaps the infusion of critical theological reflection can assist evangelism in coming to a greater clarity of its authoritative imperative, its intrinsic identity, and its goal within the divine mission which God has initiated in the Word-made-flesh, Jesus Christ.

Certainly the separation of theology and evangelism has been to the detriment of both. In these urgent times a renewal of both theology and evangelism could invigorate the church once more if we were to "unite the pair so long disjoined." We who stand with the Wesleyan tradition have in our forebears a model of unity that can inform us in this critical task.

For various reasons, four of the major presentations given at the symposium could not be included in this volume. Bishop Leontine Kelly spoke extemporaneously on "Faith Active in Love," i.e. evangelism and social witness. Wesleyan pneumatology was treated by Dr. Thomas Oden of the Theological School of Drew University; his presentation will be part of a forthcoming volume on Wesley's theology. The comprehensive proposal of Dr. Eddie Fox, Director of World Evangelism for the World Methodist Conference, will certainly have programmatic significance for that organization. Dr. Douglas M. Meeks, Dean of Wesley Theological Seminary, summarized all of the major presentations on the final morning of the symposium. These significant contributions, though not represented in this volume, are recorded on videotape and can be secured from the office of the Foundation.

Members of the symposium came from many cultural and

geographical quarters of the church—England, South Africa, Ghana, Kenya, Germany, and the Philippines as well as the United States. This was vivid witness to the universality of the Gospel. While the dominant focus of the symposium was the evangelist-theologian John Wesley, over the proceedings there assuredly hovered the shadows of more recent figures, such as E. Stanley Jones and Harry Denman, reminding the church that the evangelistic mission is an ongoing and never-ending one.

James C. Logan

CHAPTER 1

The Evangelical Imperative: A Wesleyan Perspective

James C. Logan

Why Wesley?

In an ecumenical era, is the appeal to Wesley an expression of "ecclesiastical chauvinism"? Since the early church, the necessity has existed for a hermeneutics or interpretation of the gospel in the variety of cultures and shifting changes of history. The various ecclesial traditions have stamped the ecclesial hermeneutics of the gospel in distinctive theological patterns. The Wesleyan tradition is no exception. Prerequisite to an authentic ecumenical dialogue is the necessity of a clearer understanding of the various ecclesial traditions, including the Wesleyan tradition. Without a clear understanding of the distinctive elements lying at its roots, no denomination or church tradition has a contribution to make to the on-going ecumenical conversation.

To appropriate the Wesleyan tradition in our time does not call for a repristinated Wesleyanism. Such an effort of reappropriation requires a critical dialogue with that very tradition. Rather than repeating Wesley's own words and structures of thought, which really belong to the eighteenth century, we must seek to discover trajectories from that tradition which can inform, inspire, and direct us as faithful participants in the tradition in a new day.

The Wesleyan tradition incorporated much of the biblical and ecclesial traditions of Christianity, both Western and Eastern. At the same time the Wesleyan tradition had its own peculiar distinctives. Among these is the historical fact that Methodists were a mission movement before they ever became a church. Wesleyans were originally a revival or evangelistic mission which eventually shaped itself into a church precisely to be more responsibly engaged in the mission of salvation to which they sensed they had been called. Other church traditions may trace their origins to distinctive confessional or theological patterns. Wesleyans, on the other hand, became a church not for confessional reasons but for evangelistic or missional reasons. The early Wesleyans unmistakably understood this. Francis Asbury entered in his *Journal* in 1815, one year before his death:

> The Methodist preachers, who had been sent by John Wesley to America, came as *missionaries*. . . . And now, behold the consequences of this *mission*. We have seven hundred travelling preachers, who cost us nothing. We will not give up the *cause*—we will not abandon the world to infidels.[1]

In the North American experience the early Wesleyans on the local level understood themselves to be "mission societies." That was their rationale for existence. In fact, for years after 1784 Methodists on the local level persisted in calling themselves "societies" rather than "churches" because they conceived of themselves as missions. While Methodists in the United States may not have formulated an ecclesiology, they nevertheless operated with an ecclesial consciousness. Mission was not a derivative of the church. Quite to the contrary, church was derived from mission. Mission was the central and crucial mark of the church.

Without complicated exegesis these early Methodists plainly understood themselves to be *apostolic*. Apostolicity consists in "being sent." Paul expressed the logic clearly:

> But when the time had fully come, God sent forth (*apostellein*) his Son, born of woman, born under the law, to redeem those who were under the law, so that we might receive adoption as sons. And because you are sons, God has sent (*apostellein*) the Spirit of his Son into our hearts. . . . (Gal. 4:4-6a, RSV)

God's apostolic mission through Jesus Christ is now continued through God's apostolic Spirit in the apostolic church. The church is truly a "sent people."

It is no small matter that the earliest ecclesial consciousness of Wesley and his followers was apostolic or missional. If within our own time the people called Methodists are to experience revival and renewal, the beginning will be an intentional recovery of the missionary nature of church. Such recovery will require our giving primacy to the evangelical imperative which is implicitly and explicitly Jesus Christ. In the economy of God we discern that God is a "sending God," and through Christ and the Holy Spirit the church is "sent." The logical locus of the evangelical imperative is within the very nature of the triune God.

The power of the Wesleyan revival did not arise simply from the personality of John Wesley nor merely from his organizational ability. These were important factors, but the great power of the revival was inherent in its message and, above all, in the Person whom the message bore witness. Herein is another Wesleyan distinctive—the message. One can hardly underestimate the powerful attraction of the message of universal grace. In the hymns of Charles Wesley the words which appear more frequently than any other are "all" and "love." The "pure universal love" which is God's act in Jesus Christ was freely available for "all"—no one excluded! In this John and Charles did not understand themselves to be theological innovators. In John's words, the message was "plain, old Christianity," or as he stated in the preface to the sermons, "plain truth for plain people."[2] "Plain truth," however, did not mean a simplistic message. The witness to the gospel was a rugged message of divine grace.

John Wesley rang the changes on the threefoldness of God's grace in Christ. Grace is singular because Christ in his person and work is grace. To be sure, every sermon preached did not render a systematic outline of this threefold grace, nor did every sermon include the entirety of the so-called *ordo salutis* or order of salvation—terms which Wesley himself never employed. His favorite phrase (and I believe it was carefully chosen) was "the scriptural *way* to salvation."[3] For Wesley *ordo* was too static. Grace was dynamic and could not be "ordered." In human experience, in the believer's heart, grace was the "way." Grace was not structurally contained, but dynamically operative in three modes—prevenient, justifying, and sanctifying. This simple, yet profound, message was in Wesley's mind and preaching "in place" soon after 1738.

The "way" was a radically life-changing one of proceeding, in Wesley's metaphors, to the "porch," through the "door," and into the "house." Rarely in the history of the church has a person

17

captured a synthesis of grace as did Wesley. Like the Pietists, he was concerned with "experimental" (experiential) religion. And from the early Eastern Fathers, he learned the necessity of holiness of life which he understood to be both inward and outward. Grace was rigorous. Grace radically changed persons from self-seeking to other-seeking. Grace was not passive but issued in accountable discipleship. This was no "scissors-and-paste" synthesis. What God in Christ has done *for* us, God through the Holy Spirit does *in* and *through* us. It was a mighty message of the universality of grace, no one excluded, no area of life excluded, a theology of grace composed of prepositions—*for, in,* and *through.*

The evangelistic import of the message of universal grace "free for all and free in all" should be immediately obvious. If the divine grace is already operative, preparing persons for the gospel (prevenient grace), then that same grace is universally available to all without qualifications (justification), and that same grace continues to work in the life of the believer forming persons into "faith active in love" (sanctification).

Such a message of "pure universal love" makes no distinctions of class, race, nationality or social status. One can readily understand why the marginalized and dehumanized of his day heard him gladly. Those whose self-esteem had been so degraded by the inhumane conditions of an oppressive economic and social order had ears to hear that through God's grace they were sons and daughters of worth and dignity whom God gifted and lifted up through Christ and the Spirit. Universal grace compelled Wesley, though initially he was reluctant, to the open fields, to the marketplaces, the prisons, the mineshafts, and the bedsides of those dying in poverty in the squalor of a tenement flat.

In 1744 Wesley convened his preachers for what was to become an annual occasion (the predecessor of our annual conferences). The first question raised by Wesley on this occasion was, "What may we reasonably believe to be God's design, in raising up the preachers called Methodists?" The answer given marks still another of the Wesleyan distinctives. Wesley saw the evangelical mission to be "to reform the nation, more particularly the Church; to spread scriptural holiness over the land."[4] The definition of evangelical mission had a formal similarity to the definition of grace. Prevenience, justification, and sanctification are not stages. The prevenient grace of Christ continues to operate even though one may experience justifying and sanctifying grace. The relationship between the functions of grace is not so much sequential as dialectical. The same applies in the definition of the evangelical mission. Reform, social and ecclesial, are not separate from the spread of "scriptural holiness." The evangelical mission is not sequential but dialectically whole.

Forty years later at the Christmas Conference in Baltimore the American Methodists were asked the same question and virtually the same response was evoked: "To reform the Continent, and to spread scriptural holiness over these lands."[5] In the *Large Minutes* during Wesley's lifetime the answer was reprinted with only slight and inconsequential variations until in British Methodism the *Discipline* of 1797 read:

SECTION I. The Design of God in sending the Methodist Preachers.
Q.1. In what view may the Methodist Preachers be considered?

The answer was given as follows:

A. As Messengers sent by the Lord, out of the common way, To provoke the regular clergy to jealousy, and to supply their lack of service, towards those who are perishing for want of knowledge: and above all to reform the nation, *by* spreading scriptural holiness over the land.[6]

Note the transposition of either the semi-colon or conjunction "and" into the infinitive "by." The dialectic of mission had been broken. Where historically "reform" and "conversion" had been one integral whole in defining the Christian mission, now conversion was made instrumental to reform. History repeated itself on the American scene less than three decades later. Bishop William McKendree made the same substitution in the Episcopal Address to the General Conference of 1816.[7]

There was a certain genius in Wesley's ability to forge a dialectical synthesis. He would not "traffic" with a one-dimensional message of grace. On the fundament of prevenient grace, Wesley steadfastly insisted on the utter inseparability of justifying grace and sanctifying grace. Regeneration, or the "new birth," is the critical connecting link between justifying and sanctifying grace. The synthesis of grace involves both event and process; for this reason, sanctification—growing in grace—is understood to begin at the moment of new birth. In both, the syntheses of grace and of mission, Wesley strongly insisted upon justification *and* sanctification, faith *and* works, conversion *and* social engagement. This is, without boast, a Wesleyan distinctive. When the dialectic of grace is severed we have either antinomianism (the modern equivalent is "anything goes") or a works righteousness (the modern equivalent is compulsive self-justification). When the dialectic of the missional norm is torn apart we have the all-too-frequent separation of evangelism from nurture, from church reform, and from social responsibility.

The rehearsal of the dialectics of grace and mission is intentional. The Wesleyan heritage in its earliest days possessed a grasp of the wholeness of the gospel as grace active in mission. In our time we have a plentitude of truncated gospels, inside the church and out. A recovery of the trajectory of wholeness, both of grace and mission, could be a mighty corrective to current social accommodations of the gospel. Wesley's message was no superficial gospel catering to the whims of the moment. It was a whole gospel for persons, church, and society.

Methodists stand squarely in a tradition which is both evangelical and catholic. An evangelism which is less than this fails to do justice to the fullness of the gospel of Jesus Christ. We stand in a tradition of the church seeking to be apostolic. We, therefore, stand under a divine imperative. God has entrusted to us a Story to be told and lived. If we are faithful to that mandate, as stated in the 1988 mission statement, *Grace Upon Grace*—if we act as instruments of God's grace—lives can be changed by grace, the church can be formed by grace, and the world can be transformed by grace.[8] Such is the promise of Wesley.

The Evangelical Imperative

To this point we have not specifically defined "imperative." It has been important to re-examine our roots before we address directly this issue. To be sure scripture does not speak the precise language of "imperative." Rather, terms like "send," "command," "witness," and "empowerment" by the Holy Spirit are generally employed. In recent mission and evangelism writings increasing attention has been given to one form or another of the Great Commission. The four Gospels and Acts have the Great

Commission in slightly different versions. They all have in common the dominical summons to herald, to witness, or to make disciples.

As widely used and embraced as the Great Commission in one form or another is today, this has not always been the case. The reformers did not view it as binding, claiming that it had been delivered to the Apostles and fulfilled by them. On the other hand, whereas the reformers did not view the texts as binding, no biblical texts appear more frequently in the Anabaptist confession of faith than the Matthean and Markan versions of the Great Commission. The Anabaptists were the first to make the commission mandatory for all believers. The person really to be credited with putting it on the map, so to speak, was William Carey in his 1792 tract entitled *An Enquiry into the Obligations of Christians to Use Means for the Conversion of the Heathen,* in which he, with the aid of a simple yet powerful argument, demolished the conventional Reformation interpretation of Matthew 28:18-20. In other words, aside from the Anabaptists, the Great Commission did not have wide currency until the modern world missionary movement began in the late eighteenth century.

In Wesley's sermons, he makes only four references to Matthew 28:18-20 and never to the entirety of the text. The references are all to the power given unto Christ and do not move on to the mandate. Although he wrote and preached evangelical sermons loaded with passion and logic, calling persons to repentance and faith, he seemingly offers us no sermon on any form of the commission. His most explicit reference is to the Markan version, "Go ye into all the world, and preach the gospel to every creature" (Mark 16:15), in his *Explanatory Notes* where he simply comments:

> Our Lord speaks without any limitation or restriction. If, therefore, every creature in every age hath not heard it, either those who should have preached, or those who should have heard it, or both, made void the counsel of God.[9]

The scarcity of references to the scriptural passages does not indicate, however, any doubt on Wesley's part that he and his revival were under divine imperative. Being the thorough biblical student Wesley was led him to roam widely over the scriptural terrain, and it would be difficult to single out one particular scriptural passage as central to all others. The scriptures were for him the "oracles of God," and he treated all scripture as authoritative for faith and practice.

In the totality of the Wesleyan corpus the most systematic and concentrated appeal to the Great Commission is found in one of Charles Wesley's hymns:

> Come, Father, Son, and Holy Ghost,
> Honour the means ordained by thee!
> Make good our apostolic boast,
> And own thy glorious ministry.
>
> We now thy promised presence claim;
> Sent to disciple all mankind,
> Sent to baptize into thy name,
> We now thy promised presence find.
>
> Father, in these reveal thy Son;
> In these for whom we seek thy face,
> The hidden mystery make known,
> The inward, pure, baptizing grace.
>
> Jesus, with us thou always art;
> Effectual make the sacred sign,
> The gift unspeakable impart,
> And bless the ordinance divine.
>
> Eternal Spirit, descend from high,
> Baptizer of our spirits thou!
> The sacramental seal apply,
> And witness with the water now.
>
> O that the souls baptized therein
> May now thy truth and mercy feel;
> May rise and wash away their sin;
> Come, Holy Ghost, their pardon seal![10]

I have quoted the full text because it demonstrates the Wesleyan sensitivity regarding authority, commission, command, or imperative. Such authoritative imperative is always rooted in the triune nature of God as revealed in the incarnate life, death, and resurrection of Jesus Christ. There is no question but that John Wesley's passion was to "preach Christ." Charles' hymn helps to explain that passion. The trinitarian action of the Father sending Christ and the Spirit forms the grounding of the evangelical imperative and its authority. In other words the imperative is rooted in the very being of God, and is made manifest in the life, death, and resurrection of Jesus Christ.

For Wesley it was the total gospel which issued in the imperative of witnessing to the same gospel. The logic of grace is the logic of the imperative. Grace not shared is grace forfeited. Wesley's logic is illustrated in his comments on Matthew 5:13-15. "Ye are the salt of the earth"—note Wesley's comments:

> Ye—Not the apostles, not ministers only; but all ye who are thus holy, are the salt of the earth—are to season others.

"Ye are the light of the world"—again note Wesley's comments:

> If ye are thus holy, you can no more be hid than the sun in the firmament; no more than a city on a mountain—probably pointing to that on the brow of the opposite hill.
> Nay, the very design of God in giving you this light was that it might shine.[11]

For Wesley the evangelical imperative is grounded ontologically in the triune nature of God, while being revelationally grounded in the threefold manifestation of grace in Christ.

From the Wesleyan doctrine of grace one can derive three essential components of the gospel imperative. *The authority of the imperative* is rooted in the triune God's action in the incarnate and atoning Christ and the Holy Spirit. *The motive for the imperative* is experientially anchored in the prevenient, justifying and sanctifying grace of God in Christ. *The goal of the imperative* is a life having both the form and the power of holiness, a kingdom life, or a life of accountable discipleship.

Preaching Christ "In All His Offices"

From the time of the crucifixion, resurrection, and Pentecost, the apostolic witness has been that the event of Jesus Christ is God's eschatological initiation of the end-time. If the new divine order or Kingdom which Jesus proclaimed is the fulfillment of time (Mark 1:14) and the proleptic inauguration of God's final hour for the world, then so identified were word and person in Jesus that the apostolic church very shortly proclaimed," Jesus is Lord." God's plan of salvation had been brought to its fulfillment in the crucifixion, ratified by the resurrection, and made experientially alive in the present by the Holy Spirit. The confession of the Lordship of Christ was not an emotive-expressivist "love statement."[12] It was a bold, ontological claim of God's action. The New Testament kerygma witnessed to the decisive finality of Jesus Christ as the Savior and Lord of humankind. The authority of the evangelical imperative, therefore, does not lie in human experience. Faith, as the gift of God, is the medium of the authority, but faith is neither the source nor the ground of the authority. What no one or nothing else could do, God has accomplished in Jesus Christ. Hence, the Wesleyan imperative was to "preach Christ."

Lest it appear that we have strayed from Wesley's dictum of "plain truth for plain people," we should permit Wesley himself to speak:

> It is our part thus to 'preach Christ' by preaching all things whatsoever he hath revealed. We may indeed, without blame, yea, and with a peculiar blessing from God, declare the love of our Lord Jesus Christ; . . . But still we should not 'preach Christ' according to His word if we are wholly to confine ourselves to this. We are not ourselves clear before God unless we proclaim him in all his offices. To preach Christ as a workman that needeth not to be ashamed is to preach him not only as our great 'High Priest' . . . but likewise as the Prophet of the Lord, 'who of God is made unto us wisdom', who by his Word and his Spirit 'is with us always', 'guiding us into all truth'; yea, and as remaining a King for ever; as giving laws to all whom He has bought with his blood; as restoring those to the image of God whom he had first reinstated in his favour; as reigning in all believing hearts until he has 'subdued all things to Himself'; until He hath utterly cast out all sin, and 'brought in everlasting righteousness'.[13]

Christ "in all his offices" is clearly a Christological claim. Though Wesley never wrote a treatise, as such, on Christology, in certain of his sermons and elsewhere he enunciated a Christology in the Reformed tradition of the "offices of Christ."[14] The form was a "preached theology" and a "sung theology" which Wesley simply called "practical divinity."

It would be theologically too clever to press the three dimensions of the imperative—authority, motive, and goal—systematically into the "offices of Christ." This would result in an artificial separation of the offices. A Christological modalist Wesley was

24

not! As the "offices" interpenetrate and are expressed in one Jesus Christ, so the imperative has the same unity in the interpenetration of authority, motive, and goal. Christ is one in three offices. The imperative is one in three dimensions. Yet, these dimensions are not accidental nor imposed; they are derived from the "offices."

Wesley's evangelism was marked by a vision of the wholeness of authority, motive, and goal. He proclaimed Christ in his fullness: the Christ of Bethlehem (incarnation), the Christ of Galilee (ministry), the Christ of Calvary (atonement) and the Christ of Jerusalem (resurrection). A theology of evangelism would do well to check itself constantly with this criterion of the fullness of Christ.

The Christ of Bethlehem

The "offices" of Christ presuppose the uniqueness of the ontological fact of incarnation. The incarnation clearly points to the very foundation of evangelism in the nature of the "sending" triune God. The offices would lack authority, motive, and goal were it not that Jesus Christ is the Incarnate "Sent" One.

The Christ of Galilee

Christ's prophetic work is the work of the Incarnate One. He does not speak as the prophets, "Thus saith the Lord." They had been given a "word." He speaks as the Word-made-flesh. He is the Word. Wesley can speak, therefore, of "the most intimate knowledge" between Jesus Christ and the One who had sent him. In the prophetic office of speaking the divine word or law there is a fundamental unity of Jesus' word and God's will or law. Ironic as it may seem to our modern ears, the speaking of the law is itself the proclamation of grace. Law is an instrument of grace, or as Wesley on at least one occasion called it, "a sacrament of grace." To be sure, Christ in his prophetic office is not proclaiming salvation by the law, but neither is there salvation apart from the law.

The divine law convinces (convicts) sinners of sin, brings them to an acknowledgement of the need of a Deliverer, and then keeps them with Christ.[15] While the law convicts, it always brings the believer into conformity to the law through grace. In this manner

25

Wesley preserves the dialectic of prevenient, justifying, and sanctifying grace. It is the work of prevenient grace to convict sinners by the law. In justifying grace the law is transformed into "promise." Justifying grace "promises" us what we shall be. Finally, the work of sanctifying grace makes the "promise" a reality through the restoration of the divine image. Here the law serves its "third use" in keeping the believer constantly in accountable obedience to Christ.[16] In claiming the law as a means of God's grace, Wesley insists that its workings, whether legal (conviction or judgment) or evangelical (justification/sanctification), are nevertheless the necessary working of Christ in his prophetic office.

The Christ of Calvary

Obviously, the Wesleyan doctrine of grace is centered in the priestly office of Christ. The priestly office holds the prophetic and kingly offices in one common whole. The admonition to preach Christ in his priestly office confronts contemporary sensibilities with considerable difficulties. The priestly office focuses upon the sacrificial work of Christ and presupposes what the "first work of the law" in the prophetic office reveals. In stark terms this is sin in all its horrible manifestation, wrecking personal life and bringing havoc to the life of society. While Wesley sought to announce a message of Christ lovingly wooing persons rather than frightening them, he nevertheless spoke uncompromisingly of the human condition of sin and rebellion. No other word was adequate; it was sin! Wesley's scathing logic is expressed in his words to William Law:

> Say you, "To affright men from sin"? What, by guile, by dissimulation, by hanging out false colours? Can you conceive the Most High dressing up as a scarecrow, as we do to fright children? Far be it from Him! If there be any such fraud in the Bible, the Bible is not of God. And indeed this must be the result of all: If there be "no unquenchable fire, no everlasting burnings," there is no dependence on these writings wherein they are so expressly asserted, nor of the eternity of heaven, any more than of hell. So that if we give up the one, we must give up the other. No hell, no heaven, no revelation.[17]

26

While Wesley warned his preachers against a kind of "hell fire and damnation" preaching which degenerates into psychological manipulation, this did not constitute a reason for avoiding the fundamental human condition which called for God's saving action. Wesley does not permit some convenient escape for the sake of contemporary sensibilities. The message was for some as offensive in his day as in ours. The words of the Duchess of Buckingham, wife of Wesley's benefactor at Charterhouse, document this observation. Writing of the Methodist preachers, she states:

> Their doctrines are most repulsive and strongly tinctured with impertinence and disrespect towards their superiors in perpetually endeavoring to level all ranks and do away with all distinctions. It is monstrous to be told that you have a heart as sinful as the common wretches that crawl the earth.[18]

We cannot trivialize sin in either its person or social manifestations. Sin is not a human maladjustment to be treated with palliatives or therapies. Sin is the human condition before a righteous God. Wesley's logic to William Law could just as easily be reversed. No God, no revelation, no sin!

A distinction between the urgency and the authority of the imperative should be noted. The urgency of the imperative is human sinfulness. The authority of the imperative is the action of God in Christ to meet this great rupture in the order of creation. From the human side what is required is repentance and belief (though even such is not possible apart from Christ's prevenient grace). From the divine side what is required is nothing short of a divine sacrifice. The sacrifice is twofold in that it is offered *to* God and *for* humankind. In short, it is substitutionary.

Wesley states no new doctrine. To him this is the atonement as set forth in scripture and as preached by the apostolic church. No student of theology is unaware that precisely this classical formulation of the human condition and the substitutionary death of Christ has now for two centuries been subjected not only to critical scrutiny but to outright rejection. Modern preachers would prefer to proclaim a Christ who came to compliment our best rather than to redeem our worst.

If Wesley's conceptual vocabulary sounds somewhat alien to our modern ears, his denouncement of a certain kind of "gospel

27

preaching" in his day sounds strikingly contemporary:

> Why (these) "gospel preachers" so called corrupt their hearers; they vitiate their taste, so that they cannot relish sound doctrine; and spoil their appetite, so that they cannot turn it into nourishment; they, as it were, feed them with sweetmeats, till the genuine wine of the kingdom seems quite insipid to them. They give them cordial upon cordial, which make them all life and spirit for the present; but meantime their appetite is destroyed, so that they can neither retain nor digest the pure milk of the Word.[19]

The center of the priestly office is the cross. At Calvary, Christ's passive and active obedience fuse into the mighty act for salvation from sin. His action constitutes not only the imputation of pardon but the impartation of a New Birth. Justification is the grace-formed pardon imputed, new birth is the pardon imparted, and sanctification is the life. Wesley defined justification as "the plain scriptural notion . . . pardon, the forgiveness of sins." He goes further, "Justifying faith implies, not only divine evidence or conviction that 'God was in Christ, reconciling the world unto himself,' but a sure trust and confidence that Christ died for *my* sins, that he loved *me*, and gave himself for *me*."[20]

Similar to the prophetic office, Christ's priestly office includes the full threefoldness of grace—prevenient, justifying, and sanctifying. Nevertheless, for the sake of theological and experiential integrity, these functions must be held distinct and never confused:

> [Justification] is not the being made actually just and righteous. This is *sanctification*; which is indeed in some degree the immediate *fruit* of justification, but nevertheless is a distinct gift of God, and of a totally different nature. The one implies what God *does for us* through his Son; the other what he *works in us* by his Spirit. So that although some rare instance may be found, wherein the term 'justified' or 'justification' is used in so wide a sense as to include sanctification also, yet in general use they are sufficiently distinguished from each other both by St. Paul and the other inspired writers.[21]

It is a strange twist of history that Augustus Toplady, the Whitefieldian Calvinist and bitter theological opponent of Wesley, could so well summarize the Wesleyan doctrine:

28

> Rock of Ages, cleft for me,
>   Let me hide myself in thee;
> Let the water and the blood,
>   From thy wounded side which flowed,
> Be of sin the *double cure*,
>   *Save* from wrath and *make* me pure.

The sacrifice of Calvary effects the "double cure" in that it saves from the guilt of sin (justification) and saves progressively from the power of sin (sanctification). Wesley may have accounted for the founding of the church on Pentecost. He never used, however, Pentecostal language nor made any reference to Acts 2 as expressive of sanctification. The two, justification and sanctification, are moored in the cross of Christ and constitute the priestly work.

The Christ of Jerusalem

The atoning death of Christ is the ultimate ground for sanctification as well as justification. Hence, the Anselmian "satisfaction," the "sacrificial," and the penal "substitution" theories of the atonement express the priestly work of Christ and form the heart of his doctrine of salvation. The picture behind these terms is a courtroom, a verdict, and a substitutionary ransom. Sometimes neglected in Wesley, because due attention has not been devoted to the fullness of Christ in his three offices, is another picture. This is the picture of a cosmic battle against the forces of Satan and evil, and the victory confirmed in the resurrection. It could be argued that the Wesleyan passion for sanctification is minimized by the neglect of the final image of victory. Later those who would attempt to correct the neglect of sanctification would do what John Fletcher in Wesley's own time did. Sanctification was then argued and defended on the basis of the Pentecost paradigm. The danger in this is that the work of Christ and the work of the Holy Spirit are separated in an unconsciously implicit trinitarian modalism. The work which the Holy Spirit accomplishes is to bring to the heart of the believer the work which Christ accomplishes on the cross. The cross therefore is victory; the victory is announced in the early morning Jerusalem experience of the women who go forth with the evangel of the heavenly messenger, "He is not here. He is risen!" To my knowledge nowhere does

29

Wesley seek to bring these two pictures together, Christ crucified and Christ victorious. Like Luther, he simply sets them alongside each other. The closest to conjoining the two lies in Wesley's insistence upon the fullness of Christ in his three offices.

The Kingly office is the victorious office and is stressed throughout the *Explanatory Notes* and a few of the sermons. This office is crucial for Wesley's treatment of the kingdom, sanctification, and the church, to say nothing of his eschatology. The victory of the cross is both retroactive and eschatological. In the words of Oscar Cullman[22] (which harmonize with Wesley's insistence) the decisive victory over the principalities and powers has been won (D-day). They are revealed and disarmed (Col. 2:15). They no longer have power over the justified because the justified are in the process of being sanctified. The powers have not, however, been destroyed. This remains for the final eschatological victory (V-day).[23] In the meantime, Christians live with confidence in the victory achieved and still to be consummated. In hope, Christians live by faith "active in love."

Wesley's understanding of the Kingdom is essential to his proclamation of grace.[24] While recognizing that there is only one Kingdom, Wesley nevertheless sensed the necessary internal tension between the kingdom already and the kingdom not-yet: the kingdom already is "the Kingdom of Grace," while the kingdom not-yet is "the Kingdom of Glory."

The Kingdom of Grace consists in both the sanctification of persons in this life and the forming of the community of grace, which is the church. The Kingdom of Grace dawns when a person repents and believes through the prevenient and justifying grace of Christ. The Kingdom of Grace "dawns" precisely because at this moment Christ through the Holy Spirit begins to reign in human life, restoring the divine image, which is the love of God and neighbor, fulfilling the divine law, and conferring righteousness, peace, and joy through the Holy Spirit.[25]

The Kingdom of Grace, however, is not individualistic. It is profoundly communal. The church is the parable of the Kingdom of Grace. Wesley sensed in the revival the importance of the social dimensions of justification and sanctification, and provided structurally for these through the societies and classes. No one could be a "lone-ranger" Christian. The process of sanctification takes place in community of accountability. Again, grace was rigorous

in that it entailed accountability for one's discipleship in the
crucible of the class meeting. The goal of the evangelical imperative was the Kingdom experienced as sanctification and perfection, in the company of Christ's followers. A kingdom existence
is dependent upon the means of grace, ordinary and
extraordinary, while at the same time it is active in apostolic living.
A recovery of the kingly office is precisely what saves Wesley from
a highly individualistic interpretation which many of his followers
have embodied.

The Kingdom of Glory is the final blessedness for the individual within the corporate reality of a "new heaven and a new earth."
Wesley's delineation of the Kingdom in two manifestations under-
scores the teleological direction of the Christian life. Being in
Christ is not static but dynamic. In popular parlance, following
the King means "going somewhere." The Wesleyan question to
his preachers, "Are you going on to perfection?" aptly illustrates
this. Charles' hymn summarizes the eschatological, teleological
reality of the Kingdom already and not-yet:

> Love divine, all loves excelling,
>   Joy of heaven, to earth come down,
> Fix in us thy humble dwelling,
>   All thy faithful mercies crown!
> Jesus, thou art all compassion,
>   Pure, unbounded love thou art;
> Visit us with thy salvation!
>   Enter every trembling heart.
>
> Come, almighty to deliver,
>   Let us all thy grace receive;
> Suddenly return, and never,
>   Never more thy temples leave.
> Thee we would be always blessing,
>   Serve thee as thy hosts above,
> Pray, and praise thee without ceasing,
>   Glory in thy perfect love.
>
> Finish then thy new creation,
>   Pure and spotless let us be;
> Let us see thy great salvation
>   Perfectly restored in thee;
> Changed from glory into glory
>   Till in heaven we take our place,
> Till we cast our crowns before thee,
>   Lost in wonder, love, and praise.[26]

31

"Christ in his fullness" was Wesley's passion. The offices of Christ were the revelation of this fullness. Grace—prevenient, justifying, and sanctifying—was the experiential motive. The kingdom present and coming was the goal. The authority, motive, and goal of the evangelical imperative are ontologically, revelationally, and experientially grounded in the fullness of Christ through the wholeness of grace.

Conclusion

I have attempted to permit Wesley to speak in his own words and with his own logic. Albert Outler, in what is unquestionably the best exposition of Wesleyan evangelism,[27] warns us that Wesley must be read within the context of his eighteenth-century worldview. He, however, must be interpreted today in the context of a very different worldview. We, therefore, can claim no particular power or merit in the specifics of his theological vocabulary— but if we take seriously the trajectories of his vision and message, then we must reckon seriously with his logic.

Why does contemporary Methodism in the western world give so little evidence of the imperative? We are not talking about just church membership. We are speaking of apostolic zeal and witness. A recovery of the so-called Wesleyan logic which gives priority to apostolic witness over institutional formation and structure would bring into scrutiny every structure of the existing church. Are these structures "bent outward" missionally, or are they "bent inward" in institutional self-service? A recovery of the wholeness of grace would motivate the church toward a mission of wholeness for the wholeness of persons throughout the whole world. A recovery of the missional mandate would prevent us from truncating the gospel and would give both evangelism and social engagement an evangelical grounding invigorating both.

The task is greater than appropriation. As judgment begins at the household of God, so does evangelism. The field is as much within as without. Time does not permit an analysis of the attrition of the experiential reality of grace within the church. The theological analysis of the loss of grace has already been done.[28] Across our history we have slowly but surely lost the experiential vitality of the original charisma, namely, grace itself. One looks longingly for evidence of new expressions of the grace of Christ, and in the two-thirds world we see it. Here and there we find it in "neo-pagan North America,"[29] but—frankly—not often. We still look because we believe nothing less than a re-birth of experiential grace—that plentitude of grace, as Wesley called it, is the very life of persons, church, and world.

Gordon Rupp once remarked that Wesley was a pessimist by nature and an optimist by grace.[30] This is not a bad mixture. What we cannot do of ourselves, Christ's grace can accomplish working in and through us. Under the gospel imperative we look with hope for the day when the Methodists can sing with conviction and integrity:

> O that the world might taste and see
> The riches of his grace!
> The arms of love that compass me
> Would all the world embrace.

CHAPTER 2

The Revitalization of United Methodist Doctrine and the Renewal of Evangelism

William J. Abraham

Introduction

My aim in this essay is threefold. First, I shall sketch what I mean by the term "United Methodist Doctrine" and by the term "evangelism" and argue briefly a case for the importance of doctrine for the life of evangelism. Second, I shall suggest that The United Methodist Church is in a much healthier position now with respect to its doctrinal heritage than it was twenty years ago. Third, I shall argue that the continued revitalization of doctrine depends crucially on the continued renewal of evangelism within the church as a whole.

The Importance of Doctrine for Evangelism

By the term "United Methodist Doctrine" I mean that body of doctrine which The United Methodist Church has constitutionally designated as its formal standards of doctrine. It does not, therefore, refer to the doctrines which any particular United Methodist, or group of United Methodists, or even the whole of United Methodism itself, might contingently hold at any point in its history, as determined, say, by sociological inquiry. Christians of all denominations are often woefully ignorant of the doctrines normatively held by their church; United Methodists more so than most others. However, this is beside the point. The referent for the term "United Methodist Doctrine" is not sociological but broadly constitutional. It refers to those doctrines formally adopted by The United Methodist Church, acting in its legislative capacity, and thus endowed with the power to speak normatively, canonically, and officially. So likewise the term "United Methodist Doctrine" does not refer to the doctrines or theological proposals actually held or argued for by theologians, professional or otherwise, who happen to have been or now are United Methodists. In North America United Methodism has produced its own cadre of theologians; one thinks immediately of figures like Georgia Harkness, Edwin Lewis, Albert Outler, Geoffrey Wainwright, John Deschner, Thomas Langford, Justo González, Schubert Ogden, Thomas Oden, and the like. One might even argue, as Langford has done, that there is a distinctive Wesleyan theological tradition with its own unique theme or themes, its own specific ethos, its own distinctive methodology, and such like.[1] Yet again, this is not what we mean when we speak of "United Methodist Doctrine." We mean by this term those doctrines which have become canonical for the church as a whole; those teachings which have been voted on in the appropriate General Conference; that body of doctrinal material which has been formally adopted by the church through appropriate action in its courts.[2]

This is not to say that the work of a United Methodist theologian might not become canonical. In fact in 1972 The United Methodist Church came within a hair's breath of making both the doctrines and the theological methodology of Albert Outler canonical. Even now this issue is not fully resolved, as we shall see below when we look at the interpretation of the doctrinal standards of The United Methodist Church. In actual fact, however, it is very difficult for theologians to get their work accepted as de jure canonical. Whether they can or not is a contingent matter. Ironically the Roman Catholics and the Eastern Orthodox Churches have complex processes to make this possible; Protestant theologians, including United Methodist theologians, have to lean heavily on hermeneutics to attain this lofty status merely de facto. Whatever the case historically, a clear logical distinction can and should be made between standards of doctrine accepted as canonical for a church and the doctrines and theology of this or that theologian or group of theologians within that same church.

What do we mean by the term "evangelism"? Here we can be much briefer. The United Methodist Church has never defined what it means by evangelism. My own proposal, argued for at length elsewhere, is that we should construe evangelism as those acts of ecclesial ministry in which people are initiated into the kingdom of God for the first time.[3] Thus understood, evangelism is grounded in the new world order designated in the gospels as the reign of God. It has been inaugurated through the Holy Spirit in the life, death, and resurrection of Jesus Christ, and is made available now in the church and the world. In actual practice this means that evangelism will be rooted in celebration and worship, and that it will have two characteristic sets of actions associated with it. There will, first, be acts of proclamation in which the good news is preached, and shared with all and sundry; second, there will be acts of initial catechesis such as were carried out in the catechumenate of the first centuries and by the class meetings of early Methodism. Expressed very broadly, evangelism is about the making of new Christians. It designates those human acts of proclamation, sharing, and initial discipling which introduce people to the new and glorious reality brought into the world by God through the Holy Spirit in the person and work of Jesus Christ.

What then is the link between doctrine and evangelism? I think we can express it simply as follows. Commitment to some body of doctrine is a necessary but not sufficient condition of healthy forms of evangelism over the long haul of a church's life. It is not a sufficient condition for two reasons. First, because it is perfectly possible for a church to be formally and even in reality committed to a body of doctrine, and yet be totally inept in evangelism or even completely opposed to evangelism. The history of the church is so full of examples which obviously support this generalization that I need not mention them. Second, no description of human action can be a sufficient account of the causal factors essential to evangelism because entry into the kingdom of God depends crucially on the concurrent action of the Holy Spirit. Without the Holy Spirit we can do nothing; hence any attempt to make commitment to certain doctrines a sufficient condition of evangelism is doomed to failure theologically.

Commitment to doctrine is a necessary condition, however, because it is quite impossible to engage in evangelism without being committed to a body of religious teachings. Evangelism cannot take place in a vacuum. This is true both for individuals and for corporate bodies like churches. Evangelism depends for its execution on convictions about creation, human nature, sin, salvation, and the like. More generally it depends on some understanding of what the gospel is. Indeed, as Bonhoeffer so astutely observed, a church which loses its sense of the content of the gospel is much worse off than a church which goes morally astray.[4] For the loss of the gospel means in the end that there is no hope for such a body. Moral failure and disaster are precisely what the gospel addresses and ultimately cures; so a church which is without the gospel has no medicine for its moral sickness; whereas a church which still has the gospel buried deep within it always possesses grounds for hope.

This is surely one reason why churches as they have been birthed in history have developed constitutional standards of doctrine. This is not necessarily a fall into dead orthodoxy or a barren institutionalism. In fact not nearly enough attention has been given to the manifold functions of doctrinal standards. It is common among recent commentators on standards of doctrine to focus almost exclusively on standards of doctrine as a means of identity across the generation.[5] This is important but clearly not the whole story. Standards of doctrine serve many functions. They help keep a body protected from subversive teaching, they provide means of evaluating leaders, they form part of the boundary to determine who is out and who is in, they act as a catalyst for ongoing reflection, they are a crucial ingredient in ecumenical dialogue, they operate as a banner of conviction or a counsel of perfection, and they prevent bodies from falling into unhealthy extremes.

With respect to evangelism, standards of doctrine provide a stable context in which the ministry of evangelism can be thought out and developed. They identify those convictions which a particular body has found invaluable if not essential in its evangelistic activity; that is, they provide conceptual foundations a deep horizon in which a church can root and inform its ministry. They can do so in two ways: first, by actually specifying those teachings which a church considers constitutive of its identity and existence; and second, by identifying those norms against which all doctrine is to be tested. The former method is more direct: it spells out those convictions about God, creation, sin, and the like which inform the church's life and hence its evangelistic life. The latter method is indirect; in the Protestant traditions it usually identifies the scriptures as the ultimate norm of doctrine and thereby draws attention to a crucial source for reflection on the ministry on evangelism.[6]

On this reading, standards of doctrine have a thoroughly complex character. They are obviously open to all sorts of abuse when their varied functions are misunderstood or wrongly applied. They appear to impose limits to the freedom of the individual and even to the church as a whole in the long run; they seem to hamper commitment to deep theological reflection; they become irrelevant and out of date in the eyes of many; and they get used as weapons in religious wars. We are all aware of the catalogue of evils generally associated with doctrinal standards. The solution to these evils is not to abandon doctrinal standards; this is myopic and naive. The solution is to understand them more fully and more positively and to use them more deftly and more creatively.[7]

The Doctrinal Heritage of United Methodism

This is precisely the challenge which faces The United Methodist Church in the present generation. We will not be able to meet it, however, without a review of the work of the last generation in its interpretation of the doctrinal standards in The United Methodist Church.

Developments in the interpretation of the doctrinal standards of The United Methodist Church over the last twenty years have been extraordinary. For nothing less than one hundred and sixty years the forbears of the United Methodists had not formally given serious attention to their doctrinal standards[8]—so much so that by the late nineteen sixties they were not able to identify with certainty what they were, or how they were to be construed and used. The issue was compounded by a clear statement in the first restrictive rule that United Methodism did have doctrinal standards which could not be changed. On the surface this confusion bespoke a thoroughly incoherent ecclesial tradition; the church had doctrinal standards but no one knew for certain what they were. Under the surface it made manifest a deep set of dilemmas some of which still remain to be resolved.

(1) At one level the confusion made manifest the incongruity between the constitution of the church and the general avowals

39

of United Methodists. The common perception of United Methodists in the twentieth century has been that United Methodists believed anything and drank beer. They gloried in their lack of doctrinal unity, priding themselves, for example, that, unlike Presbyterians with their Westminster Confession of Faith, they were not a creedal church. *Prima facie* this totally fails to fit with the possession of a set of Articles of Religion and the First Restrictive Rule. However unlike other ecclesial bodies the forbears of United Methodism may be, this kind of contrast is inept and inaccurate.

(2) At another level the confusion drew attention to the question of how United Methodism intended to relate its own distinctive doctrinal heritage, as highlighted in the writings of Wesley, to the wider heritage of the Christian tradition. This was made particularly acute because of the deep ecumenical impulse in the Wesleyan tradition. It raised the issue of the center of gravity in doctrine. Was it to be located, say, in one's doctrine of God, or in the material of the ecumenical creeds, or in the *ordo salutis* as worked out by Wesley? Where was this to be located and why? Without answers to these kind of questions it is difficult to enter into serious ecumenical dialogue.

(3) At another level the confusion brought to light the thorny issue of the grounding of specific doctrines. How far was this in fact addressed in those documents which might plausibly be construed as the doctrinal standards? Should United Methodism be seen as fundamentally a Protestant body, a proposal supported by Article V of the Articles of Religion, by Article IV of the Confession, by the generally Protestant tenor of several articles, and by sundry material in Wesley? Or should United Methodism be seen as more a Catholic body, a construal supported by the concentration of patristic material in the Articles and Confession, and by the appeal to tradition in Wesley? Or should United Methodism be seen as offering a hybrid of Christian and Enlightenment traditions, an interpretation suggested by the sundry and unorganized references to scripture, tradition, experience, and reason?[9]

(4) At yet another and perhaps the deepest level of all the confusion inherent in the late sixties and early seventies posed the question of how any Christian body which had roots that antedated the Enlightenment could come to terms with the challenges

of modernity. Could Methodism maintain both its fundamental intellectual identity and its ongoing relevance at the same time? *De facto* United Methodism has within its own womb given birth to a variety of doctrinal and theological strategies which in one way or another attempted to face up to the intellectual needs of its members and its changing context.[10] United Methodism was from the start deeply enculturated, and it prided itself in lauding many of the values, like freedom, autonomy, and critical rationality, which were the benchmark of modernity. Moreover, its intellectual leaders acutely felt the tension, which the Enlightenment celebrated and emphasized, between the cognitive commitments of the classical Christian tradition and the content of much modern theorizing about history and the world. This precipitated a quest for an identity which would not just be doctrinal but theological in nature. That is to say, it called for an account of how United Methodism conceived its own theological task in the modern world. If there was one problem which lay at the root of the confusion among United Methodists in the early seventies, then this is surely one of the most likely candidates for this coveted position.

Given such a complex set of dilemmas it will come as no surprise that different interpretations of what happened at the General Conference of 1972 abound. As I see it, this is what happened.

The query about what constituted the doctrinal standards was resolved by identifying these clearly as the Articles, the Confession, and Wesley's *Sermons* and *Notes on the New Testament*. Their authority, however, was eviscerated by treating them as strictly non-juridical, as landmarks in our complex historical heritage, as foundation documents, as subject to historical interpretation, and as radically contextualized in a one-sided version of the apophatic tradition. This way of identifying the status of the doctrinal standards provided the context for resolving the problem of the relation between the classical tradition of Christendom and the Wesleyan emphasis. It was solved by insisting on a common core and a set of United Methodist distinctive beliefs. Presumably this simply specified in a nuanced way the context of the standards.

The problem of the grounding was resolved by means of the famous Wesleyan "quadrilateral." Scripture, tradition, reason, and experience were recommended as the doctrinal guidelines of

The United Methodist Church. Within this an effort was made to do two things: first, to specify the content of tradition; and second, to develop a working account of the relation between the four elements. All this in turn provided the context for resolving the tension between past doctrinal identity and contemporary theological reflection and expression. The primacy clearly belonged to ongoing theological reflection. United Methodist identity was to be secured by the way in which one did theology rather than by what one believed doctrinally. United Methodist identity was relocated not in the content of what one believed but in the process of how one came to believe. As a consequence, or even as constitutive of this, United Methodism embraced a radical doctrinal pluralism as its *modus vivendi*.

If the construction of this proposal was intrinsically extraordinary, its radical reappraisal within the space of twenty years was even more so. Again I can only touch on the crucial highlights. Ostensively what the 1988 General Conference did was tidy up the material decisions of 1972. Thus it made more explicit the basic Christian affirmations shared with other churches. Likewise it tidied up the content of the distinctive Wesleyan emphases. At another level it sorted out the much debated question of the referent for our "present existing and established standards of doctrine."[11] This could have been a nightmare to resolve, in that there developed a crisis for the church when it was argued that these did not at all refer to Wesley's *Sermons* and *Notes*. The solution was a stroke of ecclesiastical genius: the *Sermons* and *Notes* were treated as *de facto* canonical but made *de jure* subsidiary to the Articles of Religion and Confession of Faith. Furthermore, the Conference action of 1988 cleared up the vexed question of the primacy of scripture, making what was implicit much more explicit, while retaining a commitment to tradition, reason, and experience. In so doing, it retained the challenge to engage in ongoing doctrinal and theological reflection which would attend to the concerns generated by various human struggles for dignity, liberation, and fulfillment, by various ethnic constituencies, by the praxis of mission and ministry, and by ecumenical and interfaith dialogue. Within this call to theological reflection an attempt was made to chart a clear distinction between doctrine and theology. The doctrinal affirmations assist in the discernment of Christian truth in ever-changing circumstances, while theology includes the testing, renewal, elaboration, and application of our doctrinal perspective.[12]

Clearly all these moves contributed in their own way to removing the suspicion that United Methodists had opted for doctrinal indifference when they embraced an identity which focused primarily on the method or process of doing theology, rather than on any agreed doctrinal consensus. Doctrinal indifference was countered by being much clearer about the role of the Articles of Religion, the Confession of Faith, and the *Sermons* and *Notes*, by making more explicit the relation between scripture and the other three elements of the quadrilateral, by dropping all talk of theological pluralism,[13] and by insisting on a distinction between doctrine and theology. All this is to my mind an enormous gain. Yet in one crucial respect it is deeply defective. It fudges the issue of the core of United Methodist identity. Is identity to be located in a body of doctrine, in a particular theological method, or some combination of both? The impression is that it is to be found in the last of three options, but nowhere is this matter clearly addressed. If it is to be located in the third option, then it rests on a deep misunderstanding and an even deeper confusion.

The misunderstanding is to think that the use of the quadrilateral entailed a commitment to theological indifference. On the contrary, the quadrilateral was intended to preserve theological integrity and theological liveliness. Its fundamental function was to call the church as a whole to engage in critical theological reflection of the highest order. This was conceived in terms of the use of the elements of the quadrilateral. The practical result of this was also clear: it would lead to precisely the doctrinal pluralism which was celebrated in the 1972 document. However, doctrinal pluralism does not at all entail theological indifference; it is simply an appeal for toleration of radically diverse doctrinal proposals within a single ecclesial body. Indeed a community which is indifferent to theology will not be doctrinally pluralistic, for, by definition, it will not produce any statements of doctrine at all; those who do not care about theology will not be very likely to write Christian doctrine.

How then did the issue get framed in terms of indifference? The answer to this question takes us to the heart of the deeper confusion which still permeates the territory. It was framed in terms of indifference because the use of the quadrilateral

43

inevitably leads to doctrinal pluralism. It results in radically different proposals as to the content of Christian doctrine. Theologians are in the business of producing normative accounts of what Christians are to believe about God, creation, sin, salvation, and the like. Moreover, these are exactly the matters which are covered in the doctrinal standards of the church. So a church which makes the quadrilateral the foundation and benchmark of method in theology, and thereby embraces the challenge of rigorous theological reflection, cannot avoid the embracing of radically diverse doctrinal positions. These doctrinal positions will compete with each other for allegiance, and they will also compete with the content of the official doctrinal standards of the church. To the normal observer this looks perilously close to doctrinal indifference, in that it does not matter what you believe, so long as you use the right method to get what you believe.

The deep confusion that lies buried in this is the claim that what makes one a United Methodist is the commitment to the quadrilateral. If we know anything, we know that this is not the kind of material which is the central concern and content of the constitutional standards of doctrine. The quadrilateral is a working hypothesis about method in theology, derived from interaction with the Wesley corpus by the one of the greatest Methodist scholars of the twentieth century. It was effectively Albert Outler's attempt to solve tangled questions that crop up in the prolegomena of conventional systematic theology in the western branch of Christendom. As such it deserves our deepest respect and attention. It merits the kind of critical assessment which any theological proposal deserves. What it does not deserve is to be treated as an essential element in our constitutional standards of doctrine.

The quadrilateral does not merit this status for two very good reasons. First, because it was never proposed and endorsed by the constitutional process which identified the standards of doctrine in the first place. In fact those involved would not even have framed the issue in these terms. Moreover, although it is clearly rooted in aspects of the *Sermons* and *Notes*, it is precarious in the extreme to argue that it is constitutive of the *Sermons* and *Notes*.[14] Second, it does not merit this status because it is riddled with problems.[15] At its heart it involves a fatal running together of a reduced account of the canons of ecclesial identity with the norms of Enlightenment epistemology. To express the matter

44

graphically, it is a hastily contrived shotgun wedding between scripture and tradition, the bride provided by the church, and reason and experience, the bridegroom provided by the European Enlightenment. So on neither historical nor theological grounds should the quadrilateral be granted the same status granted to the doctrinal standards.

What is ultimately at stake here is how we are to construe all the material in the *Discipline* which falls outside the doctrinal standards themselves. This includes the material on our doctrinal heritage, on the doctrinal history, and on our theological task. Am I suggesting that this should be summarily dumped and set aside? On the contrary, I think that it should be taken with the utmost seriousness. However, all this material works at the level of midrash and interpretative commentary. These materials represent the mind of the church on the nature and function of our doctrinal standards, as regulated by General Conference in the latter half of the twentieth century. They therefore deserve to be read, mulled over, and digested. In my own judgment these materials are now indispensable pedagogically. They provide exactly the kind of suggestions which can help bring the doctrinal standards to life, and they provide an invaluable introduction to their content and function in the life of the church. As the conclusion to the section on our theological task points out:

> Evangelism, nurture, and mission require a constant effort to integrate authentic experience, rational thought, and purposeful action with theological integrity.[16]

The material outside the doctrinal standards is an invaluable aid along these lines. In fact they enhance the position of the church. They put the church in a much richer state than it was in the early seventies when there was so much confusion and uncertainty. They are, then, invaluable guidelines for doctrinal and theological reflection within the church as a whole. They cannot and should not, however, be anything more than that. They cannot at present be construed canonically, and they should not in the future be construed theologically, as the core of United Methodist identity. Nor can they be asked or expected to fulfill the functions which the doctrinal standards fulfill. They can at best be an aid to our theological reflection and a source for the enlivening of those standards in the life of the church at large.

Revitalizing Doctrine by Renewing Evangelism

How can a church revitalize its doctrinal standards? More specifically how can United Methodists best appropriate the Articles of Religion, the Confession of Faith, and the *Sermons* and *Notes*? There is no easy answer to this question. In a moment I shall look to the place that the renewal of evangelism can have in this process. Before that I would like to mention three preliminary suggestions which deserve mention.

First, I think it would help enormously if the General Conference appointed a standing commission on doctrine. This would continue the invaluable conversation which has developed over the last twenty years. There is just too much unfinished business and too many loose ends; and more business and additional loose ends are sure to appear in the future. We need an ongoing process which can act as an advisory clearing house for the church at large and which can make appropriate materials available from time to time.

Second, far more attention needs to be given in seminary teaching to the doctrinal standards, to General Conference action and midrash thereon, and to the whole sweep of theological reflection in the Wesleyan tradition. At the moment this is far too marginal to be taken seriously. Moreover, its fruitful potential for introducing students to the whole gamut of theological disciplines in the academy has not been adequately exploited.

Third, a major effort needs to be made to introduce the laity at large to the doctrinal standards and the literature they have evoked. It is ludicrous to think that laity will seriously engage in the appropriation of doctrine or in theological reflection upon it or around it, if they are left in the dark and given no opportunity to be engaged with this material. There are hosts of educated and motivated laity who would be fascinated by United Methodist doctrine and by theological reflection related thereto, if these were properly taught; they would also find their ministry and service deeply enhanced.

We are now ready to push this further by noting the intimate and reciprocal role there is between the revitalization of United Methodist doctrine and the renewal of evangelism. They key to this is to recall the close connection that existed between evangelism and doctrine in the birth of Methodism itself.

Methodism began in part as an evangelistic movement in the womb of the western church. It did not begin as a movement of theological reform; that is, it did not begin by positing some lacuna in doctrine or set of doctrines and insist that the church needed to be reformed in the light of these. Nor did it begin as a quest for the primitive church where one starts from scratch and wipes out the history of the church as irrelevant.[17] The early Methodists found themselves in the midst of a deep spiritual awakening, and in the providence of God were driven to take the gospel into the fields and to establish in the faith those who were converted. So it began in the womb of the church; it situates itself, therefore, in the catholic faith of the church as modified by the Anglican Reformation. However, its own evangelistic labors had deep cognitive consequences. The Wesleys and their cohorts, in order to make sense of their experiences and their ministries, had to engage in the kind of profound theological reflection which brought to birth themes and convictions that lay buried in the scriptures and tradition. We can leave to historians the detailed etiology of these matters, but the final outlines are remarkably clear. They found expression in the articulation of such themes as prevenient grace, justification, new birth, assurance, and sanctification. The recent discussion about the meaning of United Methodist doctrine is entirely correct then to insist on both the common faith of the church and a set of United Methodist distinctives as the constitutive components of United Methodist doctrinal identity.

The development of some such set of doctrines is to my mind inevitable. Any movement which is to become a church or even to last more than a couple of generations cannot avoid summing up its convictions in terms of doctrine, polity, liturgy, and the like. There is a kind of inner logic of question and answer which requires the elaboration of doctrinal schemes and the handing over of these to future generations. Methodism is no exception to the processes we can see at work in the early church and in the Reformation traditions. There is no necessity about exactly how this will happen, but that it will happen seems to me causally inevitable. This in turn poses its own set of problems. Chief among them is that later generations often do not share the profound spiritual experiences which propelled the development of doctrine in the first place. This is clearly the case in wide tracts of all

47

the churches with respect to the doctrine of the trinity, for example. The profound experiences of the Holy Spirit which in part lie behind the doctrine of the trinity are ignored or written off as religiously pathological. It equally applies in the case of doctrine of justification by faith in the Reformation churches. In this instance the sense of sin and alienation essential to a deep grasp of this doctrine is missing.

The long-term effects of this process of erosion are obvious in a tradition. It loses the ontological moorings of its doctrine. It gets separated from those realities without which received doctrine becomes for the most part boring theological archeology. A deep alienation sets in. Negatively this is expressed in terms of impatience with the past and in terms of critical analyses which have no sympathy for the deeper inner spirit of the tradition. Positively it is expressed in terms of a quest for action and relevance which tends to focus on this or that aspect of the tradition without taking the full measure of its content. This in turn hastens the demise of the original doctrines. They become treated with increasing suspicion until one reaches the point where they are forgotten or even despised.

This is not wide of the mark as a description of the dilemma which faces United Methodists with respect to their doctrinal standards. Much of United Methodism has become exactly what Wesley feared it would become, namely, a culturally established sect which knows the form but not the power of religion. Its grasp of the deep ontological realities so essential to a living tradition and to fruitful theological reflection has been eroded and whittled away. So much so that its doctrinal standards have become *de facto* irrelevant. Outside the elite circle of scholars who work on them they are unknown. Moreover, many of the theological endeavors of United Methodists have become an exercise in unfruitful self-criticism, a search for some methodological miracle that will turn water into wine, selective appeal to developments in other parts of the globe, and a quest for intellectual relevance which is often deeply intolerant of classical forms of Christian tradition. Traditions which are reduced to such straits will survive for a time, but they have very limited guarantees of existence. Perceptive observers over a decade ago began to see the writing on the wall. Only the blind and obdurate can now ignore it.

This is precisely why the revitalization of doctrine linked to the renewal of evangelism is so important. It could well be a matter of life or death for United Methodism. On both scores we have made enormous progress over the last twenty years. As I argued above, the debate about doctrine and theology has been enormously fruitful. We have been shocked into acknowledging that the claim that United Methodists can believe anything and drink beer is historical and theological nonsense. We have been forced by the evidence before us to admit that the common assumption, so magnificently expressed by Albert Outler, that United Methodists found their identity in a hypothetical proposal in the prolegomena to systematic theology rather than fundamentally in a body of doctrine, was a deeply illuminating mistake. We have been awakened from our indifferent doctrinal slumbers and find ourselves exposed to a fascinating and brilliant deposit of doctrine and theological midrash, aided and abetted now by a first-class scholarly edition of Wesley's *Works*. And all this has happened when we have been mugged by statistics, when we have been scandalized by the corruption of current television evangelism, and when we are now beginning to take evangelism with a seriousness which both our heritage and the subject itself require of us.

The renewal of evangelism is so obviously linked to the continued revitalization of our doctrine that all I need to do is make the connection explicit. The crucial issue is this. Evangelism is not a matter of saving the denomination by schemes of church growth. Evangelism is a matter of discovering the new world order which has come from God in the power of the Holy Spirit through Jesus Christ. The church is required to share this good news in word and deed with the whole world and to develop forms of Christian initiation which will give folk a chance to survive against the world, the flesh, and the devil. This is not all the church does in response to the dawning of God's kingdom, but it is what it should do if it is to be serious about evangelism.

The link between this and doctrine is clear. It is in encounter with this gracious and deeply mysterious reality mediated in Word, sacrament, liturgy, and holiness that the church rediscovers the truths which lie buried in its doctrinal heritage. It is in this encounter that it will in part see the point of the doctrine of the trinity and the other elements which United Methodists share with church as a whole. It is equally in this encounter that it will see the value of the distinctive doctrines which were hammered out in human history by our fathers and mothers in the faith. It is in this encounter also that United Methodists will best develop their own doctrinal and theological midrash and find a way to make their own unique and manifold contribution to the cognitive treasures of the pilgrim people of God.

CHAPTER 3

Praeparatio Evangelii:
The Theological Roots of
Wesley's View of Evangelism

Ben Witherington III

Introduction

While one could easily spend considerable time analyzing the historical or practical bases of evangelism in the ministry of Wesley, it is the aim of this study to examine the theological roots of his view of evangelism.[1] These theological roots go down into the very heart of Wesley's faith, his basic assumptions about life within and outside of Christ. G. R. Cragg reminds us that "the particular emphasis of his theology derived from his preoccupation with evangelism. He included all the traditional elements of the Christian system of belief, but he so arranged them as to bring into the sharpest relief the doctrine of salvation."[2] In other words, Wesley's evangelism shaped how he viewed and presented his theology. The converse is however also true, and it is the aim of this study to examine only the most salient of the theological roots which ground Wesley's view of evangelism.

We are not here concerned with Wesley's methods of evangelism but rather with the Biblical and theological views that gave him the impetus and rationale for taking up the tasks of an evangelist. In order to examine these theological underpinnings a good deal of summarizing will be required, for all of the topics to be covered here deserve and most have now received whole scholarly monographs devoted to them. We will begin by examining briefly John Wesley's epistemology, followed in turn by a study of Wesley's view of the authority and character of the Bible, his hermeneutics, his soteriology, and finally his eschatology. This will be followed by a summary of the relevance of these various roots for understanding Wesley's view of evangelism, and some final comments on our own modern approaches to that task.

Epistemology and the Knowledge of God

Discussions of Wesley's epistemology normally begin and end by acknowledging Wesley's life long indebtedness to John Locke. Typical of such assessments is the conclusion of Richard Brantley to the following effect:

> John Wesley's method, if not always self-conscious, is assuredly present throughout his writings; his defenses of faith are enhanced by Locke's experimental idiom, which though hardly so pervasive in Wesley's works as, say, his scriptural reference is nonetheless so clearly a major feature of them as to demonstrate that besides being syncretic and steeped in tradition his theology *articulates* his understanding of empiricism.[3]

While there is no denying the depth and durability of the indebtedness to Locke, a good deal more can and needs to be said on the subject. In the first place, like empiricists such as Locke, Wesley does assume the general reliability of sense perception. This is indeed a crucial assumption for Wesley, not least because Wesley did not believe in innate ideas but held that all knowledge comes to us from outside ourselves. This general position, when applied to the religious realm, meant for Wesley that a person does not inherently have any knowledge of God. Such knowledge must be proclaimed or taught to that individual, or must be learned by observation.

Wesley is not rightly called an empiricist, however, if by that one means that he believed that the *only* kind of data that exists is empirical data, data that can be seen, smelled, touched, tasted, or heard with the physical senses. In fact Wesley believed that human beings had two sets of senses—the physical and the spiritual senses:

> And seeing our ideas are not innate, but must all originally come from our senses, it is certainly necessary that you have senses capable of discerning objects of this kind: Not those only which are

52

called natural senses, which in this respect profit nothing, as being incapable of discerning objects of a spiritual kind: but spiritual senses, exercised to discern spiritual good and evil. It is necessary to have the hearing ear, and the seeing eye, emphatically so called; that you have a new class of senses opened in your soul, not depending on organs of flesh and blood. . . .[4]

These spiritual senses he sometimes called the spiritual inlets of the soul, and he frequently drew an analogy with the condition of a child in the womb. A person prior to spiritual birth is like a child in the womb—s/he may hear things but not distinctly. The womb surrounds him or her, as a veil between that person and the outer world. So too with persons prior to spiritual birth—the spiritual world is all around them but they cannot distinctly perceive it so as to grasp or understand it. The person outside of Christ has his or her senses clogged by sin, apart from the grace of God. Without that renewing grace, the individual cannot know, much less serve God.[5]

Wesley's theory of spiritual sense does not derive directly from Locke, but rather probably from Peter Browne who also drew on Locke and the Cambridge Platonists among others.[6] Furthermore, Wesley did not believe that the person outside of Christ was totally bereft of the grace of God.[7] Everyone has at least enough "preventing" grace from God that s/he has a conscience. Wesley insists that conscience is not a natural human faculty, inherent in the soul, but rather a gift of God's prevenient grace working in a person even before s/he comes to Christ. Therefore, while the natural condition of a person outside of Christ is that their spiritual senses are clogged and they are in a condition of being *non posse non peccare*, everyone has at least enough prevenient grace to have a conscience and be able to respond positively to the grace already working in them.

Rex Matthews ably sums up Wesley's views on these matters as follows:

> . . . the analogy which Wesley draws between the physical senses and our experience of the physical world through them, and the "spiritual senses" of faith and our experience of the spiritual world through them, is precise and exact. Lacking the requisite 'spiritual senses' and consequently lacking any experience of the 'things of God', it is impossible for 'men of reason' (alone) to employ their reason in the religious realm: no senses, no sensory experience, no

53

apprehension, no judgment, no discourse and consequently, no knowledge of God. What is required, says Wesley, is that they have 'a new class of senses' opened up in their souls, through the gift, from outside them, by God's grace, of faith. What is required, in other words, is that they be 'born again'. . . . And it is only *after* this transformation that it is possible, according to Wesley, for one to have any direct experience of spiritual reality, and consequently, to arrive at any knowledge of God.[8]

One must not make the mistake of confusing prevenient with saving grace. The former is only preparatory to the latter, and in fact the latter does not inevitably follow from the former for one may stifle the work of prevenient grace in one's life. For Wesley, salvation does not happen outside of Christ, and more particularly not outside the experiences of justification and the new birth which are available only through faith in Christ. Wesley's epistemology goes a long way toward explaining why evangelism was so critical to him. His translation of Romans 10:13-15 in the *Notes* sums it up well:

'For whosoever shall call upon the name of the Lord shall be saved.' But how shall they call on him in whom they have not believed? And how shall they believe in him of whom they have not heard? And how shall they hear without a preacher? But how shall they preach unless they be sent? As it is written, 'How beautiful are the feet of them who bring the good tidings of peace. . . .'

If persons have no innate ideas of God then they can only come to know God in a saving way through the proclamation of the Good News to them.

'Homo Unius Libri'

Wesley has been hailed by both conservatives and liberals as a champion of their own views on the Bible and its authority. The matter becomes even more complex when one tries to assess Wesley's view of the relationship of Scripture to reason, experience, and tradition—the so-called quadrilateral. Furthermore, the literature on Wesley's view of the Bible is growing more voluminous all the time.[9]

The place to start in these matters is with Wesley himself. In a letter to William Warburton, then Bishop of Gloucester, Wesley replies to various of the Bishop's views as they are espoused in a book entitled *The Doctrine of Grace*.[10] At one point Wesley quotes Warburton as saying: "But how did he inspire Scripture? He so directed the writers that *no considerable error* should fall from them."[11] Wesley in rebuttal says: "Nay, will not the allowing there is any error in Scripture shake the authority of the whole"? This is of course a rhetorical question, but it makes clear that Wesley, unlike the Bishop, thinks there are no errors in Scripture, and to admit there are any errors in any part of the Bible shakes the authority of the whole corpus. This letter was written in Nov. 26, 1762, when Wesley was already 59 years of age. It is not the product of a naive and impetuous young man.

In 1776, Wesley made this comment in his *Journal* on a tract called *The Internal Evidence of the Christian Religion* by Soame Jenyns:

> If he is a Christian, he betrays his own cause by averring that 'all Scripture is not given by inspiration of God, but the writers of it were sometimes left to themselves, and consequently made some mistakes.' Nay, if there be any mistakes in the Bible, there may as well be a thousand. If there be one falsehood in that book, it did not come from the God of truth.[12]

It is also possible to go back to an earlier date and find a similar view. For example, in the preface to Wesley's *Explanatory Notes on the New Testament*, he affirms his view that the Bible is divinely inspired in its entirety and adds: "And the language of His messengers also, is exact in the highest degree: for the words which were given them accurately answered the impression made upon their minds: and hence Luther says 'Divinity is nothing but a grammar of the language of the Holy Ghost.'"[13] In the same preface he says quite plainly "The Scripture, therefore, of the Old and New Testament is a most solid and precise system of divine truth. Every part thereof is worthy of God; and all together are one entire body, wherein is no defect, no excess."[14] This was written in January of 1754, and other statements to the same effect could be amassed,[15] but the point by now is clear enough.

For John Wesley the Bible is the Word of God, fully inspired in all parts, and without error in whatever ways it intends to speak the truth. He regularly calls the Bible the oracles of God, because he sees the divine author as the primary one. It is hardly surprising that Wesley held such a view of the Bible, for he has assented to the Anglican formulation that "all Scripture was given by the inspiration of God,"[16] a formulation based on 2 Timothy 3:16. It is interesting that in his comment on that verse he adds, "The Spirit of God not only once inspired those who wrote it, but continually inspires, supernaturally assists, those that read it with earnest prayer."[17] In short Wesley believes in a double theory of inspiration, both of the Biblical author and of the believing prayerful reader of Scripture.

Wesley's theory of the inspiration of Scripture is not, however, a purely static and mechanical one. He says that God allowed the human authors to use their own languages, styles, abilities, superintending them in regard to the truthfulness of their utterance.[18] He points out in his *Notes* on 1 Corinthians 7:25 that sometimes the Biblical author wrote by means of a "particular revelation" but sometimes s/he drew on the light s/he received in general from the indwelling presence of the Holy Spirit. In short, while in some cases we may talk about a process involving dictation, in other cases God's truth has revealed in a more general or indirect fashion. In his comment on 1 Corinthians 14:32 he remarks: "The impulses of the Holy Spirit, even in men really inspired, so suit themselves to their rational faculties, as not to divest them of the government of themselves, like the heathen priests under their diabolical possession."[19]

When Wesley comes to a problem in Scripture, such as in the genealogy in Matthew 1, he simply states that if there is any error then it is to be credited to the Biblical author's source not the Biblical author himself or herself:

> They acted only as historians, setting down these genealogies, as they stood in the public and allowed records. Therefore they were to take them as they found them. Nor was it needful they should correct the mistakes, if there were any. For these accounts sufficiently answer the end for which they are recited. They unquestionably prove the grand point that Jesus was of the family from which the promised Seed was to come.[20]

This may seem to be an exercise in exegetical gymnastics, but Wesley does feel it necessary to give what he sees as a "plausible explanation" for a possible problem in the text of Scripture. This is caused by his view that Scriptures always tell the truth, even apparently if that means truthfully recording an error in one's source.

It would be both anachronistic and in fact inaccurate to simply label Wesley an eighteenth-century version of a fundamentalist. Wesley never engaged in an argument about the inerrancy of the *autographa* of Scripture, which is where the debate has been joined in the late nineteenth and twentieth centuries, especially in certain Reformed circles.[21] Furthermore, Wesley had a very high view of human reason, and was by no means an anti-intellectual, affirming much of what he had learned from the scientists, philosophers, and noted authors of his day. For example, Wesley strongly endorsed the view that the earth orbits the sun, not vice versa. When he sought to explain why it is that Scripture might seem to suggest otherwise, he said "As for those scriptural expressions which seem to contradict the earth's motion, this general answer may be made to them all, that the scriptures were never intended to instruct us in philosophy, or astronomy; and therefore, on these subjects, expressions are not always to be taken in the literal sense, but for the most part accommodated to the common apprehension of mankind."[22] In short Wesley is capable of explaining the paradox using the idea of accommodation coupled with a distinction between what Scripture *teaches*, and what Scripture touches. In the latter case, he allowed for phenomenological use of language, in regard to the sun rising and setting.

There is even some evidence that Wesley was both cognizant of and disposed to draw on the first attempts at historical critical study of the Bible that were just coming to light in the eighteenth century.[23] It is quite clear from his preface to his *Notes on the New Testament* that he endorses text criticism, never hesitating to follow a Greek manuscript that he thinks is nearer the original reading than that used by the translators of the Authorized Version, and on occasion he will offer his own fresh translation of a text as well. Nevertheless, Wesley's very high view of the inspiration, authority, and truthfulness of Scripture should not be overlooked. This led him to take Scriptural statements like Acts 4:12 very seriously. If the Bible said there was no other name given under heaven by which human beings are to be saved other than the name of Jesus, Wesley was disposed to accept what he called the plain, literal sense of the text. This in turn affected his approach to evangelism.

Evangelism was not for Wesley an exercise in informing people of what was already true about themselves regardless of whether or not they repented and believed in Jesus as the Christ. Rather it was part of the necessary effort to seek and save those who were truly lost apart from Christ, as the Scripture mandated. Wesley frequently used the phrase "Jews, Turks, and infidels" to refer to those whom he did not see as properly called Christians. Wesley believed that his view of the full inspiration of the Scriptures, both Old Testament and New Testament, was one of the main things that distinguished himself and other Christians from the aforementioned three groups.[24] These conclusions about Wesley depend in part on examining Wesley's hermeneutics and his soteriology, especially in regard to the matter of the scandal of particularity, and to the former of these subjects we must now turn.

Hermeneutics and the Quadrilateral

Wesley's principles of interpretation have been helpfully summarized by Albert Outler:

> It was . . . a matter of hermeneutical principle that Scripture would be the court of first and last resort in faith and morals. This was the entire Scriptures too, and not just a biblical anthology; his view of the canon . . . was of a whole and integral revelation, inspired by the same Holy Spirit who continues to guide all serious readers into its unfathomable truth, parts and whole together. And it was from this basic doctrine of biblical inspiration that his main principles of interpretation were derived—all five of them. The first was that believers should accustom themselves to the biblical language and thus to the 'general sense' of Scripture as a whole. This general sense is omnipresent throughout the canon even if not equally so in every text; there is a 'message' in every part of Holy Writ, and it is always the same in essence. This leads to a second rule, adapted from the ancient fathers and from the Reformers as well: that the Scriptures are to be read as a whole, with the expectation that the clearer texts may be relied upon to illuminate the obscurer ones. There is no authority above Scripture from which a more definitive interpretation of revelation maybe sought. . . . Moreover despite the fact that he had his favorite texts and passages in both the Old and New Testaments he had no 'canon within the canon'. This holistic sense of biblical inspiration suggested his third

hermeneutical principle, that one's exegesis is to be guided, always in the first instance, by the literal sense, unless that appears to lead to consequences that are either irrational or unworthy of God's moral character as 'pure unbounded love.' Then, and only with caution, the exegete may seek for an edifying allegory or analogy, but only within the terms of the analogy of faith. A fourth hermeneutical rule follows from his doctrine of grace and free will: that all moral commands in Scripture are also 'covered promises' since God never commands the impossible and his grace is always efficacious in every faithful will. His last rule is . . . that the historical experience of the church, though fallible, is the better judge overall of Scripture's meanings that later interpreters are likely to be, especially on their own. Thus radical novelty is to be eschewed on principle.[25]

This summary is in some respects like the earlier one offered by W. M. Arnett.[26] Arnett, however, adds a further insight. He points out how Wesley stressed the importance of interpreting a text in its context. Wesley warned that "any passage is easily perverted, by being recited singly without any of the preceding or following verses. By this means it may often seem to have one sense, when it will be plain by observing what goes before and what follows after, that it really has the direct contrary."[27] Generally speaking Wesley eschewed a form of proof-texting that ignores the context of a Scriptural statement.[28]

There is however more to be said about Wesley's appeal to the *analogia fidei*, the so-called general tenor of the whole of Scripture. For Wesley that "general tenor" in fact had a rather specific soteriological slant to it. Consider what Wesley says in the *Notes* on Romans 12:6:

> 'Let us prophesy according to the analogy of faith'—St. Peter expresses it 'as the oracles of God;' according to the general tenor of them; according to that grand scheme of doctrine which is delivered therein, touching original sin, justification by faith, and present, inward salvation. . . . Every article therefore concerning which there is any question should be determined by this rule; every doubtful scripture interpreted according to the grand truths which run through the whole.[29]

This meant that all was to be interpreted in light of the *ordo salutis* as Wesley understood it, or according to the heart of the Gospel as Wesley preached it.[30] Thus while, unlike Luther, Wesley never disparaged any part of the Scriptures, nevertheless he makes hermeneutical moves that suggest that all the Scriptures should be seen in the light of a particular soteriological trajectory only explicitly traced in the New Testament. This trajectory is arrived at by a certain sort of combining of insights from several of the Pauline letters (especially Galatians and Romans) and the Johannine letters (especially 1 John).

Wesley was not above using the technique sometimes called spiritualizing of the text, but I know of no cases where he does this at the expense of, or as a means of supplanting, the literal sense of the text. An example of this technique can be found in the sermon "The Signs of the Times." Here he first recognizes and affirms the literal meaning of Matthew 11:4-5, but shortly there-after says, "I appeal to every candid, unprejudiced person, whether we may not at this day discern all those signs (under-standing the words in a spiritual sense) to which our Lord referred to John's disciples 'The blind receive their sight.'"[31] Wesley thus made clear here that he was departing from the simple literal sense of the text. It is possible that this hermeneutical move is an example of what Wesley claims when he said: "I apply no Scripture phrase either to myself or any other without carefully considering both the original meaning and the secondary sense, wherein (allowing for times and circumstances) it may be applied to ordinary Christians."[32]

Further light on this subject comes when we examine closely Wesley's "Address to the Clergy." In the course of urging the importance of studying the Bible in its original languages, and the value of being well-versed in a host of collateral subjects such as history and ancient literature, he implores his audience to have an extensive knowledge of the whole of the Scriptures both in regard to its context and its content. He then adds:

> In order to do this accurately, ought he not to know the literal meaning of every word, verse, and chapter, without which there can be no firm foundation on which the spiritual meaning can be built? Should he not likewise be able to deduce the proper corollaries, speculative and practical, from each text; to solve the difficulties which arise and answer the objections which may be raised against it; and to make a suitable application of all to the consciences of his hearers?[33]

This passage suggests that Wesley believed that every text has a spiritual or deeper meaning, or at least that Wesley believed every text has deeper spiritual significance and application which can only be discerned if one first understands the literal meaning of the text. This suggests a degree of sophistication in Wesley's hermeneutical method that is often overlooked.[34]

In regard to the Old Testament, Wesley believed in reading it in the light of the New Testament, for he operates with a theology of progressive revelation. This approach occasionally leads to the reading back of some aspects of the New Testament into the Old Testament, but usually Wesley eschewed such a practice.[35] The theology of progressive revelation did however lead Wesley to see the Old Testament as essentially a book that requires a sequel. In itself the Old Testament is inferior to the New Testament because it does not explicitly reveal the means of salvation in Christ. More revelation is given in New Testament and thus more is required of Christians than was required of God's people in the Old Testament age.

Wesley put it this way while commenting on 2 Peter 2:19: "As is the difference between the light of a lamp and that of the day, such is that between the light of the Old Testament and of the New."[36] In his sermon on "Christian Perfection" he added:

> Therefore we can not measure the privileges of real Christians by those formerly given to the Jews. 'Their ministration' (or dispensation) we allow 'was glorious' but ours 'exceeds in glory.' So that whosoever gleans up the examples of weakness recording in the law and the prophets, and thence infers that they who have 'put on Christ' are endued with no greater strength, doth 'greatly err, neither knowing the Scriptures nor the power of God.'[37]

Wesley, however, was certainly no Marcion, for he made quite clear that the Old Testament should be used as a source of reproof, correction, and instruction, as 2 Timothy 3:15-17 urges.[38] Indeed his use of the moral law in the Old Testament drew heavily on the Puritan use of it, as a sermon like "The Original Nature, Property, and Use of the Law" shows. It is telling however that what Wesley called the analogy of faith, the theme or trajectory of thought by which the whole of Scripture should be evaluated, is in essence a New Testament theme or trajectory.

61

W. H. Mullen rightly reminds us that Wesley's "method of biblical interpretation might be summarized as soteriologically activated and pragmatically implemented."[39] This is exemplified by the fact that Wesley was willing to assert that the whole Bible preaches Christ. Yet he does not mean by this that Christ can be literally found under every rock in the Old Testament. Rather,

> To preach Christ, is to preach what he hath revealed, either in the Old or New Testament; so that you are then as really preaching Christ when you are saying, 'The wicked shall be turned into hell, and all the people that forget God,' as when you are saying, 'Behold the Lamb of God, which takes away the sin of the world!'[40]

Here the point is that Christ is the author of Scripture, and thus that we should preach all that he has revealed from Genesis to Revelation.

A good deal more could be said about Wesley's hermeneutics in general but at this point we want to discuss Wesley's view of what has come to be called the Quadrilateral. Ted Campbell, in an important recent essay has urged that the phrase the "Wesleyan Quadrilateral" be seen for what it is—a modern Methodist myth.[41] In particular Campbell stresses that the quadrilateral as a fourfold source of *authority* is a modern notion, especially indebted to the works and influence of Outler. It does not derive from Wesley himself. Such a critique is not without some precedent, for William R. Cannon in 1942 argued that Wesley reasserted the idea of *sola Scriptura* against the Deists, not some sort of quadrilateral.[42] The quadrilateral is never articulated as such by Wesley.

Furthermore, Campbell points out that when Wesley talked about "tradition" he uses this term in a negative sense to critique Roman Catholics and others who rely on "merely human" traditions. Part of what in modern times has been called tradition, Wesley called "Christian Antiquity." It is also true that from time to time he appeals to the doctrines and worship practices of the Church of England. In short, Wesley drew on Church traditions in a rather limited way, almost exclusively confined to material from the fourth century A.D. and earlier on the one hand, and from the Anglican Church on the other hand. To this one may add that he drew on Protestant commentators of various denominational persuasions that were more nearly his historical contemporaries in the preparation of his notes on the Bible.

That Cannon was right can be shown from a variety of Wesleyan texts. Wesley, like various of the Reformers before him, affirmed the concept of *sola Scriptura* if by that one means there is only one final authority, one *final* arbiter of truth, at least in the realm of what one would call religious knowledge and especially in regard to what one needs to know in order to be saved. Consider, for example, what Wesley said in the sermon, "The Witness of Our Own Spirit."

> But the Christian rule of right and wrong is the Word of God, the writings of the Old and New Testament: all which the prophets and 'holy men of old' wrote 'as they were moved by the Holy Ghost'; . . . .This 'is a lantern unto a 'Christian's 'feet, and a light in all his paths'. This alone he receives as his rule of right or wrong, of whatever is really good or evil. He esteems nothing good but what is here enjoined, either directly or by plain consequence. . . . Whatever the Scripture neither forbids nor enjoins (either directly or by plain consequence) he believes to be of an indifferent nature, to be in itself neither good or evil: this being the whole and sole outward rule whereby his conscience is to be directed in all things.[43]

Here Wesley was speaking about ethical matters, but in fact his views are no different on theological matters. In a letter possibly written to John Clayton on March 28, 1739 he said: "I allow no other rule whether of faith or practice, than the Holy Scriptures."[44] In an even more emphatic and revealing remark in a letter written at a considerably later period in Wesley's life he said: "Now you and I are bigots to the Bible. We think the Bible language is like Goliath's sword, that 'there is none like it.'"[45] Wesley insisted that the Bible be the litmus test of all religious truth. If a person was arguing with Wesley about some controversial point Wesley would say repeatedly: "show me by plain proof of Scripture." This phrase, or one closely similar to it such as "to the law and the testimony," one finds peppered throughout Wesley's works.[46]

One final example will serve as well at this point. In a tract entitled "Popery Calmly Considered" Wesley said: "in all cases, the Church is to be judged by the Scripture, not the Scripture by the Church. And the Scripture is the best expounder of Scripture."[47] In Wesley's opinion, compared to Scripture there are no other giants in the land.[48] In this sense Wesley certainly affirmed the idea of *sola Scriptura*.

Whatever else one may want to say, there is no basis in Wesley for treating reason, experience, or even Christian antiquity as authorities on an equal plane with Scripture. Scripture, while not being the sole *source* of all truth, was certainly taken to be the final *arbiter* of truth on all matters which Scripture addressed. It is an open question whether Wesley would want to call even reason an "authority" or "rule" *per se*. At the same time, while Wesley was happy to talk about an infallible Scripture, he was well aware of both its need to be properly interpreted and of the fallibility of its various human interpreters. This meant that one must both consult and rely upon the best human commentators in one's study of the Scripture. Thus Wesley affirmed the value of what we call tradition, particularly exegetical tradition if one is to under-stand God's word. However, that tradition was to be critically sifted in the light of Scripture.

An interpretation or tradition was to be accepted only if it could either be confirmed in Scripture, or was a logical conse-quence or development of what Scripture said. This was no novel approach. Rather, Wesley simply affirmed his Anglican heritage in this regard: "Now it is a known principle of the Church of England, that nothing is to be received as an article of faith, which is not read in Holy Scripture, or to be inferred therefrom by just and plain consequence. . . ."[49] The way one discerned whether a tradition was true or not was this: "I lay this down as an undoubted truth—The more the doctrine of any Church agrees with Scrip-ture, the more readily ought it to be received. And on the other hand, the more a doctrine of any Church differs from Scripture, the greater cause we have to doubt it."[50]

Thus far Wesley may sound as though he could be accused of bibliolatry. This is to overlook two important factors. Wesley, unlike some of the earlier Protestant Reformers, was a true child of the Enlightenment. He had a very high view of the usefulness and general reliability of human reason. Second, into the tradi-tional Anglican triad to which one might appeal to make a point (Scripture, teachings of the Church, and reason) Wesley added a fourth—experience. Outler was quite right to say "It was Wesley's special genius that he conceived of adding 'experience' to the traditional Anglican triad, and thereby adding vitality without altering substance."[51] Neither Church teachings on doctrine and worship, nor reason, nor even experience was seen as an independent authority as Scripture was, but the witness of each was valued and frequently relied upon.

The primacy of Scripture, and even an affirmation of a form of the idea of *sola Scriptura*, did not prevent Wesley from drawing on these sources to confirm, compliment, supplement, or elucidate the Bible. What these sources were *not* called upon by Wesley to do was "correct" the Bible.[52] Rather, they might correct false interpretations of the Bible or confirm interpretations that might be difficult to accept otherwise.

This conclusion can be made clear in regard to the testimony of experience by two quotations. The first reveals that if Christian experience seemed to contradict a particular interpretation of a passage of Scripture, then one is to question neither the Scripture nor the validity of Christian experience but rather the *interpretation* placed on the relevant Scriptures. In his *A Plain Account of Christian Perfection* he says: "If I were convinced that none in England had attained what has been so clearly and strongly preached by a number of Preachers, in so many places and for so long a time, I should be clearly convinced that we had all mistaken the meaning of those scriptures."[53]

Debatable interpretations of Scripture needed confirmation, and Wesley was willing to say it needed to be confirmed by Christian experience. In his discussions with Peter Böhler about justification and inward assurance of salvation we find a very revealing admission by Wesley:

> When I met Peter Böhler again, he consented to put the dispute upon the issue which I desired, namely Scripture and experience. I first consulted the Scripture. But when I set aside the glosses of men, and simply considered the words of God, comparing them together, endeavoring to illustrate the obscurer passages by the plainer passages, I found they all made against me, and was forced to retreat to my last hold, 'that experience would never agree with the *literal interpretation* of those Scriptures.' Nor could I allow it to be true, till I found some living witnesses to it.[54]

When Wesley was convinced he had found such Christians who had the experience of justification and inward assurance of salvation his objections were at an end. Here the testimony of Christian experience is seen to be decisive in overcoming Wesley's reluctance to accept a literal interpretation of certain Biblical

65

texts. It may be well to add that what Wesley meant by experience is not simply human experience in general, as for instance we might mean when we use the expression "experience teaches us." He was referring the vast majority of the time to Christian experience, and within those parameters to specific sorts of Christian experiences—namely soteriological ones (e.g. the experience of the new birth, of assurance of salvation, of entire sanctification). His appeal most often was not to common sense but to a rather specific sort of Christian sense or experience.

This brings us at last to the place Wesley gave to reason. It is not difficult to find evidence that Wesley believed not only that the Christian faith was a rational one, but that reason played an important role in it. Even a cursory reading of *An Earnest Appeal to Men of Reason and Religion* makes this abundantly evident. Further, Wesley in his most important sermon on reason exclaimed: "Now of what excellent use is reason, if we would either understand ourselves, or explain to others those living oracles! And how is it possible without it to understand the essential truths contained therein."[55]

Reason is seen as an essential faculty for the Christian, and its proper use is of paramount importance. Its main use in Wesley's view was as a means of understanding, whereas the main cognitive benefit of Christian experience is to confirm or even to confute inwardly and personally what we have come to understand. To put it another way, knowledge of God both comes through spiritual experience and is confirmed by spiritual experience. It is generally clear that Wesley believed human reason to be usually reliable or trustworthy in most matters—" . . . in all duties of common life, God has given us our reason for a guide. And it is only by acting up to the dictates of it, by using all the understanding which God hath give us, that we can have a conscience void of offense towards God and towards man."[56]

Rex Matthews has helpfully summed up the way Wesley views reason and its function in human life:

> (1) Knowledge whether of the spiritual or the material world, depends upon the working of human reason. (2) Reason is "a faculty of the human soul" which has three functions: "simple apprehension," "judgment," and "discourse". . . . (3) Reasoning (or discourse) on any subject presupposes true judgments already formed. (4) the forming of true judgments depends on the

apprehension of clear, fixed, distinct, and determinate ideas. (5) There are no innate ideas: all ideas must originally come from sensory experience. Therefore: (6) If there is no sensory experience, there can be no apprehension, and so no judgment, and no discourse or "reasoning," and consequently, no knowledge.[57]

There are however clear limits to what reason can do. Wesley said: "Although it is always consistent with reason, yet reason cannot produce faith in the Scriptural sense of the word."[58] "Secondly, reason alone cannot produce . . . scriptural hope, whereby we 'rejoice in the hope of the glory of God; that hope which St. Paul in one place terms, tasting of the powers of the world to come. . . ."[59] "Thirdly, reason, however cultivated and improved, cannot produce the love of God . . . neither can it produce the love of our neighbor. . . ."[60] This in turn means that reason cannot produce virtue which flows from the disinterested love of God and neighbor, nor happiness since apart from Christian faith, hope, and love there can be no true human happiness. In short reason can not be a substitute for Christian experience which is caused by the work of the Holy Spirit in the individual. Yet it is equally true for Wesley that Christian experience is finally in accord with true reason and reasoning. To decry reason is mere enthusiasm in Wesley's view. It is to undercut an essential basis of Christian faith, for one cannot believe in something that one does not at least in part understand. One must have both Christian understanding and experience to live a life pleasing to God.

What, then, can be said of the quadrilateral? First, there is no place where Wesley speaks of Scripture, reason, tradition, and experience together, not even when he is discussing the question of authority in the Christian life. The closest example seems to be found in the title of his lengthy treatise on Original Sin, where he speaks of a joint appeal to Scripture, reason, and experience.[61] When he speaks of the matter of authority he says plainly: "I therein build on no authority, ancient or modern, but the Scripture. If this supports any doctrine, it will stand; if not the sooner it falls the better."[62] Or again, "The Scriptures are a complete rule of faith and practice; and they are clear in all necessary points."[63]

Thus, what we call the quadrilateral was surely for Wesley no equilateral, nor was it merely a mobile in which Scripture was the largest of the four elements. Furthermore, Wesley does not merely assert the primacy of Scripture as an authority. It is no mere *primes inter partes* for him. Rather it is clear that whatever authority reason, tradition, or experience may have they are not on the same plane as that of Scripture, not least because none of these other elements are seen as infallible.

A better model for construing the relationship of these four elements in Wesley's thought is as follows. Scripture is clearly central, and the final arbiter of all truth on which it discourses. What we have come to call tradition, reason, and experience should be seen in a two-fold fashion, First, they are windows on the central truth of Scripture, indeed necessary windows without which we would be unable to see into the Word of God. As Oswalt says, "while Reason, Experience, and Tradition provide the interpretive keys to the meaning of that Authority, they never stand on their own, independently of it, nor are they allowed to nullify it."[64] Second, reason, tradition, and experience for Wesley should be seen as avenues through which the central truth of Scripture can be expressed. Yet these three play different roles. By and large reason aids in the understanding of Scripture. Tradition functions in this way as well, providing information that may help in the proper interpretation of Scripture, but it also can serve the function of showing how Scripture has been and can be properly applied or expanded to meet new situations and contexts. Finally, the basic role of experience is to confirm the truth of Scripture in the believer's life, inwardly and personally.[65]

We would be amiss if we did not make clear what it is that links Scripture, Christian antiquity, reason, and experience in Wesley's thought. It is the Holy Spirit. We have already noted that Wesley had a theory of double inspiration. The Holy Spirit not only inspired the Biblical writer, that same Spirit illuminates and guides the believer's reason to properly understand the Word. But even more than this the Spirit is the agent which conveys and applies the truths of Scripture in the believer's life, whether that truth be the assurance of salvation or something else. It is the Spirit which creates faith, hope, and love in the believer by means of what Wesley called grace—the transforming power of God. These personal spiritual events are usually what Wesley means by "experience." Finally, it is the Spirit which guides the believer's reason to properly assess the value and truth content of tradition.

It is hardly surprising that Wesley was often accused of being an "enthusiast," the eighteenth-century buzz word for a religious fanatic. It was Wesley's views about the Spirit and its "witness" that made many rationalists both within and outside the Church break out in a rash. We would do well to thoroughly reassess Wesley's pneumatology if we wish to truly understand him. Certainly for Wesley proper evangelism could not take place unless the Spirit moved, however good our techniques might be, for it was the Spirit using the preacher as a vehicle to transform the human heart.

Suffice it to say that there is a place in Wesleyan theology for the use of all four elements in the modern quadrilateral as we undertake the tasks of evangelism. It would be a mistake, however, to underestimate how singularly crucial and central a role Wesley believed the Bible should play in this vital undertaking.

Soteriology and the Optimism of Grace

For Wesley the essential focus and function of the Scriptures was salvation. We are all by now very familiar with what Wesley said in the preface to his *Sermons on Several Occasions*:

> I want to know one thing, the way to heaven; how to land safe on that happy shore. God himself has condescended to teach the way; for this very end he came from heaven. He has written it down in a book. O give me that book! At any price give me the book of God! I have it: here is knowledge enough for me. Let me be *homo unius libri*.[66]

Wesley's assumption about the soteriological focus and function of Scripture affects not only the sort of hermeneutical moves he made in handling the Scripture, but the sort of information he believed one should expect to find in Scripture. The Bible is not, in Wesley's view, a compendium of all knowledge, but rather a collection of the historical, theological, and ethical truth one needs to know to be saved. In this more limited field of knowledge, the Bible is believed to be both completely true and fully trustworthy.[67] We have also noted how for Wesley the *analogia fidei* or general tenor of Scripture has to do with the *ordo salutis*.

Here we must consider Wesley's view of the work of Christ on the cross and the scope of salvation. When one deals with Wesley one deals with one form of the scandal of particularity so far as

69

the question of salvation is concerned. Outler was quite right that soteriology is at the heart of everything Wesley thought in regard to matters of evangelism.[68] In Wesley's view, those outside of Christ were lost and needed saving. Whatever truth, even religious truth, that might be found in other religions, salvation did not come through such truths.

If soteriology was believed by Wesley to be at the very heart of the Bible and of Christian faith, then the atoning death of Christ was at the very heart of that soteriology and as George Cell has said was "the burning focus of faith" for Wesley.[69] Wesley himself affirms that

> nothing in the Christian system is of greater consequence than the doctrine of the Atonement. It is properly the distinguishing point between Deism and Christianity . . . the only question with me [is] What saith the Scripture? It says, 'He was wounded for our transgressions and bruised for our iniquities'."[70]

And in his sermon on "The Means of Grace" Wesley says that "We allow farther that the use of all means whatever will never atone for one sin; that it is the blood of Christ alone whereby any sinner can be reconciled to God, there being no other propitiation for our sin and uncleanness."[71]

To those like William Law who protested the idea of propitiation Wesley responded:

> It is certain, had God never been angry, He could never have been reconciled. . . . Although therefore, I do not term God, as Mr. Law supposes 'a wrathful being,' which conveys a wrong idea; yet I firmly believe He was angry with all mankind, and that he was reconciled to them by the death of His Son. And I know he was angry with me till I believed in the Son of His love; and yet this is no impeachment to his mercy, that he is just as well as merciful.[72]

Wesley was reticent to involve himself in lengthy debates about various theories about *how* or *in what way* the death of Christ is atoning, but there were two things about which he was adamant: (1) the *fact* that Christ's death was the only necessary and sufficient means to atone for human sin; and (2) the scope of the finished work of Christ on the cross was broad. It was not God's design that any should perish, but rather that all should obtain eternal life. Christ's atoning death was *sufficient* to cover the sins of the world, *however* it was only *efficient* for those who believed in Christ. It is also true that the penal substitutionary view of atonement probably best describes Wesley's own views, for he clearly holds to a work of propitiation on the cross.

What Wesley said in the sermon, "God's Love to Fallen Man," is fairly typical of his thinking. In this sermon he quotes 1 Peter 2:24 and the Book of Common Prayer's Communion liturgy to the effect that " . . . we could not have loved him . . . [without his] 'bearing our sins in his own body on the tree,' and 'by that one oblation of himself once offered making a full oblation, sacrifice, and satisfaction for the sins of the whole world.'"[73] J. Deschner is also right that Wesley seemed especially indebted to Anselm in his view of the roles the humanity and the divinity of Christ both play on the cross.[74]

In one sense Wesley was a universalist—he believed in the universal scope of Christ's atoning death *in principle*. Furthermore, he believed that prevenient grace was also a benefit of the cross and thus even non- or pre-Christian people receive some benefit from Christ's atoning work.[75] Nevertheless, Wesley did not believe that one derived *saving* benefit from that death *unless* one appropriated those benefits through faith in Christ. Sermons like "The Great Assize" make abundantly evident that at the end of the day Wesley did not believe that all in fact *would* be saved. Thus the task of evangelism was of paramount importance. There was a lost world out there that could be saved, for God had not decreed in advance that any were unredeemable. Whether they would be saved depended on the proclamation of the Gospel and the response to that proclamation.

Eschatology and the Future of Evangelism

Our penultimate section in this essay must reflect on one of the most neglected areas of Wesleyan studies—Wesley's eschatology. Outler was fond of exhorting us to pay more attention to the later Wesley, and with good reason.[76] Some important aspects of Wesley's theology and preaching only come to the full light of day during the last four decades of Wesley's life. This is particularly the case in regard to Wesley's eschatology, which begins to become clear in the *Notes on the New Testament* which were largely composed while Wesley was ill in 1754–55, is further elucidated in the important sermon "The Great Assize" which was published in the summer of 1758 and included in the 1771 edition of the standard four volumes of Wesley's sermons,[77] and then appearing in close succession the sermons on "The Mystery of Iniquity" (May/June 1783 in the *Arminian Magazine*), on "The General Spread of the Gospel" (July/August, 1783 in the *Arminian Magazine*), and then finally on "The Signs of the Times" a sermon written and preached Aug. 27, 1787 which appeared in the Arminian Magazine the following spring.

What these resources show us is a mature Wesley who was increasingly interested in reflecting not merely on what may be called realized eschatology (the matters of the finished work of Christ both in history and in the present life of believers) but also on future eschatology—the return of Christ, the final judgment, the new heaven and the new earth, and also the events which would lead up to and be harbingers of the return of Christ.

If one begins with the *Notes on the New Testament*, one must also begin by keeping steadily in view the degree of debt Wesley has and admitted to having to a variety of earlier commentators on the Scriptures including Matthew Henry, Matthew Poole, John Guyse, John Heylyn, Philip Doddridge, and most especially J. A. Bengel.[78] This is an interesting and ecumenical collection of sources that is typical of Wesley's wide scope of reading and use of diverse resources.[79]

Wesley however made clear in his Preface to the *Notes* that he is indebted to Bengel above all others:

> But no sooner was I acquainted with that great light of the Christian world . . . Bengelius, than I entirely changed my design, being thoroughly convinced it might be of more service to the cause of religion, were I barely to translate his *Gnomon Novi Testamenti* than to write many volumes upon it. Many of his excellent notes I have therefore translated; many more I have abridged. . . .[80]

Close attention to the manner in which Wesley used Bengel by A. W. Harrison, among others,[81] has shown that while Wesley was heavily indebted to Bengel, he was no mere slavish copier of Bengel. He felt free to omit and amend Bengel where he chose so to do. The assumption then must be that when we come across something in Wesley's *Notes* that reflects a use of Bengel, we must assume it is because Wesley endorses Bengel's view on this or that matter, or at least he takes Bengel to be more likely correct than others.

This conclusion is confirmed in Wesley's own remarks in the Introduction to his comments on the Revelation. After admitting that he had for a long time despaired of understanding the prophecies in the Revelation, then he added that when he read Bengel's two great works (the *Gnomon*, but more particularly his *Ekklarte Offenbarung Johannes*, from which Wesley mostly draws here) "these revived my hopes of understanding even the prophecies of this book: at least many of them in some good degree."[82] In the same place Wesley makes clear that he does not undertake to defend all that he found in the *Ekklarte Offenbarung* but the "most necessary of his observations" he has undertaken to translate and to abridge. In short, what he includes here, he thinks is the best and most likely of Bengel's observations.[83]

It is necessary to make this plain for several reasons. First, Wesley, unlike various of his illustrious forbears who were Protestant reformers (including Calvin and Luther), not only dared to comment, but commented at length on the book of Revelation. Indeed Wesley in his *Notes* commented more on the Book of Revelation than any other single book in the NT canon, with the exception of his favorite Gospel—Matthew, and his favorite source on "primitive Christianity"—the book of Acts![84] Second, when we get to the comments on Revelation 9–13, we discover that Wesley reproduced Bengel's schema which includes the likelihood that 1836 is the time when the millennium will happen and the final events of human history will be ushered in.[85]

It might be possible to dismiss this as a mere reproduction of some speculation that Wesley found more plausible than other speculations except for two things: (1) Wesley was not generally given to speculative theology, but rather "plain truth for plain people"; and (2) when one investigates the later sermons of Wesley he drew on some of the ideas found in his *Notes* on the Revelation and assumes them to be true. Several examples will make this plain.

In the Sermon on "The Great Assize" Wesley warned his audience: "For yet a little while and 'we shall all stand before the judgment seat of Christ'."[86] In his sermon on 2 Thessalonians 2:7 entitled "The Mystery of Iniquity" he said that the mystery of iniquity is at work even now, even in the Churches of the

Reformation and thus he asked the question: "Is not this the 'falling away' or 'apostasy' from God foretold by St. Paul in his Second Epistle to the Thessalonians?"[87] This age of apostasy, even in the Church, is to be succeeded by a time where there is a general spread of the Gospel throughout the earth and Wesley opined: "And have we not farther ground for thankfulness yea and strong consolation in the blessed hope which God has given us that the time is at hand when righteousness will be as universal as unrighteousness is now?"[88] On this same theme the important sermon, "On the General Spread of the Gospel," which takes as its text Isaiah 11:9 ("The earth shall be full of the knowledge of the Lord, as the waters cover the sea") strongly suggests that the rise of the Methodist movement in Oxford in the 1730s and the spread of Methodism throughout the British Isles, and into America and elsewhere should be seen as the beginning of the fulfillment of Isaiah 11:9. Indeed Wesley, in a triumphalist mode said that Luther's belief that a revival only lasts a generation at most has been proved to be untrue in the case of the Methodist movement which had been going on and advancing for well over 50 years when he wrote "The General Spread of the Gospel."[89]

While Wesley allowed: "There will then very probably be a great shaking . . . [nonetheless] I can not induce myself to think that God has wrought so glorious a work to let it sink and die away in a few years. No; I trust this is only the beginning of a far greater work—the dawn of 'the latter day glory'."[90] The sermon concludes:

> All unprejudiced persons may see with their eyes that he is already renewing the face of the earth. And we have strong reason to hope that the work he hath begun he will carry on unto the day of the Lord Jesus; that he will never intermit this blessed work of his Spirit until he has fulfilled all his promises; until he has put a period to sin and misery, and infirmity, and death; and reestablished universal holiness and happiness, and caused all, the inhabitants of the earth to sing together 'Hallelujah!'[91]

In the much neglected sermon, "The Signs of the Times," Wesley clarified further how he viewed the times in which he lived. Though the sermon takes as its text Matthew 16:3, the theology found in this sermon draws heavily on Romans 11. In particular Wesley wished to assert that people have no excuse "for not discerning the signs of these times, as preparatory to the general call of the heathens? What could God have done which he hath not done to convince you that the day is coming, that the time is at hand, when he will fulfil his glorious promises; when he will arise to maintain his own cause, and to set up his kingdom over all the earth?"[92] In short, Wesley believed that his own time was the time immediately prior and preparatory to God's fulfilling the promise to bring in the full number of the Gentiles (Rom. 11:5) which in turn was prior to the salvation of "all Israel" as well (Rom. 11:26). Wesley is emphatic on this point—"I appeal to every candid, unprejudiced person, whether we may *at this day* discern all those signs (understanding the words in a spiritual sense) to which our Lord referred to John's disciples."[93]

At the very least it seems proper to draw the following conclusions: (1) Wesley thought it very possible, even likely, that the Methodist movement was part of the final great spreading of the Gospel throughout the earth that would precede the return of Christ. In short he believed in a golden age of evangelism preceding the end. This does not precisely correspond with later post-millennial speculations not least because Wesley's interpretation of Revelations 20 led him to expect a double millennium after Christ returned, and also he allowed that 'yet to come was a "great shaking" amongst believers'.[94] (2) In view of the fact that not all people had heard the Good News, and the end of the period when proclamation was possible might not be long off, there was a definite note of urgency (as well as of triumphalism) added to Wesley's approach to evangelism. It was in short a form of the classic exhortation "Repent for the reign of God is at hand." Whatever the merits of the thesis that Wesley in his early days advocated a sort of realized eschatology that focused almost exclusively on justification and sanctification, this thesis does not do justice to the mature Wesley, and in particular, Wesley in the very twilight of his career.

Conclusion: The Presuppositions of Proclamation

We have attempted to show that the theological roots of Wesley's view of evangelism are varied and somewhat complex. At the risk of oversimplifying the matter, we have seen that Wesley's epistemology in itself provided a strong impetus towards the task of evangelism. If there were no innate ideas of God, then religious truth had to be conveyed for human beings to know about it. Wesley's view of the Bible, which affirmed that the Scriptures were the very oracles of God, when coupled with his hermeneutical approach that stressed that one should take the plain or literal meaning of the text unless it implied some absurdity or contradicted some other clear portion of Scripture, led him to believe that it was the Bible people must hear proclaimed if they wished to be saved. It was the one book which could be counted on to tell the truth on how one may be saved. Furthermore, that same Bible in various places stressed that there was no salvation outside of Christ, making evangelism all the more an urgent task.

Yet it was not a task without good hope of success, for Wesley's soteriology led him to believe that God did not desire that any should be lost, but rather God provided an atoning work in Christ's death which was sufficient to cover the sins of the world. If the Gospel would only be proclaimed throughout the earth, then all peoples would have the opportunity, and with the aid of prevenient grace the means, to respond to the call to find salvation in the person and work of Christ.[95]

Wesley's eschatology also led him to believe that God would prosper the work of evangelism, even leading to a general spread of the Gospel prior to the return of Christ. Though in general he did not place a lot of stock in date-setting, Wesley did believe that the return of Christ *could* happen reasonably soon, especially if it was true that "the mystery of iniquity" was already at work both in the Church and in the world, and the time of the full number of Gentiles coming into the Church was soon to be at hand. This belief, especially in Wesley's later life, added a note of urgency to his exhortations that all Christians should in one way or another be devoted to and even involved in the spreading of the Good News.

The lessons to be learned from Wesley in these matters are numerous, but I should like to tentatively offer just a few. Much more important than style or technique to Wesley was the theological and ethical substance of evangelism. Indeed Wesley saw an ornate style as positively a hindrance to good evangelism in most cases. Rather there ought to be a commitment to "plain truth for plain people." If we hope to be successful in the tasks of evangelism then we must pay more attention to the substance of the proclamation, and not merely dwell on issues of style or strategy.

Furthermore, a general commitment to pluralism, in which everyone proclaims what is right in his or her own eyes, is hardly likely to get the job done. Lacking a coherent message about Christ to proclaim, the Methodist Church is likely to continue to appear to the world as a group that speaks out of both sides of its mouth. Rather, we must build on the good start made in the 1992 *Discipline* by making clear that Methodists do not merely have a way of doing theology and praxis, they have a unique and even powerful theological voice with which they may proclaim the Good News.

Geoffrey Wainwright and Albert Outler rightly insist that the only way forward is by means of a reappropriation of our past Christian theological heritage and in particular our Wesleyan heritage.[96] We need a center and source of theological and ethical unity in the midst of our diversity. At present we are only in the stage of the recovery of our heritage, through such projects as *The Works of John Wesley*. It is too soon to say what impact this will have on Methodism, and what use will be made of all these scholarly endeavors. It may be hoped, that among other things it will lead us to a form of proclamation that involves our really taking up the hermeneutical task of grappling with the deep and rich substance of Biblical revelation. May that substance become our sustenance as it was for Wesley, so that we may say of ourselves as well that we are people of that one great Book.

Furthermore, Wesley no doubt would urge us to think globally, dreaming big dreams of a world united in Christ. This was because he believed that the intent of God, the scope of the atonement, and the insistence on having the world as one's parish led one to think in the broadest possible terms in these matters. Wesley would not however have encouraged a false resolution of the scandal of particularity. Faith in Christ was necessary in Wesley's view for salvation. The character and basis of evangelism changes radically if it amounts to no more than informing people of what is already true about them, not only objectively in Christ but subjectively quite apart from faith in Christ. As Joe Hale says of Wesley:

His preaching was a consistent hammering home of four "alls" (*all* need to be saved; *all* can be saved; *all* can know they are saved; and *all* can be saved to the uttermost). . . . He was *not* enamored by novelty nor a devotee of the notion that because something is new, it is true. In all that transpired between John Wesley's reluctant visit to the society in Aldersgate Street where he felt his heart strangely warmed' and the time of his death in his City Road house fifty-three years later, he was an evangelist. No other objective he pursued came close to his passion to see a rebirth of vital religion. He was convinced that the message of unmerited grace offered a different life to people and that new Christians drawn together in small disciplined classes could bring change in the nation.[97]

A commitment to a particular Gospel, or better said a Gospel of Christian particularism, like that which Wesley preached, does not however require us to be committed to the sort of narrow-minded approach that suggests that Christians have a corner on all religious truth. Far from it, since surely all truth is God's truth where ever it may be found. It does, however, commit us to the recognition that inter-faith dialogue is just that—a dialogue between faiths that differ on various matters, including the means of salvation. At the end of the day, Christians and others will surely have to agree to disagree on various important matters, while still being able to recognize important areas of concord and shared values as well. This is simply a matter of intellectual honesty.

In point of fact, all three of the major monotheistic world religions have a scandal of particularity with which they need to come to grips. Devout practicing Jews believe they are God's chosen ones in a way that is not true of other peoples. Devout practicing Christians believe that Jesus is the unique savior of the world. Devout Moslems affirm that Mohammed in a unique way is God's true prophet and that earlier forms of monotheism must be reinvisioned through the true and perfect revelation found in the Koran. These claims are at crucial points not reconcilable. Any theology of Christian evangelism that does not look long and hard at what it is willing to say is theologically and ethically a given and what is not a *sine qua non* of the Christian faith, is taking up the task of a disciple without first assessing the cost. This is especially the case in a world that becomes more of a global village every moment.

Hale's remarks also remind us that Wesley would not have been satisfied with an evangelism that did not entail a transformation not only of the hearts but also the very daily lives of the people who responded to it. Salvation must not be so narrowly defined that it amounted only to either a salvation of souls, or merely to an improvement of the physical circumstances in which one lived. When *both* structural reformation and spiritual renewal took place in the community of faith, Wesley believed the larger society would see a witness of the Christ-like character all human beings are called to model.

Wesley's vision was that human transformation including the transformation of the structures of human society was to happen by reformation within, not by revolution against the society. In Wesley's view, the chief means of improving society was by converting people to Christ and thus changing their character. It is an open question how much the Church, especially in the West in the late twentieth century, simply models a conforming to the larger culture's values and agendas, and how much it still holds forth the transforming vision of a community transfixed and transfigured by the saving work of Christ.

The question of the Church's priorities must also be put. Wesley reminds us that the early Church was essentially a missionary venture, which also, as a by-product, was in the business of nurturing those who are already Christians. The modern Church by contrast overwhelmingly spends its time and money not on evangelism and mission ventures of various sorts, but on nurturing itself. Wesley was famous for asking pointed questions and in this case he might well ask us "How is it that you have taken food out of the mouths of the poor and spiritual food away from those who have never heard of Christ, in order to spend endlessly on the upkeep of buildings and programs that only really benefit yourselves? In what way is the self-sacrificial love of Christ modeled by this sort of behaviour?"[98]

Finally the question of practicality also arises. Wesley's view of the structures that serve the people of God was a pragmatic one. He believed in using what worked, and changing what didn't. The problem for western Methodism at the close of the twentieth century is that it has so sacralized its structures it has made it difficult if not impossible to change. Buildings have become "churches," instead of the Biblical vision where only the people of God, or in particular the people of God gathered, is the *ekklesia*. The "edifice complex" of the Western Church, including Western Methodists, has meant that the task of evangelism becomes difficult if not impossible to implement. With an ever-shifting population, we end up having people where there are few church buildings, and church buildings where there are few people.

Because of being so tied to our buildings we are not flexible enough to be truly itinerant and move with the shifts in population. On the global scale of things, the fact that we Western Methodists often put seventy percent or more of our budget into the maintenance of our own buildings makes it very difficult to adequately fund many worthy projects ranging from the relief efforts of UMCOR, to the Africa University, to traditional missionary work.

Those of us who are Western Methodists must also ask ourselves, is Christ calling us to a Gospel of conspicuous consumption or of self-sacrificial giving? Certainly Wesley called his first followers to live a *simple* life style and so free up one's resources to help others both materially and spiritually. This sort of lifestyle evangelism, especially in an America where materialism is seen as a virtue not a vice, is of critical importance as we look toward the new century.

Though Wesley's thoughts on evangelism need to be carefully and critically sifted so we may see whether and in what way they may apply in our situation, it must be said in closing that it appears that it is not so much the case that Wesley's ideas have been tried and found wanting, as that we have ceased to try and apply them in any consistent way. Were we to do so, we too might rediscover what it means to claim the world as our parish.

CHAPTER 4

Proclaiming the Gospel of Grace

Kenneth L. Carder

Introduction

A hint of hesitation marked my initial approach to the task of addressing the issue of Wesley's evangelical preaching. My first, unspoken response, was a question: What does one who has always been involved in the ministry of the local church have to say to respected Wesleyan scholars and renowned connectional church leaders? Upon reflection, however, I concluded that my hesitation exposes a dangerous chasm which this volume of essays can help to bridge—a chasm between the church and the academy, and the church and connectional agencies. Unless the academy, the local church, and connectional structures converge in the proclamation of the gospel of grace, the whole evangelistic enterprise is likely to fail from either an irrelevant intellectualism, or a pietism without substance, or an institutionalism without either intellect or piety. So, I have concluded that pastors are a necessary part of this dialogue.

To discuss theology and evangelism in the Wesleyan tradition without a focus on the proclamation of grace in the context of the local community of faith would be a contradiction. Wesley's own grace-warmed heart, his interest in "practical divinity," his preoccupation with "holiness of heart and life," and his conviction that God had raised up the Methodists as means of reforming the nation and the church prevent evangelism and theology from being mere topics of intellectual debate, or programmatic schemes for institutional growth, or homiletical styles polished to appeal to the masses. Evangelism and theology in the Wesleyan tradition have to do with presenting the gospel of God's grace in all of its redeeming and transforming dimensions. Wesley believed God wills that all should be *saved, redeemed* and *shaped* by God's grace revealed and mediated in Christ. Whether they are saved depends partly upon proclamation, response, and nurture in community. Consideration of the proclamation of the gospel of grace is, therefore, a necessary component of any serious discussion of evangelism and theology in the Wesleyan spirit.

Wesley as Proclaimer

John Wesley's enormously productive ministry as evangelist, theologian, missionary, prophet, writer, teacher, administrator, and witness/friend to the marginalized all evolve around his central identity and role as a *preacher*. In his Journal, July 28, 1757, he wrote: "About noon I preached at Woodseats, in the evening at Sheffield. I do indeed live by preaching."[1] Even before he left England for America he wrote in a letter to John Burton, "My tongue is a devoted thing."[2] He considered *preaching* the principal means by which converts are gathered into Christian fellowship and nurtured in faith and holy living. Wesley considered that the primary business of apostles, evangelists, and bishops in the early church was to "preach the Word of God."[3] For Wesley, preaching served two basic purposes: to convert and to nurture. It would appear that his oral sermons, which were extemporaneously delivered without notes, a technique he learned at Oxford and practiced as early as November 10, 1734,[4] were for the purpose of proclamation and invitation. His written sermons, according to Albert Outler, were for the purpose of teaching and nurture.[5]

The primary source for understanding Wesley's theology is his preaching. His *Sermons on Several Occasions* remain among the standards for United Methodist doctrinal grounding and theological exploration, and they were important tools by which early Methodists were nurtured in the faith. Wesley described "the best method of preaching" as: (1) to invite, (2) to convince, (3) to offer Christ, (4) to build up, and "to do this (in some measure) in every sermon."[6] Since Wesley preached to people on the move, it was important that every sermon proclaim the essential gospel. Therefore, Wesley's sermons usually contain a synopsis of the essence of his gospel message.

He considered the particular "Methodist way of preaching Christ" as the reason for the growth of the Methodist movement. The essential elements of "the Methodist way of preaching" included a "plain style" as contrasted with a classical style which depended upon image, intricate, philosophical reasoning, and evidences of classical education; and it included an emphasis on salvation by faith, preceded by repentance, and followed by holiness.[7] Wesley considered the matter of *style* in preaching as a moral issue. He wrote, "I dare no more write in a 'fine style' than wear a fine coat. . . ."[8] Although a learned man, he was willing to forego any outward show of learning so as not to detract his readers or listeners. He wrote in "The Preface" to the first volume of *Sermons on Several Occasions*:

> I design plain truth for plain people. Therefore of set purpose I abstain from all nice and philosophical speculations, from all perplexed and intricate reasoning, and as far as possible from even the show of learning, unless in sometimes citing the original Scriptures. I labor to avoid all words which are not easy to be understood, all which are not used in common life; and in particular those kinds of technical terms that so frequently occur in bodies of divinity, those modes of speaking which men of reading are intimately acquainted with, but which to common people are an unknown tongue.[9]

Style for Wesley was no substitute for substance, and one could speculate as to Wesley's commentary on the contemporary emphasis on images and narratives designed to communicate to a generation accustomed to dramatic television images and clever sound bites. One could be sure that Wesley would be unimpressed with clever sermons without theological depth designed to entertain the masses.

The effectiveness of Wesley's preaching, however, lay not in the sermon's literary style or the eloquence of the preacher. Historians agree that he was not the most exciting or eloquent preacher of his time. Wesley's own explanation for the lasting influence of his preaching was that he preached "Christ in all his offices," plus the Methodist system of pastoral care and Christian nurture which formed the people into a community that provided support and accountability.[10] Preaching was not a "hit and run" operation; instead, it was re-enforced by the societies and class meetings in which converts were taught the faith, nurtured, admonished, and held accountable.

The Theme of Wesley's Preaching

Albert Outler summarized Wesley's effectiveness as a preacher in these words: "More than anything else it was Wesley's *message* that struck home: people not excited by his eloquence were moved by his vision of the Christian life and his gospel of universal redemption."[11] The heart of Wesley's preaching was a lively sense of God's grace at work at every level of creation and history in individuals and communities. Central to his own life and preaching was "the order of salvation," how individuals and communities experience the fullness of God's prevenient, justifying, and sanctifying grace. Holiness of heart and life was what he desired for himself and all people, and his preaching reflected such a passion formed and driven by the grace of God. His proclamation included an emphasis on law (Christ's commands) and grace (Christ's promises). He confronted people with God's judgment as a call to turn toward God's justifying and sanctifying grace.

Wesley's preaching elicited the most positive response among the poor and marginalized. His message of universal redemption and sufficient grace in all and irresistible grace in none opened the door for men and women who had been marginalized by eighteenth-century English society. The poor were excluded from the political process and from many of the protections of common law. Victims of social and economic dislocation were relegated to the outskirts of the great cities and the mining communities in Cornwall and the North. Exploitation and deprivation stripped them of dignity and self-respect and many escaped in drunkenness and sensuality. Wesley went among this new underclass, warned of the judgment of God and proclaimed a gospel of justifying grace which bears fruit in holy living. He gathered those who responded to the gospel of grace into new groups in which each person found acceptance, a new sense of dignity, and a community which held them accountable.

Wesley's preaching was heard by the poor partly because of his relationship with them. He preached equality among God's children, and his love for the poor provided fertile soil in which preaching the gospel of grace took root and flourished. Whereas Whitefield and most of the other evangelists found their constituencies largely among the rising middle class and lesser nobility, Wesley planted the Methodist societies in pockets of poverty and nourished them with the gospel of justifying and sanctifying grace. In a letter to Dorothy Furly, dated September 25, 1757, he declared: "I love the poor; in many of them I find pure, genuine grace, unmixed with paint, folly, and affectation."[12] To Ann Foard he wrote in 1769: "I *bear* the rich and love the poor; there, I spend almost all my time with them."[13] The poor, therefore, were not only beneficiaries of Wesley's proclamation of grace, they were channels of that grace to Wesley. The poor and marginalized helped to shape the central theme of his preaching: God's prevenient, justifying, and sanctifying grace which transforms individuals and societies.

Challenges to Wesley's Proclamation of Grace

The Methodist way of preaching grace, however, was in jeopardy in Wesley's own lifetime. Proclaiming the gospel confronted several threats, which continue among the twentieth-century heirs of the Wesleyan revival. One of the threats originated with the so-called gospel preachers. These "gospel preachers," Wesley believed, emphasized the promises of Christ without the commands. They preached grace apart from law, justification without sanctification:

> The gospel preachers, so-called, corrupt their hearers; they vitiate their taste, so that they cannot relish sound doctrine; and spoil their appetite, so that they cannot turn it into nourishment; they, as it were, feed them with sweetmeats, till the genuine wine of the kingdom seems quite insipid to them. They give them cordial upon cordial, which make them all life and spirit for the present; but, meantime, their appetite is destroyed, so that they can neither retain nor digest the pure milk of the word.[14]

Wesley described one such preacher, James Wheatley, as one "who never was clear, perhaps not sound, in the faith. According to his understanding was his preaching, an unconnected rhapsody of unmeaning words, like Sir John Suckling's 'Verses, smooth and soft as cream / In which was neither depth nor stream.'"[15] Wesley considered such preaching of grace without law deadly even

85

though it received popular following. Such popular preaching, according to Wesley, harms the preachers by fostering personal exaltation and self-righteousness, and it harms the hearers by substituting superficial religiosity for sound doctrine and holy living and by creating temporary excitement without sustaining power.

In a "Letter on Preaching Christ," dated December 20, 1751, Wesley gives his most concise and provocative challenge regarding grace. He makes a rather strained and potentially misleading distinction between "preaching the gospel" and "preaching the law." He defines preaching the gospel as "preaching the love of God to sinners, preaching the life, death, resurrection, and intercession of Christ, with all the blessings which, in consequence thereof, are freely given to true believers."[16] Preaching the law, on the other hand, is "explaining and enforcing the commands of Christ, briefly comprised in the Sermon on the Mount."[17] Wesley contends that the right method of preaching is this:

> At our first beginning to preach at any place, after a general declaration of the love of God to sinners, and his willingness that they should be saved, to preach the law, in the strongest, the closest, the most searching manner possible; only intermixing the gospel here and there, and showing it, as it were, afar off. After more and more persons are convinced of sin, we may mix more and more of the gospel, in order to 'beget faith', to rein into spiritual life those whom the law hath slain; but this is not to be done too hastily either.[18]

Preaching the law, according to Wesley, avoids "healing the wounds of the people lightly." Although he affirms that "the law is not to be preached as the cause of their acceptance with God but the fruit of such acceptance," it appears, on the surface at least, that the law is the prelude to grace. However, Wesley's concept of "covered commands" avoid the trap of making the law as the prelude to justification. For Wesley, all commands of Christ are "covered" by God's grace which empowers us to live the commands. The commands, then, are part of the promises and privileges of grace, rather than preconditions for grace. Furthermore, preaching the law avoids limiting grace to justification and a superficial pious narcissism which substitutes subjectivity for holiness of heart and life. As he expressed in "Thoughts Concerning Gospel Ministers": Who is a gospel preacher? "Not every one that preaches justification by faith; he that goes no farther than this, that does not insist upon sanctification also, upon all the fruits of faith; upon universal holiness, does not declare the whole counsel of God, and consequently is not a Gospel minister."[19]

Wesley further avoided legalism in his emphasis on preaching the law by stating explicitly that the preacher is "to declare, explain, and enforce every command of God; but, meantime, to declare, in every sermon, (and the more explicitly the better), that the first and great command to a Christian is, 'Believe in the Lord Jesus Christ'; that Christ is all in all, our 'wisdom, righteousness, sanctification, and redemption'; that all life, love, strength, are from him alone, and all freely given to us through faith."[20] The *commands of Christ,* therefore, are *gifts of a relationship with Christ.*

The "gospel preachers" of Wesley's day preached a love of God which failed to include the judgment of God. Theirs was a "cheap grace" which made no demands and which ignored God's wrath. In other words, grace without law, promises without commands, removed the dimension of accountability to God and the broader community. Membership in the societies, however, was open to all, "who desire to flee from the wrath to come." Wesley knew that without a clear sense of accountability to God, preaching grace loses some of its transforming power over persons and structures. Some of Wesley's assistants, and possibly Wesley himself, at times, went to an extreme in preaching God's wrath at the expense of God's love. Wesley warned that leaning to such an extreme results in the loss of the joy of faith. He contended that preaching the "terrors of the Lord to those who know they are accepted" is folly; "for love is to them the strongest of all motives."[21]

Another hindrance or obstacle to the preaching of grace faced by Wesley and the eighteenth-century Methodists is identified in Wesley's sermon dated July 2, 1789, "Causes of the Inefficacy of Christianity." The Christian gospel has within it the seeds of ineffectiveness. Christian faith leads to diligence and frugality, which in turn often result in wealth and worldly success. Wealth and success then lead to the presumption of self-sufficiency and independence. In other words, affluence and success made the early Methodists less responsive to the gospel of grace. It is at this point, where Wesley bemoans the growing unresponsiveness of the long-time Methodists of his era, that contemporary preachers of grace face their most formidable challenge, at least in the American church.

Obstacles to Preaching Grace in the Contemporary World

Contemporary American preachers of grace confront a secular culture in which both law and grace have been severed from theological roots. Traditional theological concepts of salvation, works righteousness, the judgment of God, and justifying and sanctifying grace have been replaced with their secular counterparts. Self-esteem, self-fulfillment, self-actualization, peace of mind, and the gospel of prosperity are contemporary substitutes for salvation. Success, achievement, winning are secular versions of works righteousness. Salaries, titles and degrees, scores on standardized academic and psychological tests, prestigious positions and political power are the outward and visible signs of personal worth and well-being. Failure is feared more than sin; shame and embarrassment for not measuring up are more painful than guilt. And a just God who holds people accountable is relegated to the superstitious past or to the unsophisticated religious fringes.

Grace when preached in contemporary American culture tends to be little more than narcissistic self-indulgence or a form of superficial self-acceptance based on the illusion of "I'm okay and you're okay." Hope, in this secular version of salvation through success and self-fulfillment, emerges from a blind optimism based on thinking positive thoughts and an escapist lifestyle, rather than being considered a gift from God who shares the world's tragedy and transforms crosses and tombs into doorways into a new heaven and a new earth. In our culture, happiness results from having, and Wesley's notion that happiness and holiness are inextricably linked is foreign to dominant modern Methodist thinking.

The institutional church has been captured by the secular value of success, achievement, power, and prominence. The current survival mentality and preoccupation with statistical growth are evidences that The United Methodist Church defines itself more as a social institution competing for its share of the religious market than as a community of grace devoted to personal and social transformation through living out God's graceful vision for the world. Preaching is judged more by its ability to attract the masses than by its theological integrity. The sociology of church growth has replaced the theology of personal and social transformation. It is indeed a sad commentary on the state of contemporary preaching that United Methodist preachers are more familiar with pop sociology than with the theology of John Wesley. This preoccupation with institutional power and statistics contributes to preaching that is heavy on institutional promotion and narcissistic self-help and light on individual and communal salvation.

Another obstacle to proclaiming grace in contemporary American culture is the presence of a political, economic, and technological triumphalism. Recent events in eastern Europe and what was the Soviet Union, coupled with military conquests in Grenada, Panama, and the Persian Gulf have reinforced an idolatrous notion that salvation results from having a superior political and economic system supported by technological sophistication and military might. This triumphalism was expressed by a president of the United States in a State of the Union address. He said, "By the grace of God we won the cold war." Then he proceeded to immediately extol the power of the American military. Is the "grace of God" to be casually reduced to rhetoric by which we sell our political agendas? A culture that worships regularly at the altars of political and economic ideologies and military conquest has difficulty hearing a message about the transforming and renewing power of unconditional, suffering love freely given to all people. People who everywhere are valued for what they know, what they produce, how they look, and where they fit in have enormous difficulty hearing, much less believing, a message about self-worth rooted in being claimed and empowered by the holy and loving God. When the religious airwaves are filled with slick messages of hope based on "be happy attitudes" and success through positive thinking, it is near impossible to hear a word of hope from a cross or a graveyard. But the difficulty of the task of preaching grace makes it all the more important. In this culture, the word of grace is a prophetic word for it challenges the prevailing values. In the proclamation of a gospel of grace the evangelist and social activist join voices.

Preaching Grace Today

How is the gospel of grace to be preached today? Here we can learn from Wesley without imitating him. First, grace in its full dimensions must be the central underlying theme of our preaching. A recovery of our theological and doctrinal moorings is necessary. Wesley was asked "Why is it that people under our care are no better?" He responded that the chief reason is "because we are not more knowing and more holy."[22] He proceeded to admonish the preachers to study at least five hours every day and devote time every day to prayer and reflection. The current trend among pastors and congregations is to devote prime time to institutional maintenance and administrative tasks, and the hierarchy of the church tends to reinforce and support such use of time. In my thirty years as a pastor I have had one district superintendent and one bishop to admonish me to study. I have yet to have any connectional leader seek to hold me accountable for the theological integrity of my preaching. Wesley held his preachers accountable for the understanding of and proclamation of the gospel of grace. He was not timid about challenging a preacher who substituted appealing platitudes for sound doctrine. If grace is to be preached, *preachers must know* from personal experience and intellectual discernment *what grace is*, be supported in their preaching of it, and be expected to exhibit theological integrity. If the gospel of grace is to be proclaimed, it will be done by preachers who take such a gospel with utmost seriousness. And, local congregations must be vital centers of doctrinal clarification and theological exploration.

Second, proclaiming prevenient, justifying, and sanctifying grace requires that the preacher be aware of the secular form in which the need for that gospel is couched. The consequences of salvation sought through success and achievement and triumphalism are the same as those resulting from works righteousness—alienation, stress, meaninglessness, shame—which masks guilt, self-justifying behavior, and the marginalizing of persons who fail to measure up. Middle-class, upwardly mobile, success-oriented adults and youth who comprise our church membership are a fertile evangelistic field for the message heard and experienced of an identity rooted in God's gracious gift and a life devoted to living out that identity.

Third, the proclamation of the gospel of grace must be supported and lived out in the structures of the congregation's life. Recovery of small groups in which unconditional love and accountability are experienced is necessary in order for preaching to have sustaining power. Covenant disciple groups, Bible study groups, and support groups are all hopeful signs. The inclusiveness of a church's fellowship provides a climate for experiencing the depth and breadth of grace as barriers crumble and diversity becomes a means of nurture and a prophetic witness to a fragmented world. Church growth based on homogeneity must, therefore, be resisted as a deterrent to the proclamation of the gospel of grace.

Fourth, a relationship with the poor and marginalized is necessary if we are to preach effectively the gospel of grace. The poor may be the means to our salvation. Wesley's own relationship with the poor helped to shape his preaching. The poor and marginalized, which is one of the fastest growing segments of the world's population, may be our best hope for the recovery of the message of grace.

The church that I served for several years before my election to the episcopacy is being changed by a small group who gather on Thursday evenings for worship. Most of the thirty to forty who attend live in the streets and local shelters. They come to the soup kitchen each week and are greeted by a staff of volunteers and one of the clergy. Preaching to these persons represents a challenge to those of us who every Sunday preach to middle-class, well-educated, predominantly professional persons who comprise Church Street's membership. But those services are among the most grace-filled which I have ever experienced. Permit me to share a couple of incidents that have altered my own experience of grace and the preaching of it.

One cold winter evening a man came to the service barefoot. Immediately we all noticed. The more affluent among us began to scurry around to find shoes for him. We couldn't find any in the church. The stores were closed, so we couldn't go out and purchase them. Another man who lives in low-income housing and who joined Church Street, went to the shoeless man and said, "Take my shoes. I have another pair at home." He did spontaneously what those of us who have several pairs of shoes never thought of doing. Why? He knew what it was to be shoeless.

91

He identified with the one with no shoes. The sermon that night was infused with new power because grace created a climate of divine presence and power.

During the Thursday service each week, there is a period of community prayers. On a typical evening these were among the petitions: Royetta, whose children are in custody of the Department of Human Services because she doesn't have the mental or financial means to care for them, prayed: "O God, help my children's new parents to love them better than I can." Eleanor, who staggers because of brain damage, said: "Lord, make people stop treating me like I'm drunk when I stagger." Fred pleaded: "O Lord, help me get through another day without drinking." A professor at the university then prayed: "O God, thank you for your grace which makes us all your children." The sermon that night was from 1 John 3:1-2, "Beloved we are God's children now; it does not yet appear what we shall be but when he appears we shall be like him for we shall see him as he is." The prayers preached grace before the preacher said anything.

Recovery of an ongoing, personal relationship with the poor may be the best means of proclaiming the gospel of grace in this age. Wesley believed the biblical theme that God is among the poor. It is the poor who strip us of our idols of self-sufficiency, achievement, and success and put us in touch with grace.

Further, proclaiming grace in a generation of secular works righteousness involves identifying idols more than preaching the law. Wesley is correct in insisting that grace and law, promises and commands, are part of the same fabric. However, an emphasis on the commands of God in this secular age will only be dismissed as moralism or treated as another means of being successful; or it will intensify shame and fear more than motivate authentic repentance. A more effective homiletical approach is the identification of the success orientation as the counterpart of preaching the law, providing insight as to how grace heals our whole narcissistic orientation, and sharing God's vision of life and the world transformed by grace. Preaching which avoids false dichotomies between grace and law, faith and works, and which maintains "promises" and "commands" as indivisible manifestation of Divine Grace will counter the "cheap grace" and "the gospel of prosperity" heard too frequently in our culture.

Finally, proclaiming the gospel of grace requires that

preaching focus on the transforming reality of grace in the lives of persons and societies rather than reducing preaching to a means of institutional promotion. Growth based on preaching "cheap grace" or in the words of Wesley "Promises without commands," or growth based on clever and entertaining sermons will be at best shortlived and at worst demonic. Wesley compared the rapid growth and equally rapid decline of the societies led by the "gospel preachers" with the societies in Yorkshire under the care of John Nelson:

> From the beginning they [those under Nelson's care] had been taught both the law and the gospel "God loves you; therefore, love and obey him. Christ died for you; therefore, rise in the image of God. Christ liveth evermore; therefore, live to God, till you live with him in glory. This is the scriptural way, the Methodist way, the true way. God grant that we may never be turned away therefrom, to the right hand or to the left.[23]

Conclusion

Preaching the gospel of grace has always been a primary and formidable task of the church. One of the earliest proclaimers of grace wrote: "God decided, through the foolishness of our proc-lamation, to save those who believe" (1 Cor. 1:21, NRSV). Both the method and the message have always seemed foolish by the prevailing culture. Proclaiming the gospel in the latter decade of the twentieth century faces no less formidable obstacles than were confronted by Paul in the first century or Wesley in the eighteenth century.

Preaching grace effectively today calls for a renewed emphasis on theological depth, integrity, and accountability on the part of church leadership. If grace is to be proclaimed in its personal and prophetic power, the emphasis at all levels of church leadership must shift from the survival mentality and success orientation of institutionalism to faithfulness rooted in grateful response to God whose grace seeks the transformation of the world.

Bringing together diverse representatives from the church's academy, bureaucracy, and local congregations to struggle with theology and evangelism in the Wesleyan tradition has the poten-tial of contributing to the renewal of Methodism's mission of reforming the nations, beginning with the church, and spreading scriptural holiness throughout the lands. God grant that it will be so!

CHAPTER 5

Reflections on the Essence of and Methodology for Global Evangelization

H. Mvume Dandala

Introduction

It was two or three years ago that the Institute for World Evangelism stressed the need for the development of a theologically based evangelistic thrust both for us as a world Methodist community as well as regional Methodist communities. It was emphasized that theological thinking with regards to evangelism needed to be reinforced at theological schools, and that theological reflection occasions should be encouraged for seminary professors with a distinct aim to focus them on holistic evangelism and their role in the resuscitation of an evangelistically focused outreach by our church. It is thus a real privilege for one to be involved in a venture which shares the same sentiments.

It is appropriate, I believe, for me to begin by explaining my choice of the term evangelization over against the term evangelism, because for me the implications are pertinent for what we do globally. In essence, there are three major concerns that are raised by the term evangelism.

The first concern is that in our age of ideologies evangelism can easily be construed as yet another "ism." This in turn increases the chances for unnecessary blockages in the minds of those we wish to introduce to Christ. As Karl Barth argued strongly for the distinctiveness of Christian faith over against "religions," I believe it to be essential for the character of the Gospel to be kept as distinct as possible from ideologies.

The second concern is closely linked with the first, in that very often the Church, especially the local church, has been tempted to view evangelism as a recruitment strategy for increasing membership. While this may be one of the spin-offs of evangelism, it is unacceptable to see evangelism in these terms. The disadvantages are clear. Churches look at evangelism as a project for certain periods in the calendar of the church, and for the rest of the time they carry on with their internal projects as if they have no obligations to the work outside their structures. In this way evangelism becomes a seasonal activity, which can be set in time boundaries. This further raises problems of theological definition. What exactly do we mean by evangelism? The general response is often that evangelism refers to the "verbal" proclamation of the word, with the purpose of bringing people into the faith community. I believe evangelism to be concerned about the total transformation of the world for God. The usage of the word evangelization seeks to stress a continuous process whose ultimate goal is not simply larger churches, but the transformation of the world.

The third concern is that the transformation of the world is indeed a process that is more than the transformation of individual people, even though it recognizes the centrality of human beings in creation and for the process of global transformation itself. It is beyond dispute that the life and behavior of humans is inextricably linked to processes that are outside that individual person's scope of activity. If the intention of evangelism is thus to lead the whole of creation, including human beings to attain holiness in Christ, perfection as Mr. Wesley put it, the question is whether the transformation intended can happen only as we focus on individuals, or the entire creation, in our evangelism. I wish to argue in favor of the latter: a focus on the entire creation. To achieve this, our thinking has to be in "process" terms, hence my choice for the word evangelization.

In sum, the challenge before us is for an approach to evangelization that will demonstrate the "supra-ideological" character of the Gospel of Jesus Christ, that will give rise to a zeal for the transformation of the world for the purpose of reconciliation between God, humankind and the entire creation. The question before us is whether the Church of Christ can respond realistically to this kind of challenge. I believe it can, and the World Methodist Council has currently chosen to embark creatively on this venture.

The Motive and Intention for Evangelization

There are five elements that constitute the motive for evangelization.

(1) *A sense of compulsion.* The first is a sense of compulsion to share the gift of the Gospel, the sheer wonder of the person of Jesus Christ. Eddie Fox and George Morris refer to this sense of compulsion as "God's Idea." It is God's idea that the good news be shared, and this leaves the followers of Jesus Christ no option but to share the good news.

(2) *Divine encounter.* God is in a constant encounter with his people wherever they are, urging them all the time to find a response to Himself. God's encounter does *not* begin at the moment of evangelization. John Wesley had a central focus in his theology of salvation and that was the doctrine of *prevenient grace.* Briefly put, this doctrine states the saving work of Christ begins with the first dawning of grace in the soul.[1] In other words, even before we are moved to repentance, the grace of God is reaching out to us. "Christ died for us while we were yet sinners and that is God's own proof of his love towards us" (Rom. 8:5). Prevenient grace in the English of Wesley's time means the grace of God moving out ahead—preparing the way, going before the Christian. So the Holy Spirit is striving with all people, to convince them that Christ is the Savior. He is already at work in the life of all men and women. We are being called to co-operate with the Holy Spirit in this work. It does not all depend upon us—we have to learn how to take the work of the Holy Spirit seriously and how to rejoice in the fact that God goes before us and that we are privileged to be considered to be worthy of being called into a co-operative partnership in establishing God's rule and kingdom on earth. This in turn necessitates a humility in the evangelist facilitating dialogue with those being approached with the Gospel, precisely because of the acknowledgement of prevenient grace.

(3) *Translation.* In essence the Gospel is about the happening of God's will in a way that is understandable to God's creation.

The incarnation is God's self-revelation through Jesus, by taking upon Himself flesh. It is a process of translation into terms that we can understand. Evangelization thus has to be transnational. It has to demonstrate the good news in the language and context of the people to whom it is preached. Lamin Sanneh correctly argues that to practice translation is not simply a strategy for evangelization, but is the essence of the Christian gospel.

(4) *Service.* The basic premise for evangelization is that we work because God is already present and at work among God's people. God has promised to be constantly present with the people (Matt. 1:23, John 1:14, Rom. 8, etc.). God's presence is inseparable from the witness to God and the divine salvific activity. This in turn implies that evangelism is more than just the verbalization of the good news. Rather it is also the demonstration or actualization of God's presence among God's people through Christ. This demands of the evangelizing church an active commitment to service. In a servant church, the Gospel becomes credible as it expresses itself not only in words, but also in liberating and empowering action whether the people respond to it or not.

(5) *Fulfillment.* The fulfillment of evangelization is in the unity and reconciliation of the entire creation in the Godhead (Eph. 1:1-9, Rev. 21:1-5). It is indeed correct to say that the goal of evangelization is not just personal salvation, which may be seen as a form of selfishness and which makes Christ the means and not the end, but the consummation of all creation in Christ. It is in this context that personal salvation is located.

These five factors indeed give rise to questions that continue to bother those who are keen on evangelization. First, they seem to blur the distinction between evangelization on one hand, and mission on the other. Second, they leave one uncertain of what to do with people belonging to religions other than the Christian faith. Third, this implies that evangelization is more than what it does for people, but rather involves the whole of creation. We will attempt to examine those implications separately.

Evangelism and Mission

In the zeal for winning souls, great damage is often done to the cause of evangelization by keeping evangelization rigidly clear of mission. Credible scholars like David Bosch, who are committed to a recognition of the link between these two, unwittingly create a situation where zealous evangelists easily choose to concentrate on proclamation at the expense of the holistic nature of the gospel and evangelization. Such zealous evangelists equipped for the corresponding distinction between evangelism and mission allow evangelization to be identified with popular revivalism which often ignores the wholeness of evangelization as the manifestation of God's activity in the whole of creation. The truth is that the theology and practice of evangelization cannot and should never be treated as distinct from that of mission. Evangelization is another form and expression of the same commitment to God's mission. When a distinction is allowed, the consequences are unfortunate. We end up with a mission that on one hand does not see the need for the emphasis on the name of Jesus as Lord and Savior; a mission that ends up being no more than sheer humanism. On the other hand, we end up with an evangelistic activity that produces religious freaks with no real sense of responsibility to empower creation to deal with what Paul refers to as powers and principalities, as well as self-justifying Christians ready to judge arbitrarily the world and split it between believers and nonbelievers, an unfortunate act that was to be used as a forerunner to colonial expansionism.

In evangelization we declare that Jesus is Savior and Lord, that He is the center of God's Kingdom precisely because it is in Christ's life, teachings and actions that the Kingdom is personalized. His message of the arrival of the Kingdom is validated by his life, his teachings and actions.

The Kingdom of God and the person of Christ explain and fulfill each other in such a way that we cannot speak of God's Kingdom without Christ, or Christ without God's Kingdom. Origen's declaration that "Christ himself is the Kingdom" is indeed valid. David Bosch of the University of South Africa notes that when mission and evangelism are separated, evangelists often preach an entirely uncontextualized and disembodied Gospel. They frequently employ all kinds of psychological and rhetorical devices to persuade people to accept their specific message. People are then indeed challenged to repent and come to faith, but often the challenge is issued in terms of those areas of life where conversion will not be too costly. That evangelism will take on these features is, in a sense, a foregone conclusion, in view of the fact that the *churches* into which new members are invited are usually compromised in the surrounding culture, particularly in societies where the pastor is considered to be in the employment of the congregation and thus dependent on the parishioners' goodwill and support.

This kind of evangelism calls upon people to adopt a life-style which is defined almost exclusively in micro-ethical and religio-cultic categories. A case in point is J. Waskom Pickett's classic, *Christian Mass Movements in India*.[2] Pickett measures successful evangelism in terms of "attainments" in eleven areas: (1) knowledge of the Lord's Prayer, the Apostles' Creed and the Ten Commandments; (2) Sunday observance; (3) full membership in the church; (4) church attendance; (5) frequency of the church services; (6) support for the church; (7) freedom from idolatry, charms and sorcery; (8) abstaining from participation in non-Christian festivals; (9) freedom from fear of evil spirits; (10) Christian marriage; and (11) abstinence from use of intoxicating beverages. Where these characteristics manifest themselves in people, so the argument goes, evangelism has been successful.

In this approach all the *positive* elements have to do with narrowly defined religious and micro-ethical activities, and all the *negative* ones (those from which Christians should *abstain*) with the world. There is no reference whatsoever to any positive attitude to or involvement in the world, where liberation should have implications on the social and political front. There is a sharp break.

To all this we must say that, whenever the church's involvement in society and with the rest of creation becomes secondary and optional, whenever the church invites people to take refuge in the name of Jesus without challenging the dominion of evil, it becomes a counter-sign of the kingdom. It is then not involved in evangelization but in counter-evangelization. When preaching exclusively a message of individual salvation, the church is offering cheap grace to people and in the process this demeans the gospel. The content of our gospel then is—in the devastating formulation of Orlando Costas—"a conscience-soothing Jesus, with an unscandalous cross, an other worldly kingdom, a private, inwardly spirit, a pocket God, a spiritualized Bible, and an escapist church. . . ." If the gospel is indeed the gospel of the *kingdom*, and if the kingdom is "the detailed expression of [God's] caring control of the whole of life," then we are concerned *in our evangelism* with a God whose "nature as king (is) to . . . *uphold justice and equity*, to *watch over the circumstances of the entire creation, of strangers, widows and orphans*, and to *liberate the poor and the prisoners*."[3] It is in the bond between mission and evangelization, or service and proclamation that the gospel becomes a valid and relevant message for our global needs.

Evangelization and the Other Religions

There is evidence that religions other than Christian faith are consciously seeking to be perceived as missionary religions, recruiting members for themselves and even deliberately positioning themselves in some countries to control government mechanisms so as to ensure a growth for themselves equal to the growth of Christianity in the Constantinian era.

The immediate temptation for the Christian church is to position itself to compete vigorously with these religions for more membership. While this may sometimes be unavoidable, it is important for the Christian Church to do a self analysis which will assist in guiding its strategy and actions, especially in evangelization. Karl Barth, of course, reminded the church that Christian faith is not just another religion, it is then compelled to compete with the other religions as if it were participating in some form of divine beauty contest. We need to be wary of falling into this trap. In the book of Job we encounter Satan forcing Job to view faith in God in this fashion. In the very first chapter of the Book of Job (1:9-10, NEB), we hear Satan say to the Lord God:

> Has not Job good reason to be God-fearing? Have you not hedged
> him round on every side with your protection . . . ?

This, then, is Satan's explanation for the phenomenon of religion. People serve God for what they get out of religion. Religion pays dividends. This and this alone is the reason for Job's piety.

Satan's religious logic is not unfamiliar in our own time, even among Christians. So we often find that Christianity is marketed in a "things-go-better-with-Jesus" wrapping, that preachers tell us it pays to be a Christian. In other words: the moment religion ceases to pay dividends, it forfeits its very reason for existence. Religion is a matter of give and take: if I pay homage to God, I want something for my trouble in return, otherwise there is no point in it. Why serve God if God does not fulfill the divine side of the deal? This can become an arena of the tussle between Christian faith and the other religions.

Yet evangelization needs to rediscover the *centrality of the cross*—the power to be weak—as the key to challenging the world to contend with the gospel. Belief in God is not grounded in what one might get out of it, but one believes in God because one can not do otherwise. One follows Christ not because Christ is so powerful, but *in spite of the fact that Christ is so weak*. This is the essence of the cross.

The apostle Paul's second letter to the Corinthians illustrates this point clearly. Throughout the letter, he struggles with two issues: the thorn in his own flesh, and the controversy with the "super apostles" who are arguing that Paul is weak and inefficient in his ministry, whereas they are powerful and successful. Paul learns the hard way. He gradually develops the courage to be weak. He accepts the thorn in his flesh. And he opposes the impressive arsenal of his opponents with very weak and simple weapons: patience, truth, love, weakness, service, modesty, and respect. And towards the end of his letter he makes one of the most astounding claims ever made in religion: "It is when I am weak that I am strong." He says this on the basis of his experience of Christ who has taught him: "My grace is sufficient for you, for my power is made perfect in weakness" (2 Cor. 12:9).

It is this message he teaches the church in Corinth, a church which is sorely tempted to follow the "high road" offered by the super apostles, the road of success and power, and progress, the road of providing the validity of the Christian faith by conducting a divine beauty contest. Paul teaches them about the validity of paradox, about a God who, in spite of being all-powerful, became weak and vulnerable in his Son, about a Christ who, in spite of the fact that he could ask to dispatch twelve million legions of angels to rescue him from the cross and destroy his crucifiers, stayed on the cross and prayed: "Father, forgive them for they do not know what they are doing."

Nowhere has this life in paradox been portrayed more

102

profoundly than in Paul's words in 2 Corinthians 6:8-10:

> ... we are the impostors who speak the truth, the unknown men whom all men know; dying we still live on; disciplined by suffering, we are not done to death; in our sorrows we have always cause for joy; poor ourselves, we bring wealth to many; penniless we own the world.

It is this life in paradox that gives him the courage to be weak and the power to continue his ministry. So he writes in 2 Corinthians 4:8f:

> Hard-pressed on every side, we are never hemmed in; bewildered, we are never at our wits' end; hunted, we are never abandoned to our fate; struck down, we are not left to die. Wherever we go we carry death with us in our body, the death that Jesus dies, that in this body his life may reveal itself, the life that Jesus lives.

It is thus not to success that evangelization calls the world, but to servanthood—serving others, counting others more important than oneself. The cross thus becomes the supreme parable of the kingdom, its happening, its values, and its sign. This is proclamation and demonstration held together tightly.

The Supremacy of the Cross

Evangelization must more than just seek to draw large numbers of followers for Christ. It must bring Christ to the Center as the primary criterion against whom creation should measure itself. He is not only a measure, but the essence of existence by virtue of the substance of his mission as expressed in the event of the incarnation. While it is imperative that the Christian Church take seriously the soteriological significance of the life of Jesus in its entirety—his life, actions, and teachings—evangelization nonetheless must continue to find its emphasis on the theology of the cross precisely because it is here that the teachings and actions of Jesus find ultimate expression.

Taken together, the three atonement theories of Ireneaus (cosmic victory of Christ), Anselm (satisfaction or legal) and Abelard (sacrificial love, contemplation, and moral adjustment), begin to provide criteria that can be used in responding to or interpreting a context for the formulation of an evangelical response. It can be argued that globally, albeit in a generalized way, there is evidence of:

- reactionary behavior among the powerful nations that overwhelms smaller nations—what Martin Luther King, Jr. refers to as the nations' drum major instinct, a desire to be the super nation;

- criminal tendencies born of this sense of super ego; and

- rampant poverty, disease, and injustice.

- The three theories effectively say that neither evil powers, (cosmic powers have been subdued: Ireneaus), divine anger (neither is there divine retribution: Anselm) nor human self-deprivation (Abelard) have power to rule over us anymore. These in Christ have been destroyed, and therefore there is room for all to become as God meant them to be.

On reading these varying contexts and determining the expressions of sin (a state of absence of brotherhood and love in interpersonal relationships) as well as the activity of God (opportunities of reconciliation), the evangelist offers Christ as the clearest divine expression of God's activity, not in opposition to the encounters the people have had with God through other religions perhaps, but rather as an enhancement of what they were already seeing, albeit dimly, because God precedes the evangelists. Paul tried this in Ephesus; and for that matter this is the current dialectic between Judaism and Christian faith. This experience provides the model for evangelization. Yet even more, evangelization must see itself as a vehicle for the salvation that leads to the transformation of a broken and self-destroying creation.

Evangelization and Creation

Wesley spoke about Methodists as being one family wherever they are. That statement was in a sense prophetic. The ailments of the world have brought us to realize more and more how globally inter-related we are. In South Africa there is currently a lively debate as to what has given rise to the sudden commitment to the jettisoning of Apartheid. Currently the continent of Africa has to contend with the real threat that as relations between the East and the West begin to thaw, these continents may begin to focus on the Far East economically to the detriment and dearth of the African economy. Wesley was right. He should have gone on to say that the entire world is one family: the issues we have to grapple with are the same. Besides the natural disasters, human-made disasters are ravaging not only relations between nations and continents, as depicted in ideologies with origins from the East and West, but also the natural world as well. Alan Walker shared with us in London in 1988 how a group in Australia has started in the name of God to ask questions about the morality of their mineral exploitation ventures.

Hardly a week goes by without a reference in newspapers to the pending ozone layer destruction. A serious reflection on the ravages of hunger and poverty in countries like Ethiopia convicts one of the shallow relationships between humankind and God's creation. The problem is global, and it is more than just between person and person or nation and nation. It is not only between humanity and God but also between humanity and everything that God has done and stands for. Failure to recognize this can only lead to shallow evangelization with no theological respectability, credibility or integrity. We are *one family* living in *one home*, planet Earth. Together and individually we have responded to God negatively, a condition that the theological tradition has called sin. I fear an evangelization that may dull and make obscure our corporate responsibility to God, His *one* family over generations and our *one* home.

The Method of Evangelization

The subject of debate between traditional theology and liberation theology, which essentially is in the understanding of revealed truth as contained in the scriptures, ought to be recognized also as essential for a proper development of the methodology of evangelization.

Simon Maimela of the University of South Africa captures the debate in the following terms: "Traditional theology holds that theology ought to begin, methodologically speaking, with some 'eternal' or 'revealed' truth enshrined somewhere (or better 'out there') in the Bible, a truth that ought to be brought down to the human sphere and applied there." Liberation theologians, on the other hand, according to Maimela, "have raised serious objections against this traditional understanding of the relation of theory to practice." They argue that there is no direct access to such an ideal truth in itself, independent of human action in relation to it.[4]

This debate has direct implications for both the understanding and the method of evangelization. Traditional theology has informed the traditional method of evangelization, in the sense of bringing in the gospel as a prepackage put together outside the context of the recipient, and *only* applied to that context. Maimela effectively claims that theology must be an interpretation of actions that emanate from an encounter between God and humans in their context, with such analysis informed also by the God/person encounters in other contexts, especially those in Biblical records.

Evangelization then becomes the articulation, announcement and bringing into being of God's action as perceived in the context of proclamation, and understood in the context of the universal activity of God, as primarily evidenced in the scriptures. The role of evangelist therefore primarily becomes that of a *reader* of the Acts of God in his/her contemporary context: these in turn are examined in the light of the biblical context, as well as that of universal and historical faith experience. It is this that formulates an intelligent message of the good news to proclaim and obey.

Maimela immediately recognizes that to base theology on "the partial and engaged readings of the germinal events of Christianity, as liberation theology does, raises the problem of truth." As a response to this, however, he asserts that

> . . . in reality humans as historical beings can never hope to *have the ultimate truth*, which only God possesses, because the correspondence between historical truth and "heavenly" truth remains an eschatological hope. In the interim, humans have to work with the only truth they know, namely this historical, penultimate truth gleaned from divine impingement on their lives. Such a historical, non-platonic truth can never be a neutral and uninvolved idea separable from an effective and transformative action. Put differently, a historical truth remains a functional one; *it is a truth that really works and is effective in transforming the world and untruthful human relationships*. At stake here is the claim that a truth to be worthy of the name of things resides in the divine or human mind.

Rather it must be the truth that in practice really works, is effective and proves itself in the dynamics of the historical process by achieving demonstrable results such as liberating humans from bondage, oppression, and self-deification, that is, from all untruth (sin).[5]

As the truth that involves and carries humans with it, it emerges naturally out of their social context or praxis, where it is experienced, responded to, and embodied and has real transformative results. For if truth is not felt personally and is not recognized as the truth that intends to transform us, then it will not be able to liberate us from untruthful (sinful or oppressive) social conditions. The upshot of this is the contention that knowing the truth, biblically speaking, is inseparable from doing the truth, for one cannot really encounter divine truth and remain unaffected by it, either being transformed and carried by it or being repulsed by it. This follows from the fact that knowing the truth and doing the truth belong together.

This way of conceiving the truth finds support in the New Testament, especially in the Johannine emphasis on doing the truth, where knowing and doing the truth belong together (John 8:44-47; 1 John 3:17-18, 4:20-21). In other words the true knowledge of divine truth is invariably radiated through actions as people try to witness to this truth among them, live in it, and are involved in its transformation dynamics. This is the wholeness of mission of which evangelization is an essential part.

I want to conclude by saying that the World Methodist Council's Division for Evangelism is to be commended for recognizing the value of contextually based evangelism in its global evangelistic strategy. Yet, on the other hand, we need to double check if our emphasis on evangelism is as strongly located in *mission* as it should be.

CHAPTER 6

Evangelism and Religious Pluralism in the Wesleyan Heritage

G. Howard Mellor

Introduction

A discussion about the Christian faith in a plural world should begin by recognizing that our first response needs to be one of repentance. There has been too much evidence in ecclesiastical history that the laudable ideal of winning the world for Christ has also been tainted by the structure of power, the desire for control, and the longing for wealth.[1] Repentance is appropriate because (to take an example from my own context) when people from the new Commonwealth came to Britain, they were not welcomed by many English people. We should be ashamed to note that Asians have very little experience with British people as a people of prayer and devotion. Indeed, the Christian Church is seen by them as being corrupt and Western culture as decadent.

The focus of this essay is evangelism, considered in the context of religious pluralism and from the perspective of the Wesleyan heritage. The interface between evangelism and religious pluralism brings into sharp focus the issues in each discipline. First let us note some of the issues that affect or irritate that interface.

The Cultural Setting

The speed of travel and its widening availability to people in the West, as well as the enforced movements of people through war, hunger, and disease, has meant the presence of people of other faiths in every culture. It is very difficult to say today, as did

Wesley, that "the Mahometans . . . are in truth a disgrace to human nature and a plague to all that are under the iron yoke."[2] In all of our major cities are people of other faiths who are quite clearly good citizens, decent human beings, whose emphasis and love of family life, hard work, and morally respectable lives are often a testimony to those who see themselves as belonging to a Christian country. It is this very plurality of culture which has assisted the rise of the ideology of pluralism. "If what matters about religious beliefs is not the factual truth of what they affirm, but the sincerity with which they are held . . . then there are certainly no grounds for thinking that Christians have any right—much less any duty—to seek conversion of these neighbours to the Christian faith."[3]

Lesslie Newbigin points out that not only do we live in a plural culture, but it is "pluralist in the sense that this plurality is celebrated as something to be approved and cherished." "Pluralism is conceived to be a proper characteristic of the secular society, a society in which there is no officially approved pattern of belief or conduct."[4]

A Shift In Philosophy

The issues of truth and its nature have been a matter of debate for centuries, but the influence of philosophical thinking from the eighteenth-century philosophical revolution initiated by Descartes and Locke is now all-pervasive in our culture, not least in the written and visual media. The dominant philosophical trends of the Enlightenment, in turn, have led to secularism and modernity. Lesslie Newbigin has carefully charted the roots of pluralism, seeing their genesis in the work of Descartes and his cry, *cogito, ergo sum,* which in turn gave rise to a distinction between thinking reality (*res cogitans*) and reality extended in space (*res extensa*). Newbigin concludes that in our culture today "skepticism about whether our senses give us access to reality is the background of major philosophical thinking since Descartes."[5] Therefore we are left to ponder whether our Christian faith is an "experiment in living," one of the available "worldviews," or a "coherent and emotionally satisfying picture of reality."[6]

A Divergence in Theology

Despite the confident call by John R. Mott, as Chairman of the 1910 World Missionary Conference in Edinburgh, that Christians should unite "For the evangelization of the whole of this multitude," the stage was already set for the withdrawal by evangelicals from the newly-born ecumenical movement.[7] This polarization has remained through most of this century and despite there being accommodating ripples between the World Council of Churches' Consultation on Evangelism at San Antonio, and Lausanne II in Manila, one could not confidently predict that the two movements would jointly sponsor a conference on world mission.[8]

It has become commonplace to categorize different theological approaches to religious pluralism as exclusivist, inclusivist, and pluralist. We shall use this typology of views here, even though they are somewhat blunt instruments.

Exclusivism has historically been the dominant position of the Christian church. It maintains that the central claims of Christianity are true, and where these claims are in conflict with those of other religions or philosophies, the latter are to be rejected as false. This would be represented by the Lausanne Covenant, which in paragraph 3 states: "We also reject as derogatory to Christ and the gospel every kind of syncretism and dialogue which implies that Christ speaks equally through all religions and ideologies . . . to proclaim Jesus as 'The Savior of the World' is not to affirm that all people are either automatically or ultimately saved, still less to affirm that all religions offer salvation in Christ, rather it is to proclaim God's love to the world of sinners and to invite everyone to respond to him as Savior and Lord in the wholehearted personal commitment of repentance and faith. Jesus Christ has been exalted above every name: we long for the day when every knee shall bow to him and every tongue shall confess him Lord."[9] More recently Harold Netland in *Dissonant Voices* has given a well reasoned defense of the exclusivist position.[10]

Inclusivism, like exclusivism, maintains that the central claims of the Christian faith are true, but adopts a much more positive view of religious pluralism than does exclusivism. The revelation of God in Christ is held to be in some sense unique, normative,

111

and definitive, but it is claimed that God is also actively revealing and providing salvation through other religious traditions as well. There is a tension in holding these truths together, which is reflected in the writing of Pietro Rossano, Secretary of the Vatican Secretariat for Non-Christians: "As for the salvific function of these religions, namely, whether they are or are not paths to salvation, there is no doubt that 'grace and truth' are given through Jesus Christ and by his spirit (cf. John 1:17). Everything would lead one to conclude, however, that the gifts of 'grace and truth' do reach or may reach the hearts of men and women through the visible, experiential, signs of the various religions."[11] Karl Rahner, whose influence has been enormous in this century, is best known in missiology for his writings about the "anonymous Christian." By this he argues that a person could be regarded as anonymously or implicitly Christian and thus benefit from salvation, even without having any contact with the preaching of the gospel or the visible church. The implication would be that any person of faith, any faith, would be included as an "anonymous Christian."[12]

Pluralism rejects entirely the premise that God's revelation in Jesus Christ is in any sense unique or definitive and therefore parts company both with exclusivism and with inclusivism. John Hick and Paul Knitter, in publishing *The Myth of Christian Uniqueness*, intended it to serve as a kind of "crossing of a theological Rubicon." They hoped for a rejection of both exclusivism and inclusivism and in the essays they "were exploring the possibilities for the pluralist position—and moving away from insistence on the superiority or finality of Christ and Christianity toward a recognition of the independent validity of other ways."[13] Paul Knitter explains "that Jesus is unique, but with a uniqueness defined by its ability to relate to—that is, to include and be included by—other unique religious figures." He views Jesus "not as exclusive or even as normative, but as theocentric, as a universally relevant manifestation (sacrament, incarnation) of divine revelation and salvation."[14] The devotional statements of certain faith he views as the "love language" of devoted people.

John Hick considers that the variety of religions is not only inevitable but desirable because of the variety of human types and needs.[15] He is very skeptical that we have any reliable knowledge of the historical Jesus as being truly God. Jesus is the man infused

112

with God who dramatically impacted those around him.[16] While it is quite proper for Christians to be devoted to Jesus, he wants recognition to be given also to the object of devotion for others.[17]

The Privatization of Religion

Newbigin has delineated as one of the chief characteristics of the Enlightenment the sharp distinction between the public realm of facts and the private world of values, opinions, and preferences. It is assumed that truth belongs to the public realm of facts, particularly the physical sciences, and not to the private world of relative issues such as values and preferences. In the private world, Newbigin asserts, questions of truth and falsity are not relevant. The implications of this to our discussions are spelled out by Newbigin: "In contrast to traditional societies, modern western society leaves its members free, within very wide limits, to adopt and hold their own views about what is good and desirable, about what kind of life is to be admired, about what code of ethics should govern one's private life."[18] As a natural extension of this, it is assumed by a large number of Christians that the principle of pluralism applies here also. The rival truth-claims of the different religions are not felt to call for argument and resolution; they are simply part of the mosaic—or perhaps one should say, kaleidoscope, of different values that make up the whole pattern.

Religion, as a result, has become not a matter of truth, but a matter of taste. The primary questions seem to have less to do with Christian faith and more to do with buying a suit, for the primary question is no longer "Is it true?" but "Does it fit?" Indeed, it follows that religious pluralism is not only welcome but essential, for what fits one person does not necessarily meet the need of another.

The Plurality of the New Age

Religious pluralism is set to increase at an exponential rate, due to what is popularly called the New Age Movement. The New Age is definitely not a religion, nor is it a belief system in the traditional sense, and it is certainly not a cult. There is nothing to join, it does not have a headquarters, and New Age people might be doing literally anything. Its gurus are much more likely to be from the theater than from theology, e.g. Shirley MacLaine, the colorful high priestess of New Age, who has popularized the practice of "channeling" (or spiritualism) in several best sellers. The 1960s "Age of Aquarius" was always regarded as the preserve of the long-haired, open-sandalled, wholefood-eating, joss-sticks-burning curiosities who read the works of Eastern mystics. Now New Age is big business. It is fashionable to be green and spiritual, which all evangelists and apologists should note. For to point someone to Christ, is in fact to point to the one in whom all things have their being (John 1:3, Col. 1:15-17), whether created or invisible.

The New Age has a bewildering variety of options. Color analysts, transpersonal psychologists, and New Age musicians abound; university courses in consciousness studies compete for customers with Eastern gurus and Gnostic priests. They claim to offer personal transformation and self-discovery through therapies that range from healing with crystals, past life recall, and advice from entities in outer space or some other spirit world. That most are concerned about the future of our polluted planet is revealed by their membership in environmental pressure-groups, pilgrimages in remote places, or attunement to Gaia, the earth goddess. The Californian New Age Directory, *Common Ground*, states: "There are undoubtedly as many paths to personal transformation as there are people . . . whether a resource is useful to your personal transformation is a matter of attunement—it is a matter of resonance between what the resource is and who you are at this moment in time."[19]

Clearly the New Age, without creeds and demands, is finding a ready response to those longing for a spiritual reality, without moral imperatives. They are assuming that it cannot be found in a Christian church tainted by hypocrisy, division and alignment with the power structures in society.[20]

The Arrogance of Affirmation

A certain hope in Christ as Savior of the World is seen as both arrogant and intolerant. The most influential contemporary critic of the traditional or Chalcedon Christology is John Hick, who quite clearly sees the implications of this orthodox teaching in relation to a plural world: "If Jesus was literally God Incarnate, and if it is by his death alone that men are saved, and by their response to him alone that they can appropriate that salvation, then the only doorway to eternal life is Christian faith. It would follow from this that the large majority of the human race so far have not been saved."[21] There are an impressive group of theologians and missiologists who take Hick's line in relation to this scandal of particularity. Dr. Diana Eck, who is Professor at Harvard and Moderator of the WCC Program of Dialogue, speaks of the astonishment of a Hindu at the idea that God had only one incarnation, and continues: "this exclusive understanding of revelation, which speaks of it as an event of the past and imprisons it in the first century, is also folly to many Christians."[22] Stanley Samartha, the distinguished Indian theologian, writes of the precarious nature of human existence and the present situation of social unrest, environmental pollution and the threat of nuclear disaster: "since this is a threat to all humanity, to proclaim that one religious tradition has the only answer to such a global problem seems preposterous."[23]

There is not only the danger of theological arrogance, but also of national arrogance. The inter-religious issues are often compounded by inter-racial ones; since we are all aware that racism infects us so deeply, there are strong emotional reasons for regarding religious pluralism as something to be accepted and welcomed. Lynn De Silva, a pioneer in Buddhist-Christian dialogue, writes: "People of all faiths have a vital role to play in bringing about racial harmony, since it is acknowledged that the government alone cannot achieve this end by legislation and other measures."[24]

We do well to remind ourselves that the Christian message is endowed with a doctrine of creation in which humankind is made "in the image of God." It would follow logically that those so created have the ability to think, decide and act for themselves. To be committed, then, both to the integrity of the Christian message, as well as the integrity of others to decide, should be sufficient caution against arrogance on the part of Christians.

I have tried briefly to sketch a wide range of theological reflection which, as we have seen, leads Christian theologians, missiologists and practitioners to a variety of conclusions on how to act and react as Christian missioners in a plural world. We are left asking the question: "Where can we find help to begin to point us in the right direction?" As Methodists coming boldly from the evangelical tradition, we shall look first at some of the biblical material and then reflect on our Wesleyan heritage before attempting some conclusions.

What Guidance Does the Bible Offer?

Colin Chapman at Lausanne II in Manila reminded his evangelical audience that they have "tended to emphasize passages in scripture which present other religions in a very negative light."[25] There are clear passages which show Yahweh as a jealous God: "I am the Lord your God . . . you shall have no other gods before me" (Exod. 20:2-3). During the Exodus, God brings judgment on the gods of Egypt (Num. 33:4). The Israelites are warned from Canaanite religious practices, "because every abhorrent thing that the Lord hates they have done for their gods" (Deut. 12:31). The Psalmist is in turn clear that, "all the gods of the peoples are idols, but the Lord made the heavens" (Ps. 96:5).

Similarly we can find uncompromising attitudes in the New Testament. Jesus' initial response to the Syro-Phoenician woman seems very sharp and uncompromising, though her persistence is rewarded (Mark 7:24-30). To unbelieving religious leaders he answers: "You are of your father, the devil" (John 8:44). In Lystra, Paul has to explain to those who think he and Barnabas are gods that they should "turn from these worthless things to the living God . . . " (Acts 14:15).

However, is this the total picture? Kenneth Cracknell points to Genesis 1–11 as containing a picture of the nations in which Yahweh is concerned with all the nations: "Genesis 10 teaches that the expansion over the then known world of the peoples is within the purposes of God."[26] This is echoed by the Psalmist: "For all the nations belong to you" (Ps. 82:8). The claim in Malachi 1:11 is even more shocking: "For from the rising of the sun to its setting my name is great among the nations, and in every place incense is offered to my name." The prophet is telling his hearers that sacrifices offered by their pagan neighbors are more acceptable than their own ritual, carelessly followed and evidently devoid of commitment.

There are many to whom the God of Abraham communicates. Job has no dealings with Israel, but has personal dealings with

Yahweh (Job 38:1; 40:1; 42:1). Amos knew that the Lord had moved the Philistines and Syrians according to his purpose (Amos 9:67). Isaiah knew that Assyria would be the instrument of God's wrath to a rebellious Israel (Isa. 10:6). Jeremiah speaks of God intervening in the affairs of the nations. Jonah, the reluctant missionary, finds that the people of another nation are far more willing to respond to Yahweh than his own people. Indeed, he is offended at their complete obedience and at God's willingness to be merciful.

The New Testament picture is challenging also. Jesus commends the centurion for his faith: "I tell you, not even in Israel have I found such faith" (Luke 7:9). There is the striking example of Peter's conversion from being a racist and separatist to being the open and inclusive Peter who explains his moment of disclosure to Cornelius: "I truly understand that God shows no partiality, but in every nation anyone who fears Him and does what is right is acceptable to Him" (Acts 10:34-35). The confirmation for Peter that salvation is universally available comes when the Spirit descends, following the preaching of the Christian message.[27]

Anyone approaching the scriptures with the topic of religious pluralism must have to do with John 14:6 and Acts 4:12 and the logos theology in John. We can only touch upon them briefly here. John's splendid cleverness in uniting Hebraic and Hellenistic thought, by claiming Jesus to be the logos, has also given us insight into the work of Christ in all creation and for all time. It would follow that if He is the true light which enlightens everyone, then that which has become light for anyone finds its source in Christ. As William Temple put it:

> So it may truly be said that the conscience of the heathen man is the voice of Christ within him, though muffled by ignorance. All this is noble in the non-christian systems of thought, or conduct, or worship is the work of Christ upon them and within them. By the Word of God—that is to say, by Jesus Christ—Isaiah and Plato and Zoroaster and Buddha and Confucius conceived and uttered such truths as they declared. There is only one divine light, and every man in his measure is enlightened by it.[28]

It is one thing to affirm the work of God in all creation and all cultures, and quite another to claim, as does John Hick, that the offer of salvation in any religion affords saving grace from the logos of God, Jesus Christ himself.[29] This I consider to be a bridge too far.

Many religions speak of their spirituality as "the Way" (John 14:6).[30] Let us not lose sight, though, of the fact that John, writing in a religiously plural world, is keen to express the view that Jesus is the Way; in him is truth and life, for he is the Word who has tabernacled among us; he is the exegesis of God (John 1:14); to see or perceive him is to see the Father; it is through him, the logos of God, that people will come to the Father.

The Acts incident (Acts 4:8-12) does confront us with the translation of *sozo* and derivatives as "to heal, make whole, save." The crucial thing about the context is not merely that a man is healed, but that the healing points to Jesus of Nazareth (Acts 4:8-12). Peter declares that what they call a notable sign points to the salvation found in the name of Jesus.[31]

The Wesleyan Heritage

I want to say with John Munsey Turner that religious pluralism "was just over Wesleyan's horizon."[32] Maybe as a result, teasing out the Wesleyan heritage does not in itself give us a crystal clear picture. It has been demonstrated that John Wesley was somewhat ambivalent about other faiths.[33] His earlier views on other faiths, noted above, were tempered in later life and he argues against a summary damnation of Muslims.[34] Like his contemporaries he organized religions into four categories: Christianity, Judaism, Mohametanism, and Paganism.[35] He identified a variety of pagans (Greek and Roman; the tribal religions of Africa and America; Indian religions, including Hinduism and Buddhism) and in later life "held out the hope that many of them might have found a true saving relationship with God by responding to the light that they received."[36] His view of general revelation fluctuated, but he certainly thought that knowledge of God was available to humankind either by influence or by interference, through the works of God, or directly, as prevenient grace via the "spiritual senses." This led him logically to the view that God would judge such people not by the light of Christ but by the light they had received.[37]

The approach to people of other faiths could be nowhere bettered than in the openness of "The Catholic Spirit"; "his heart is enlarged towards all mankind, those he knows and those he does not; he embraces with strong and cordial affection neighbors and strangers, friends and enemies. This is catholic or universal love." Such refreshing openness is not an indifference to all opinions, which would be the "spawn of hell, not the offspring of heaven." Wesley enjoins on the person who adopts such creative love to be securely "fixed in his religious principles, on what he believes to be the truth as it is in Jesus."[38]

In his *Journal* for 18 May 1788 we see Wesley's commitment to wide-ranging tolerance: "The Methodists alone do not insist on your holding this or that opinion, but they think and let think."[39] It is this kind of attitude and openness which so many Methodist scholars who are involved in inter-faith work have found a source of strength and direction: "For my part the openness and commitment spoken of here is the reason why I return again and again to my Methodist roots as I enter into inter-faith dialogue... Wesley himself would have recognized faith and love and hope in the people that I have to deal with and would have walked the same way with us."[40]

Wesley, then, had a remarkable capacity for openness in the pursuit of truth. Let us also recall his urgent desire, on every occasion, to "offer Christ," for all people need Christ. As he says in the best-known passage of all dealing with this topic:

> Christian faith is then not only an assent to the whole gospel of Christ, but also a full reliance on the blood of Christ; a trust in the merits of his life, death, and resurrection; a recumbency upon him as our atonement and our life, as *given for us*, and *living in us*. It is sure confidence which a man hath in God, that through the merits of Christ, *his* sins are forgiven, and *he* reconciled to the favour of God; and in consequence hereof a closing with him and cleaving to him, as our 'wisdom, righteousness, sanctification, and redemption', or, in one word, our salvation.[41]

The object of saving faith, as he regularly made clear, is Christ himself. He did not call upon people in the first place to embrace truth, but to "look unto Jesus." In that sense I suggest that Wesley had a very suitable stance for his theology and evangelism in a plural world, a mixture of openness toward people and certainty of message, which is one we would do well to follow.

Where does this place Wesley in the topology of views noted

119

earlier? My conclusion is that he does not fit easily and so I suggest the following: that he is *at* the interface of the exclusivist and inclusivist position. His Christology is exclusivist, saving faith is in Christ; but his exclusivism is not myopic. His openness to others and the pursuit of truth, his view that God would judge by the light that people had received, all move toward the inclusivist position. To place him simply in this latter category would be an injustice to his doctrine of regeneration and saving faith. Therefore I suggest he is at the interface of the two.

Sharing Faith in a Plural World

Part of British Methodism's response to *A Decade of Evangelism* is the production of *The Good News Works*[42] and there I have argued that the Methodist people are well placed to witness to their faith in Jesus among people of other faiths. It is partly to do with our history, for the mission and care and help of the people called Methodist has been to all. It is partly to do with the characteristic life of the local churches which have at their best been welcoming and opening to new people and ways.

The report *Faithful and Equal*[43] has prompted profitable discussion on racism within the church, for our hand of friendship to those of other faiths cannot be racist. We are well placed also because some of our churches are present among people of other faiths. Churches now in the Asian communities are in the right place and as a church we have a responsibility to ensure that such churches are encouraged to see the possibilities that are open to them. How then are we as Methodists, or indeed any Christian, to share our faith with those of another faith? There are a number of principles and assumptions that need now to be considered if we are to share our faith effectively.

Dialogue is a fundamental part of any kind of mission in which there needs to be openness and interaction. It is in the dialogue that we learn about people, their customs, their religious awareness, their values and basic assumptions of life. The term has been used widely to describe discussion between adherents of two different religions.

In his *Toward A New Relationship*, Kenneth Cracknell gives a thorough exploration of *dialegomal* and *dialogizomai*, affirming not only that dialogue is a word with biblical roots, but that its

primary meaning is "argue-reason-content." Cracknell emphasizes the importance that Paul placed upon dialogue, in that he
was prepared to remain at Ephesus (Acts 19:8-10) and spend over
two years in reasoning and persuading. This Paul does, Cracknell
notes, first of all in the synagogue, and then in the hall or school
of the Greek philosophers, teaching there when the school was
not otherwise in use:

> Paul at Ephesus shows us that the way of dialogue is a way of
> patience, often very time consuming. It shows us that the way of
> dialogue means meeting the other person on his or her own terms
> and really attending to what they say, believe, feel. We also see that
> it is a way seeking to share persuasively the best of our own
> conviction, to share that which has most persuasively the best of
> our own conviction, to share that which has most persuasively laid
> hold of our own minds and hearts.[44]

This raises the question of how we view the nature of dialogue.
Is it a method to win others to Christ? Or in the dialogue do we
meet as equals in the sense that neither partner needs, nor must
be thought to need, the religion, the savior of the other partner?
If we are to be open and vulnerable then, "to enter into dialogue
is not only difficult, it is dangerous . . . our faith is at stake."[45]

In this essay the term carries its missionary connotation, that
the debate, or dialogue, is a fundamental part of the missionary
task, even with the risk just noted. When in Athens, Paul starts
where people are, debating on their ground, taking up their issues
(Acts 17:17). At the Areopagus he cleverly weaves strands of their
philosophy into his address before introducing the essential
points he wants the audience to consider. He may start where they
are, but he gets to Christ in the end. Such dialogue and building
up of relationships in mutual friendship and trust over a period
of time is the only way to share faith with people of other faiths.
Reference to Athens gives me opportunity to reflect that we must
not assume that dialogue is simply a one-to-one or even a small
group experience. Paul does all this in the synagogue and marketplace, but also in the preaching arena of the Areopagus. I note
this here, for it has implications when we come to think about our
sharing and proclaiming of faith today.

My impression ten years ago was that interfaith dialogue
included a suspension of sharing Christ. A different note is
sounded by Cracknell and others more recently:

121

> For the vast majority of Christians, including those most energeti-
> cally engaged in dialogue, Jesus is not merely a background figure,
> he is central to Christian faith. Not only do the Christian dialoguers
> recognize this, but so do their Muslim, Buddhist, Shinto, Hindu
> and Jewish conversation partners. Wherever one starts . . . any
> honest dialogue between Christians and others will sooner or
> later—and in my experience, usually sooner—have to deal with the
> figure of Jesus.[46]

The British Council of Churches has helpfully distilled the
various documents from the World Council of Churches and
offered in its *Relations with People of Other Faiths* four principles of
dialogue:

> (1) Dialogue begins when people meet each other.
> (2) Dialogue depends upon mutual understanding and mutual
>   trust.
> (3) Dialogue makes it possible to share in service to the commu-
>   nity.
> (4) Dialogue becomes the medium of authentic witness.[47]

Generally in Britain, Christians have been at best hesitant to
engage in dialogue with people of another faith. Strangely, they
are more hesitant to do this than to do mission among people
with no faith. This is undoubtedly because Christians in Britain
have come to fear other faiths with their different ideas, customs,
and food. However, avoidance of relationships based on ignorance and fear is an entirely inappropriate response.

Engaging in dialogue brings an openness, interest, and sharing which is dynamic. As a Community Relations officer in the
Bolton and Rochdale District comments, "In our Inter-Faith
group we have recently discussed Salvation in the Bible and the
Quran, and What does Jesus mean to me, a Muslim? a Christian?
This group have known one another for some time and we
regularly discuss our differences and controversial areas. My
experience is that Muslims have a greater respect for Christians
who truly follow Christ."

Starting Where People Are

The doctrine of incarnation is crucial to our understanding of
evangelism with its insistence that the gospel is about a With-Us

God. If we wish to be alongside people of other faiths, whether Eastern or New Age, let us recognize that hospitality is of enormous importance. Jesus spent much time in giving and receiving hospitality and we would do well to copy this model. Unless we take time to listen, to open our homes, we shall forfeit the right to speak about our faith.

The importance of dialogue and the setting of hospitality was understood well by E. Stanley Jones and described in his *Christ of the Round Table*.[48] To his Round Table Conferences, Stanley Jones would invite about fifteen adherents of other faiths, many of them educated people such as judges, government officials, doctors, lawyers, and religious leaders, and also five or six Christians, mostly Indians. He insisted upon fairness and mutual respect in the sharing and at the beginning of each conference would say, "Let everyone be perfectly free, for we are a family circle; we want each one to feel at home, and we will listen with reverence and respect to what each man has to share."[49] This kind of openness, depth of sharing and hospitality is as important today to our missionary strategy as it was between the wars in India. Jones concludes that "no one could sit through these conferences and not feel that Christ was master of every situation, not by loud assertion, or through the pleading of clever advocates, but by what he is and does."[50]

The only way that many people are going to hear the good news of Jesus is if someone goes to them and creates friends amongst those of other cultures and faiths. Evangelism here may mean being alongside a person who cannot come to church because of the opposition of another member of their family. Women may feel hesitant about coming to church because they will undoubtedly meet men that they don't know. Therefore hospitality for women, given by women, is vital.

What Approach to Evangelism Is Required in A Religiously Plural World?

The nature of religious pluralism brings into sharp focus the problem confronting the evangelist. For evangelists "are concerned not merely to articulate a truth in such a way that another mind can grasp it, but to impart conviction in such a way that others can share it."[51] This is the area in which I have conducted most of my research into evangelistic ministry.[52] It must be quite clear that in an age of cultural and theological plurality, a directive approach to evangelism is not appropriate. George Morris and Eddie Fox discuss this in *Faith Sharing*, describing the directive approach as both information transmission or manipulative monologue. In both cases, the recipient is assumed to be passive and, in the case of the latter, often the subject of an emotion appeal.[53]

Both these cases, which I would broadly consider a directive approach, cause us to use methods which can bring compliance (by the weak) and defiance (by the rebellious and by those with any sense of their own worth) rather than facilitate a meeting of minds or effect an inner change. Such an approach would seek to control people or the situation rather than encourage their personal and spiritual development.

The third category is described as "non-manipulative dialogue"; such an approach involves a two-way process involving honest interaction through establishing a relationship between the speaker and the hearer. This is something the evangelist does "with the listener," rather than "to them." "Here the relationship between the evangelizer and the hearer approximates to that of a friend to a friend. The goal of the relationship is that of sharing love and faith with the other person."[54]

Christian evangelism must, in my view, adopt an approach which resonates with the content of that evangel. That is, it is about relationships, with a triune God, and past, present, and future relationships with other people. The research that I have undertaken suggests that we must take very seriously that no person can take or make an interior or spiritual decision for another person.

The parabolic method of Jesus gives some guidance to us in our evangelism: "In the parables, it is not so much that we are instructed by Jesus, but that we must stand with him and view life through his eyes . . . We are not told what we must see there, rather, the scene is set in sparse terms and we are invited to view what is before us."[55] By the use of parables, Jesus engaged his listeners in an inner dialogue with him. It is as if Jesus uses parables to create a window and invite his hearers not merely to look upon it, but to look through it and see the significance for themselves.

Eta Linnemann shows how the effectiveness of the parable was dependent as much upon the hearer and their response as on the skill of the storyteller: "It is the essence of a parable that there is achieved in it a *dialegesthai,* a conversation, a dialogue between the narrator and the listener."[56] Alexander Findlay notes that there is within the parables of Jesus both an element of risk and of surprise, both of which have the effect of creating a dialogue experience.[57] "The parable does not teach a spectator a lesson; rather it invites and surprises a participant into an experience."[58]

It is remarkable that Jesus takes the risk of using, to carry his urgent message, a form of communication which demands the cooperation of and deliberate engagement in the dialogue by the hearer. There is no manipulation or indoctrination there. "Anyone who risks a parable in such a situation is risking everything; but this is the only way he can win everything."[59]

I am convinced that the approach to evangelism required in our modern plural world is one which is characterized by risk and development, the kind of faith and striking openness that characterized Wesley's ministry. It will not seek to control the hearers nor their decisions. It involves freedom of participation, giving the listener the capacity to think and decide and act for themselves. Sharing will be a reciprocal relationship which embodies two-way communication, with each open to be influenced by the other.

Those engaged in such evangelistic ministry will ensure, as far as possible, that they are using words, symbols, pictures, to which the listener can relate. In a dialogue, as the listener becomes more active in the process by hearing, interpreting, thinking about the words proclaimed, an inner dialogue begins to take place. This inner dialogue not only interprets and assimilates the proclaimed word, but also allows it to challenge present thinking and assumptions. This process is not merely relevant person to person, but also has implications for preaching. My research shows that this approach is relevant to all forms of evangelistic communication, but we cannot explore that fully here. Let us note here, however, that this approach is appropriate in persuasive proclamation of the good news of Jesus Christ.

Such evangelistic ministry which, I contend, is an appropriate form of proclamation in a plural world, will be as vulnerable, as creative and as dynamic in the hearer and proclaimer as were the parables of Jesus. It was appropriate in the religiously plural culture in which Jesus ministered and in which the early church grew and is appropriate today. The evangel will be shared with conviction and forcefulness and yet in a way that does not impose belief. The need of the hearer to decide is not violated, and the need of the evangelist to declare the message is not compromised. The risk undertaken by the evangelist is no greater than that undertaken by Jesus in his parables, namely, that the hearer may think, discuss, decide, and act for him or herself. This, I propose to you today, is consonant with the Wesleyan heritage and is an entirely appropriate approach to evangelism in a plural world.

This essay opened with a recognition of the need for repentance. It might have been noted then that repentance was due for the many times, through fear or neglect, that we have failed to evangelize. Let us now pray that God will give us humility and boldness—humility as we offer Christ to others through the art of sensitive listening, both to God and those with whom we share; and boldness to proclaim "the mystery of the gospel." God grant us the joy of that kind of evangelism in our plural world.

CHAPTER 7

Wesleyan Evangelism in an Asian Context: A Case Study

Dennis C. Dutton

Introduction

The subject "Wesleyan Evangelism in an Asian Context" is problematic for me for several reasons. There is a sense in which evangelism is easier spoken than done. The way of sharing what the Lord has done for one must be so natural that it becomes part of one's Christian life. To put one's evangelistic performance into words is not easy. The responsibility of speaking about evangelism becomes even more difficult in an Asian context. Asia is a large and diverse continent, not only in a spatial sense but also in a religious, ethnic, and cultural sense. Asian countries differ also in their systems of government, economics, politics, logic, and practice of religion. The plurality of cultures and customs, languages and dialects make communication of any sort difficult even within the same nation. It would be impossible for me to do justice to the topic of evangelism in an Asian context even if I spoke in generalities. In the light of this I have chosen to narrow the scope of this essay to the context in which I live and serve. I hope that by my doing this you will find my comments helpful.

The Religious Situation in Malaysia

Malaysia is a nation located in the heart of Southeast Asia. It is a young country hardly noticed by anybody except its own citizens. Its capitol, Kuala Lumpur, with nearly a million people, is the smallest in the region. It has the rare distinction of having declared independence twice in the last 35 years. Once in 1957, when it became independent Malaya and then in 1963, when together with Singapore and the Borneo territories of Sabah and Sarawak, it became Malaysia.

The ethnic Malayas make up about fifty-three percent of the population of about seventeen million. Other indigenous ethnic groups who are not Malay make up about seven percent. Ethnic Chinese and Indians make up about thirty percent and nine percent of the population respectively. The Malays are Muslim; most Indians are Hindu; most Chinese are a combination of Buddhist, Confucianist, and Taoist; and most Punjabis are Sikhs. Christianity is the only religion that has no ethnic base of its own. Indians, Chinese, and the indigenous ethnic communities such as the Kadazans and the Dayaks in Sabah and Sarawak form the bulk of the Christian population.

Religious freedom is enshrined in the Federal Constitution of Malaysia, but Islam is the official religion of the nation. Article 3(1) of the Federal Constitution reads, "Islam is the official religion of the Federation, but other religions may be practiced in peace and harmony in any part of the Federation." Article 11 contains these provisions:

(1) Every person has the right to profess and practice his religion, and subject to Clause (4), to propagate it.
(2) No person shall be compelled to pay any tax the proceeds of which are specially allocated in whole or in part for the purpose of religion other than his own.
(3) Every religious group has the right:
  (a) to manage its own religious affairs;
  (b) to establish and maintain institutions for religious or charitable persons: and
  (c) to acquire and own property and hold and administer it in accordance with law.
(4) State law and, in respect of the Federal Territories of Kuala Lumpur and Labuan, Federal Law may control or restrict the propagation of any religious doctrine among persons professing the religion of Islam.

Evangelism in the Malaysian Context

In the Malaysian context, there are two major factors which must be taken into serious consideration when doing evangelism.

The first is the constitutional and legal limits placed on all its citizens with regard to the propagation of non-Islamic religions among the Muslims. Even radical and unorthodox Islamic teachings are not acceptable. The second pertains to the strong sentiments expressed by the people of the Buddhist, Hindu, and Sikh faiths against the attempts of Islam and Christianity to convert members of their respective groups.

The religion of Islam and Islamic affairs come directly under the control of and are regulated by an Islamic Council in each State and the Ruler, i.e. the Sultan, is the Head of the religion. Individual States and the Federation of Malaysia, over the years, have promulgated laws to address the issue of the propagation of the non-Islamic religions among the Muslim community. On the surface such laws would appear to be an attempt to control and regulate all forms of religious propagation.

An example of such legislation is Chapter XV of the Penal Code of the Federation of Malaysia, which deals with offenses relating to religion. Under this Chapter it is a criminal offense "to injure or defile a place of worship with intent to insult the religion or any class or disturb a religious assembly . . . or utter words or make gestures with deliberate intent to wound the religious feelings of any person." In 1983, a new section (§298.A) was introduced "to prohibit the creation of disharmony, disunity or feelings of enmity, hatred or ill-will, or prejudice in the maintenance of harmony or unity, on grounds of religion." While the laws of the various States differ in some minor aspects, all of them have the effect of placing a total ban on the propagation of non-Islamic faiths among Muslim people. Heavy penalties, including prison sentences, are prescribed for offenders. To date no Malaysian citizen has been prosecuted under these laws, but in 1987 a number of Christians were detained without trial under the provisions of the Internal Security Act for allegedly propagating their faith to the Muslims. Other religious communities have tended to react to Muslim and Christian missionary activities by strong protests and increased efforts to prepare their followers to withstand any attempts to convert them. In a few isolated cases there have been violent and physical attacks on church workers.

The prevailing circumstances demand serious consideration on the part of Christians in Malaysia. We seem to be caught in a dilemma. On the one hand, we are scripturally required to obey the Lord's Commission to go into all the world and make disciples, baptize them, and teach them (Matt. 28:19, 20), and on the other, we are legally obligated to take stock of the religious sensitivities of the people of other faiths who are trying to live in peace and harmony within Malaysian society. On the one hand we are under the obligation to share our faith to as many who are willing to listen, and on the other, we are expected to be law abiding and peace-loving people who should harbor no desire to stoke the fires of public disorder. Under these unenviable circumstances what is to be our Christian response?

The Response of the Christian Community

I will frame my answer to this question by examining some of the responses that the Christian community is currently engaged in. There are two that are particularly noteworthy. The first is the continuing necessity to remind all Christians of their duty to heed our Lord's call for Christians to be united. This visible coming together is in itself a form of evangelism. The second is the continuing need for the Christian leadership to be in consultation with the leaders of their faiths. Through accepted procedures and traditional Malaysian norms attempts must be made to find solutions to the race and religious problems that arise from time to time.

Unity and Harmony Among Christians

There is no need for me to elaborate too much here on the Biblical injunction for Christian unity. This has been adequately done by the ecumenical movement. In the Malaysian context it is necessary for us to constantly examine the content and practice of the Christian faith. The quest for Christian unity is not an option but a necessity for us. It is a duty which requires constant attention. Before the rest of the world can believe in the new commonwealth of Jesus Christ it is important that the Christians are united in the bond of love and harmony first. In the Gospel of John, chapter 17:21, Jesus prayed, "that all of them may be one . . . so that the world may believe. . . ." This call for unity and brotherhood reverberates throughout the Christian scriptures. Psalm 133:1 says "How good and pleasant it is when brothers live together in unity." Second Corinthians 13:11 exhorts us Christians to be "of one mind, and live in peace; and the God of love and peace will be with you." Again in Ephesians 4:3 we are told "make every effort to keep the unity of the spirit through the bond of peace." In Philippians 1:27 the Christians are reminded to "stand firm in one spirit. . . ." To this end the Christians in Malaysia have decided to close ranks. In 1983 the Christian Federation of Malaysia was envisioned and in 1985 was established. For the first time the entire Christian community in our country came under one "umbrella." The founder members are The Roman Catholic Church, the Council of Churches, and the National Evangelical Christian Fellowship. These groups, together, represent more than ninety-five percent of the Christian population of our country. This is our starting point for Christian unity. If the Church of Jesus Christ is to be taken seriously by the government and the people of Malaysia it must be able to speak with one clear voice. If the bugler gives an indistinct sound who will be ready to follow? We have purposed in the future decades to work together for both church and society through the Christian Federation of Malaysia (CFM) which facilitates closer cooperation among the churches and the search for a common identity for the Christian community.

The CFM also gives form, structure, and impetus to the ecumenical movement. Under its auspices, a National Christian Conference is held every three years. Week of Prayer for Christian Unity services are held in various centers throughout the country. Coordinated responses to public issues are better made through the CFM. The Christian community can now speak with one voice and meet with government authorities as one body. Government agencies and even the Prime Minister himself have contacted the CFM when there was a need to obtain Christian input in government programs regarding the welfare of the people in general and especially related to Christianity.

Dialogue with the People of Other Faiths

Christian thinkers have always had to wrestle with the issue of the relationship between Christianity and the other religions. It appears to me that Jesus gave dignity and respect to sincere believers whose views differed from his own. By focusing on Jesus'

131

behavior and teachings and on his interaction with the people of other religions, a basis does exist for the Christian's openness to the people of other faiths.

At the World Missionary Conference held in Mexico City in 1963 "dialogue" emerged as an articulated issue of permanent ecumenical concern. In one of its sections on "The witness of Christians to men (and women) of other faiths," it is stated that "the proper Christian approach to people of other religious convictions is one of love, respect, and patience."[1]

Martin Goldsmith, drawing on both biblical material and his own experience as one with wide cross-cultural experience, wrote: "In our Global Village, world religious communities have got to learn to live together in tolerant peace. Even if they disagreed theologically and long to see other people converted to their faith, loving tolerance, and peaceful co-existence remain essential for the welfare of our planet."[2]

Lesslie Newbigin, another Christian scholar with cross cultural experience, says that " . . . the Christian points to the Lord Jesus Christ as Lord of all men (and women). . . ." He continues:

> The church does not apologize for the fact that it wants all men (and women) to know Jesus Christ and to follow him. Its very calling is to proclaim the Gospel to the ends of the earth. It cannot make any restrictions in religion. Whether they have sublime ideals or a defective morality makes no fundamental difference in this respect. All must hear the Gospel.[3]

While we may believe that Jesus Christ is the Way, the Truth, and the Life, we must also be humble enough to admit that we are not the only ones who believe that we have the blueprint of a utopia for our country and the world. What we all can do is to bring repentance, compassion, and hope in the name of Jesus into all relationships in which we are involved.

Jesus broke down the walls of hostility which separate people from each other. There can be no unity when barriers of social status, sex, economic standing, and race are not eradicated in word and deed. Therefore, our response to the people of other faiths is to become active participants in the Malaysian Consultative Council for Buddhism, Christianity, Hinduism, and Sikhism, commonly referred to as the MAJLIS. This group was formed to ensure that there is an acceptable forum that will also provide for a civil and orderly process which will assist in the resolution of problems within a climate of sensitivity and peace. It must be noted that the Muslim community has excluded itself from this group.

The members of the MAJLIS have agreed that provocation or unfair and unjust means of propagation should be forbidden. Bigotry, the deliberate distortion of facts, ridicule, and insults are definitely out of place in our day and place. Such attitude and conduct are not compatible to true religion and are not sanctioned by the Christian faith. The path to unity must be paved with humility and hospitality, peace and justice, mutual respect, compassion and good will, in order that fellow travelers, irrespective of religious background, can travel together in peace and harmony. A declaration of understanding is now being formulated by the MAJLIS.

In some countries, religion is made a political football. It is disastrous for anyone to assume that religion can be made a sacrificial lamb at the altar of political expediency. Like the forbidden apple in the Garden of Eden, it must be resisted at all cost. To do otherwise is to court chaos and disaster. We have experienced some of these in the riots of 1969. Again the work of the MAJLIS helps to prevent religious conflict from being exploited for political advantage. Where unhappiness and dissatisfaction exist these are dealt with and dismissed in an atmosphere of amicability and mutual respect within the leadership of the MAJLIS.

It is my sincere hope that this process will be accepted eventually by *all* religious groups and that this will give rise to a truly National Religious Consultative Council which would include all religious leaders, including those from Islam, so that wider forum for religious harmony can be promoted in the country. The nation needs the efforts of all to bring about the fulfillment of a process which will project well in terms of tolerance and good will among all people. Such a forum can be the conduit through which sensitive racial and religious matters can be sifted and solved.

Methods of Evangelism in Malaysia

In order to address the issue of religious sensitivity among people of different faiths, Malaysian Christians must develop a methodology for evangelism. This must attract the potential un-believers rather than turn them away. Evangelistic methods em-ployed in Malaysia have tended to be more western oriented. Some of these methods are pushy and insistent. Much publicity goes with them. Often such methods offend the Asian sense of propriety and privacy. In general Asians are religiously devout and sensitive. They do not usually wear their religion on their sleeves. Religion is a way of life and greatly affects the way one person relates to another. It is not something that is pushed down the throats of other people. But when they or their religion are insulted and ridiculed they can become violently fanatical. This may explain why it is not usual for "Asian Religions" to have overt activities to promote and propagate their religions. Of course, converts from outside their religious community are always wel-comed. But there is in general no organized evangelistic efforts as such to win people to their religion.

Christian evangelistic activities have inadvertently brought about some changes to the way of thinking among other religious communities. Occasionally we come across Muslim or Hindu scripture verses or slogans on car stickers. The Buddhists now have "Christian style" Sunday schools.

Given the facts of increasing governmental regulations and the sensitivities of the other religious communities Christian evangelistic methods have to be carefully considered. There are some methods currently used which are neither possible nor desirable. Large scale evangelistic campaigns are still run from time to time. It is not the general practice to do so now. The government, wishing to demonstrate its good faith towards non-Islamic religions, still grants permission to hold such activities. However, strict conditions are attached to such permits. For instance when any open evangelistic campaign is planned a police permit is required. In granting the permit for such an assembly, the sponsors are required to state in their publicity materials that the campaign is "for non-Muslims only." To give credit where it is due, the government authorities have been fair in the method that they have chosen to dispense with such activities.

Christians themselves should exercise restraint and resolve in this matter to demonstrate our sensitivity to the people of other faiths. Distributing tracts which attack or ridicule other people's faith is not only unfair but is counter-productive to the Christian cause. Healing rallies have also brought adverse effects when many of the promises of healing have not materialized. There was a case when a foreign evangelist accompanied by a few of his local hosts went uninvited into the head office of the Hindu Sangam (the largest Hindu Organization) and posted on the door a written challenge to a public debate.

Christians for their part should also refrain from using the word "crusade" because of its historical overtones. Indiscriminate door-to-door "tracting" should also be reconsidered as it causes unnecessary offense especially to Muslims. Some overseas groups have been mailing tracts and scripture portions to certain targeted people including the Prime Minister himself. This inevitably gives the impression that a concerted effort to convert Muslims is being carried out. While it is true that the gospel itself gives offense by its claims and what it declares, it is the unnecessary additional burden of human insensitivity that Christians can do without. We must find ways to minimize it. We pray that good sense will prevail so that the real mission of sharing Christ can go on unhindered and unencumbered.

You may have come to the conclusion, by now, that the doors in Malaysia are pretty well closed to the gospel. In one sense that is true. We are seeing a resurgence of traditional "Asian" religions which now seek to inculcate allegiance to its particular ethnic and cultural roots. In such a situation Christianity, especially in its more "western" form, is in danger of being dismissed and relegated to the status of a foreign religion. The other religious communities are building a protective wall around their respective communities to withstand Christian encroachment on their territory. But we, as a Christian community in Malaysia, believe that the doors will always remain wide open. We believe that the power of the gospel of Jesus Christ to find its way into the heart, mind, and spirit of human beings knows no boundaries. In spite of many strong efforts to keep it out, the authentic gospel still has an appeal to individuals.

Of special encouragement to Christians is the fact that the phenomenon of spiritual rebirth is no longer confined to the youth. A growing number of adult conversions have been taking place. Spouses and parents, many in their "third age," have received Christ. In my opinion, two factors have contributed to this: (1) the faithful work of local church congregations giving holistic ministry to the whole family, and (2) the testimony of individual Christian converts in their homes and places of work. The idea of the Wesleyan cell or class group appears to be the best avenue for the practice of the discipled life. The emphasis is not on specially formulated methods or strategies nor the enormous one-shot campaigns but on the life of the local church or parish and the daily life of Christians. The message is not just the gospel reduced to a capsule of a few salient points made easy to swallow but the holistic gospel relevant and effective for the whole human person and life. What is needed most of all for our evangelism is real Christians living out authentic Christian lives in the real world. God's method is incarnational: the Way of Jesus Christ displayed in the very lives of His followers. The life of our Lord is a model of progressive humility: God became man; that man became a servant; and that servant became a sacrifice (Phil. 2). No laws or regulations nor protectionist policies can keep out the message and influence of a truly Christian life. How then do we do evangelism? Ultimately, we evangelize by the style of our life and not just by word of mouth. As we evangelize we remember that we too stand in the need of God's grace, mercy, and forgiveness.

The late Dr. D. T. Niles' definition—"Evangelism is one beggar telling another beggar where to find food"—would be most apt in our society. Let me end this section with the words of Martin Goldsmith, "The love of Christ overrides all denominational and national boundaries, binding us together in loving unity whatever our background."

The Work and Witness of the Methodist Church

The ordinary members of the Methodist Church in Malaysia continue to be faithful to the fundamental ingredients of the Lord's Commission, namely "to go," "to preach," and "to make disciples." The Methodist Church has been in Malaysia for over a hundred years. In that period of time it has built and run seventy-two schools and over three hundred churches and preaching points. The Gospel has been brought to us by missionaries from Australia, the United Kingdom and the United States. Once we were part of The United Methodist Church but now we are not sure. Since autonomy in 1968 we have progressively uncertain of our "connection" with The United Methodist Church in the USA. Becoming autonomous was as much a choice as it was an expedient exercise. With our government's attitudes towards missionaries and their unwillingness to grant "work permits" it has become increasingly difficult for missionaries to enter the country and practice their profession. However, we will find other ways by which we can maintain a fraternal relationship with our partners in mission.

It is my belief that God has used temporal powers to provide the occasion for the nationals to arise to the challenge of being His witnesses. All the three hundred or more pastors and church workers are nationals. Unwritten governmental policies are meant to restrict the building of more churches. Therefore, there is a greater need for us to find alternative places for our congregations. Thus shop fronts and houses are now being used as places of worship and centers for Christian service. A great explosion in evangelism is expected in this last decade of the twentieth century. God is opening up new doors and providing new opportunities for sharing His Gospel. It will be up to us to handle this as discretely as possible.

The Methodist Church in Malaysia has decided that, in order for every member to be an Evangelist, an Institute for Evangelism has to be established. A feasibility paper has been prepared and now awaits the approval and support of the General Conference. We have identified the personnel and completed the curriculum for this project. Now it will be a matter of getting down to the practical details of setting it up. Our target is for every Methodist to be an Evangelist.

CHAPTER 8

Good News to the Poor in the Wesleyan Heritage

Theodore W. Jennings, Jr.

Introduction

A few years back, when United Methodism was engaged in the self-congratulatory rhetoric associated with the 250th anniversary of Aldersgate, I endeavored to expose what I called the myth of Aldersgate, which had produced, in my view, a fundamental distortion of the Wesleyan heritage.[1] At the risk of repeating myself, I wish to return briefly to that discussion as a way of opening up the theme of this essay: the call for a recovery of the Wesleyan heritage of the evangelization of the poor.

Aldersgate: Wesley's Vocational Crisis

In my previous essays on the subject, I endeavored to show that Wesley himself opposes the reading of Aldersgate that would make of it *the* decisive moment either in his spiritual life or in the emergence of the movement of the people called Methodists. Wesley himself recorded in his published *Journal* the ways in which his own expectations of the Aldersgate experience were eroded, beginning in the very moment itself and continuing through the remainder of that year, until his spiritual despondency exceeded that in which he had found himself prior to his "heart-warming experience." When he reissued the *Journal*, he added a series of footnotes that disclaimed the view that he was not a Christian before Aldersgate. And when Wesley finally issued an abbreviated one-volume edition of his *Journal*, he expunged the whole story of Aldersgate. Moreover, in none of Wesley's many accounts of the origin of Methodism did he ever give any role whatever to Aldersgate.

I bring this up again here to suggest a further point. It seems to me that Wesley's spiritual malaise, so carefully recorded in *Journal* entries before and after Aldersgate, was something like a mid-life crisis (he was 35, which in early eighteenth-century England would easily qualify for middle age). More especially, Wesley was in the throes of a vocational crisis. He had known since Oxford days that the life of a parish minister was not for him, he simply did not believe it possible to be both a Christian and a parish pastor. But in spite of the consolations of the so-called Holy Club, the life of an Oxford don was insufficient for his restless spiritual energy. Hence he had desired to become a missionary in order to live and serve among the indigenous tribal peoples of England's southernmost mainland colony. For a variety of reasons this aim was frustrated and his experiences in Georgia served only to re-enforce his aversion to the life of a parish pastor.

This vocational crisis was resolved only when Wesley discovered a new vocation, one that was to energize him for another half century and more: that of an evangelist to the poor and disinherited of England. In order for this resolution to occur Wesley needed two things: a message and an audience. The message was what he was struggling for in his famous conversations with Peter Böhler. In these conversations he was groping toward a message of divine transforming grace. Even though he would have to repudiate virtually every proposition of which he became convinced in his conversations with the Moravians, still the core conviction that God's grace was sufficient to transform the life of persons was central to his development.

But by itself the emergence of this conviction did nothing to alleviate Wesley's own malaise, even after it was seemingly confirmed for him that famous night in Aldersgate Street. Something more was needed. And this something more Wesley discovered when he was lured into the experiment of announcing the gospel not to the parish churches of London, but to the multitudes of the poor and marginalized who appeared at public hangings, in market places, in the parks and byways of England.

It was only when the message of God's transforming grace became good news to the poor that Wesley's spiritual malaise gave way to vocational certainty. The holiness project that had begun in his Oxford chambers and staggered in the parish in Georgia then became the populist project that gave us the people called Methodist.

I recall this because I believe that the spiritual malaise of Methodism, which has been the subject of so much hand-wringing over the last decade or so is also, at heart, a vocational crisis that will be resolved only when we, like Wesley, discover or rediscover the congruence of gospel and its appropriate audience; only when we learn again what it means to proclaim good news to the poor, the despised, the marginalized in our respective nations, and in our world as a whole.

Wesley's Option for the Poor

In order that we may become more clear about our Wesleyan heritage in this respect, let me recall for you Wesley's own assessment of the character of the movement that he launched and directed for so many years.[2] Toward the end of his life Wesley attempted a number of assessments of the Methodist movement. Not all of these evaluations are encouraging, and I will return later to Wesley's critical appraisal of the people called Methodists. But in the sermon "The Signs of the Times" Wesley did seek to place Methodism within his own growing appreciation of history as the arena of God's saving work. In order to show that God was indeed at work in history he pointed to the Methodist movement and declared:

> And surely never in any age or nation, since the Apostles have those words been so eminently fulfilled, "the poor have the gospel preached unto them," as it is at this day.[3]

Here we should notice two related things. The first is that the mission of the people called Methodists can be accurately summarized, according to Wesley, as the preaching of good news to the poor. The second is that this is regarded by Wesley as the fulfillment of the gospel mandate itself and thus as making of the people called Methodists a true sign of the work of God in the world accomplishing the divine purpose. I will only remark that whatever may have been true of the Methodist movement in Wesley's day, by no stretch of the imagination could the character

141

of The United Methodist Church be described as the announcing of the good news to, of all people, the poor.

We cannot understand the significance of Wesley's remark here unless we bear in mind that this carrying of good news to the poor was not, for Wesley, something that just happened. It was the result of a conscious and deliberate choice. Wesley turned away from the prosperous in order to turn toward the poor. Thus Wesley can say to his critics in the established church:

> The honourable, the great, we are thoroughly willing to leave to you. Only let us alone with the poor, the vulgar, the base, the outcasts of men.[4]

And Wesley was as good as his word. He regularly reported in his *Journal* that he was alarmed by the presence of the prosperous among his audience. When he discovered them there, he would change his message to suit the occasion:

> In the evening I was surprised to see, instead of some poor plain people, a room full of men daubed with gold and silver. That I might not go out of their depth, I began expounding the story of Dives and Lazarus.[5]

And when a sermon on the rich man in hell appealing in vain for the mercy of the poor in God's reign does not suffice to drive the prosperous away Wesley himself was disposed to leave:

> Many of the rich and honourable were there; so that I found that it was time for me to fly away. . . .[6]

It would be possible to illustrate this point many times from Wesley's *Journal*. He sought out the poor, he turned away from the prosperous. There are still many who regard such a policy as perverse. But Wesley understood that it was absolutely necessary if the gospel of Christ were to be served. When he was questioned about this policy Wesley responded:

> Religion must not go from the greatest to the least, or the power would appear to be of men.[7]

Here is what we may call the theological basis of Wesley's preferential option for the poor in the work of evangelization. Those strategies that seek first to convert persons of influence and reputation are modeled after the dictates of what Wesley termed worldly prudence. They suppose that if persons of influence or even prestige embrace the gospel then the poor will seek to emulate their betters. How many missionary strategies have been built upon this foundation of sand? But Wesley knew that he was about God's work. And the work of God does not proceed in accordance with the wisdom of human calculation, but rather in accordance with the folly and the impotence of the cross (1 Cor. 1:18-25).

Religion, if it is not to be the pious form of worldliness, if it is instead to be the response to the action of God, must begin where God begins, among the poor, the despised, the oppressed, and the marginalized. Otherwise it is not a divine but merely human project. And whatever success such worldly evangelism has need not be explained as the operation of God but as the result of good public relations, market research, and customer satisfaction. Wesley understood that the means must correspond with the end, that evangelization which corresponds to the gospel must begin with the poor. What a revolution it would be if only those who speak so glibly of evangelism and church growth were to take to heart this most elementary truth of the gospel.

Wesley was far from ignorant of the plight of the poor. Indeed he made it a regular practice to acquaint himself directly with their situation. He was not content to preach to them, even though his favorite venues for preaching (open fields, market places, public hangings, etc.) made certain that he would reach them in ways closed to those who stayed within the bounds of churches and meeting halls. Instead Wesley made a point of visiting the poor and even of lodging with them.

The practice of visiting the poor on a regular and constant basis goes back to Wesley's Oxford days. He regarded it then simply as an essential aspect of that holiness without which none can see God. He could no more imagine a week without the hovels of the poor than he could a week without participation in the Eucharist. Moreover, he insisted to all who placed themselves under his direction that the visiting of the poor was an essential means of grace and an indispensable form of obedience to the command of Christ:

> The walking herein is essentially necessary, as to the continuance of that faith whereby we are saved by grace, so to the attainment of everlasting salvation.[8]

143

Wesley understood that the deep class divisions of his own society were largely based upon a studied ignorance of the life of the poor on the part of the prosperous.

> One great reason why the rich in general, have so little sympathy for the poor, is, because they so seldom visit them.[9]

Thus the practice of the visitation of the poor which he regarded as essential to Methodist discipline was a praxis that broke down the barriers between the classes so as to produce a conversion of the prosperous to the cause of the poor. An immediate consequence of this intimate awareness of the conditions of poverty was the determination to develop programs of aid for the poor:

> On the following days, I visited many of our poor, to see with my own eyes what their wants were, and how they might be effectually relieved.[10]

One level of response was the practice of "begging for the poor." Here is one illustration of this practice which comes from Wesley's 82nd year!

> At this season [Christmas] we usually distribute coals and bread among the poor of the society [of London]. But I now considered, they wanted clothes as well as food. So on this and the four following days, I walked through the town, and begged two hundred pounds in order to clothe them that needed it most. But it was hard work, as most of the streets were filled with melting snow, which often lay ankle deep; so that my feet were steeped in snow-water nearly from morning till evening.[11]

Wesley made a point of the fact that he took up collections for the needy and never for himself or his movement. The collections taken at his public meetings were not for Church buildings nor for pastor's salaries but exclusively for the poor.

Even at this level Wesley's practice far exceeded what is normally thought of as alms giving and charity. But he went much further than this. He sought to help the poor help themselves. Thus he organized clinics, cooperatives, and credit unions. The evangelization of the poor entails far more than simply preaching to people. The gospel concerns not a disembodied word but the word made flesh. And the announcement of good news to the poor must at the same time be the enactment of good news to the poor, the healing of broken bodies and the feeding of the hungry and the mobilizing of the paralyzed. If this does not occur there can be no talk of an evangelism that has anything to do with the gospel of Jesus Christ.

Wesley sought to make the welfare of the poor the criterion of every aspect of the Methodist movement. This is already obvious in his choice of venue for preaching. It is also the motivation for his work of extensive publishing of small tracts and abridgements and indeed whole libraries. It is the criterion for the building of meeting places which were to be cheap so as not to make the Methodists beholden to the rich:

> Let all preaching-houses be built plain and decent; but not more expensive than is absolutely unavoidable: Otherwise the necessity of raising money will make rich men necessary to us. But if so, we must be dependent upon them, yea and governed by them. And then farewell all Methodist discipline, if not doctrine too.[12]

Thus every aspect of Methodism was subjected to the criterion, how will this benefit the poor? Solidarity with the poor was not to be a side issue, but the test of every dimension of activity.

Before leaving this brief summary of Wesley's own concern for the evangelization of the poor let me touch on one other aspect of his preaching and practice that is critical in this regard. What style of life corresponds to a commitment to the poor? From the days at Oxford, Wesley had sought to develop a life style that would permit him to engage in solidarity with the poor. This included visitation but it also included the disciplines of frugality.

When Methodism became a lay ecumenical movement following 1738 Wesley developed his views on this question under such headings as stewardship and in specialized reflections on such matters as dress, the drinking of tea, and so on. Consider the following points:

(1) We are to be stewards "for God and the poor":

> Be a steward, a faithful and wise steward, of God and the poor; differing from them in those two circumstances only,—that your wants are first supplied, out of the portion of your Lord's goods which remains in your hands; and, that you have the blessedness of giving.[13]

(2) Everything beyond what is necessary for life belongs to the poor. God gives me what I have in order that I may give it to the poor:

> ...who lodged [this money] for a time in your hands as his stewards; informing you at the same time for what purposes he entrusted you with it? And can you afford to waste your Lord's goods. . . . Away with this vile diabolical cant! This affording to rob God is the very cant of hell. Do not you know that God entrusted you with that money (all above what buys necessaries for your family) to feed the hungry, to clothe the naked, to help the stranger, the widow, the fatherless; and indeed, as far as it will go, to relieve the wants of all mankind.[14]

(3) I am to regard myself as another of the poor:

> You may consider yourself as one in whose hands the Proprietor of heaven and earth, all things therein, has lodged a part of his goods, to be disposed of according to his direction. And his direction is, that you should look upon yourself as one of a certain number of indigent persons, who are to be provided for out of that portion of his goods wherewith you are entrusted.[15]

Given that our economic life is to be governed by the welfare of the poor, the attempt to acquire more than is necessary, and especially the attempt to consume, is in Wesley's view to be understood as robbery. Thus consumption or needless expense is simply the robbery of the poor:

> ...the more you lay out on your own apparel, the less you have left to clothe the naked, to feed the hungry, to lodge the strangers, to relieve those that are sick and in prison, and to lessen the numberless afflictions to which we are exposed in this vale of tears. . . . Every shilling which you save from your own apparel, you may expend in clothing the naked, and relieving the various necessities of the poor, whom ye "have always with you." Therefore, every shilling which you needlessly spend on your own apparel is, in effect, *stolen from God and the poor!* . . .
> I pray consider this well. Perhaps you have not seen it in this light before. When you are laying out that money in costly apparel which you could have otherwise spared for the poor, you thereby deprive them of what God the proprietor of all, had lodged in your hands for their use. If so, what you put upon yourself, you are, in effect, tearing from the back of the naked; as the costly and delicate

146

food which you eat, you are snatching from the mouth of the hungry.[16]

Wesley's view of what we would call consumerism is as strict as a commandment: *"Everything about thee which cost more than Christian duty required thee to lay out is the blood of the poor!"*[17] When Wesley speaks of stewardship he is not talking about fund raising for a middle-class institution. He is talking about the redistribution of wealth from the prosperous to the poor.

Scripture and Tradition

We have seen that Wesley's commitment to the evangelization of the poor is at the very heart of the Methodist project. This should be no surprise to those who know that Wesley was concerned with the project of realizing what he called scriptural Christianity. Nor should it be surprising to those who know of Wesley's respect for the early church fathers whose sentiments with respect to stewardship for the poor Wesley has quoted virtually verbatim in the passages from his writings I have cited above.[18]

I wish to linger for a moment over the point that there can be no evangelism that is worthy of the gospel of Jesus Christ which does not embody this preferential option for the poor, this turning away from the prosperous in order to turn to the poor. The evangel which is the theme of evangelism is the gospel of Jesus Christ, who was born as one of the homeless, whose childhood was passed as an illegal alien in Egypt fleeing tyranny, whose ministry was opposed by the religious and respectable, the prosperous and the powerful, who was rejected by these and executed among bandits as one who was subversive of the existing order.

It is not enough to say that the gospel of Jesus Christ is good news without specifying for whom it is good news. And it is completely destructive of the truth of the gospel to maintain that it is simply good news for all in the same way. Certainly the Gospels make abundantly clear that the gospel of Jesus was not good news in the same way for rich and poor alike, any more than God's work in history was good news in the same way for Pharaoh and his slaves.

147

We should recall that Jesus' message was not regarded as good news by the respectable; for they were scandalized by his consorting with publicans and sinners. The action of Jesus demonstrates that his message was good news for the disreputable and despised in a direct way and could be good news for the respectable only in so far as they were prepared to abandon their respectability and join him alongside those who were despised and rejected by society.

And the same is true of the religious. The chief priests, the Sanhedrin, even the pharisees could not see good news in Jesus' total disregard for religious custom, ritual, and sacred space. His contempt for the rituals of fasting and washing, his disdain for the temple and its tax, his disregard of the sacred institution of the sabbath meant that his message and manner were good news for the ritually impure and the religiously marginalized in a way that was received as bad news by the guardians of religiosity.

Certainly the prosperous did not hear Jesus' word as good news in anything like the way the poor and destitute of Galilee did. When one who knew something of prosperity did seek to receive the message of Jesus he was told to sell all he had and give to the poor, while the poor heard that they would be able to depend upon God in their poverty, the God who cared for sparrows and lilies of the field. And the reaction of the powerful to Jesus' message was quite different from that of the powerless. For it was the powerful who conspired in his torture and execution.

This is not to say that the prosperous and powerful, the respectable and religious, were simply and totally excluded from the reign of God. The way was open to them to take up the same way of Jesus, to renounce respectability in favor of befriending the despised, to renounce religious distinctions to stand with the sinner, to renounce possessions to follow him, to renounce power to acclaim him. The Gospels record that here and there some few did respond: the centurion who acclaimed him son of God; Joseph of Arimethea who claimed his body. They are not simply excluded, but the way they must tread is narrow indeed.

The point of this recollection of the message and ministry of Jesus is to see that Wesley's own turn away from the wealthy in order to turn toward the poor was by no means an eccentric invention of his own but is deeply inscribed in the very gospel he sought to serve. An evangelism that is not first and last good news for the poor can have nothing whatever to do with the gospel of Jesus Christ. Whatever his defects of understanding, Wesley saw this far more clearly than the denominations that claim him as ancestor.

To Evangelize the Poor

I have indicated that Wesley's ministry and mission entailed what is today called a preferential option for the poor, in which the outreach to the poor is the litmus test of authentic evangelism and indeed of honest stewardship. And I have suggested that this turn away from the prosperous and toward the poor is in truth required by the gospel that Wesley sought to serve. How do things stand with us, the inheritors of Wesley's movement? Who could conceal that The United Methodist Church has in fact chosen a quite different course, has indeed chosen to take a preferential option for the middle class and so has abandoned its Wesleyan heritage? Of course I know that The United Methodist Church has some programs for the poor. But I also know that these programs are even more marginal to our denomination than the poor themselves are in our society.

One of the ways we have distracted ourselves from an understanding of our situation in this respect has been through a misreading of the signs of the times represented by the famous, or infamous study, *Why Conservative Churches are Growing?*[19] For we have focused upon the supposed theological content of the message of so-called growing churches without noting a phenomenon of even more striking relevance, namely that many of these churches do far more than we (or any other mainline denomination) at reaching out to the poor. One of the great ironies is that those churches whose pronouncements and resolutions seem so favorable to the cause of the poor consistently marginalize the poor from their own efforts, above all from their own evangelistic efforts while churches that seem oblivious to the concrete conditions of the poor in our society are in fact devoting themselves and their resources to an outreach to the poor.

For the five years before we returned to Chicago Theological Seminary in 1992, my wife was the pastor of a small and impoverished Hispanic-American congregation in Bakersfield, California.

149

While there she launched two mission congregations among poor Spanish-speaking immigrants (documented and otherwise). In the course of that work we had occasion to reflect on the failure of The United Methodist Church to reach this huge and expanding population. At the same time it was possible to observe the work of those groups that were more successful. Let me suggest a few of the ways in which we are institutionally opposed to the evangelization of the poor.

The United Methodist Church, at least in the United States, is committed to starting new churches mainly among the affluent. The bulk of money dedicated to the purpose of new church development is devoted to the search for and acquisition of property in areas where prosperous suburbs are planned. Moreover, the iniquitous salary system of The United Methodist Church strongly discourages, where it does not prohibit, experienced pastors from being available to launch new work among marginalized populations.

The bias is overwhelming toward launching congregations in the direction of becoming self-supporting. But the assumptions for thus becoming self-supporting are entirely oriented toward the middle class who will be able to construct a middle class temple and pay the salary of a middle-class pastor. With these assumptions a middle-class congregation would have to have a good 200 members to be "self-supporting." But a congregation of the poor in order to mimic this standard would have to have in the neighborhood of 500–600 tithing members.

Where churches are unable to meet this standard of becoming self-supporting, they are eventually cut off from salary support, no matter what other indices of vitality are present, unless the slack can be taken up by ethnic minority funds. Churches among ethnic minority groups that do become self-supporting are those that deliberately determine to be churches for the middle classes of those population groups. Thus African-American and Korean-American churches for example are overwhelmingly middle-class churches, not congregations of and for the poor.

When congregations among the poor in spite of these roadblocks are begun in our inner cities they are immediately saddled with the maintenance of decaying plants abandoned by middle class flight from the cities. Thus all the money they are able to raise goes to paying the heating bills. And they are doomed to pay their share of apportionments, to move toward being able to pay their pastors and so on.

The active discouragement of work among the poor and the destitute takes many forms. When a pastor decides that there is urgent work to be done among the homeless for example, she or he will be permitted to do this work only if paid by a funding agency which will support them in a middle-class life style. Otherwise they cannot be appointed. I know of cases in my wife's conference. Their example actively discourages others from heeding the gospel call.

Now let me contrast this with another picture, that of grass roots church development characteristic of many of the so-called evangelical churches. There it is common to begin as house churches, to develop into store front operations, to have preachers who support themselves by other work and are paid little. They pay no apportionments, in consequence a surprising percentage of the money they raise goes directly to mission work thereby increasing their own sense of morale in contributing to those less fortunate than themselves. Not all of these efforts succeed by any measure. But enough do to produce a strong grass roots base for positive growth. In our case if a pastor should be successful in a congregation of the poor then he or she will be rewarded as soon as possible with a move to an affluent congregation—where the real work of The United Methodist Church goes on.

What would it mean for The United Methodist Church to develop a preferential option for the evangelization of the poor?

- It would mean that we educate ourselves about how this work is done. In United Methodist Seminaries or in Course of Study schools little attention is given to congregational development among the poor. The church growth and church development literature we produce is devoted exclusively to the tastes of the wealthy and middle class.

- It would mean an abandonment of our current salary system and a move to equal salaries among all pastors. This is already true of Methodists not infected by North American Methodism. It is even true of missionaries sent by the General Board of Global Ministries, though it is not true of other persons associated with the board. Only with a policy of modest but equal salaries will there be the possibility of an effective deployment of trained leaders.

- It would also mean an abandonment of the measures of success, including the self-defeating measure of self-supporting congregations. Instead we would ask about the vitality of congregations in carrying and enacting the good news of God's love for the least of these.

- It would mean the orientation of our publishing programs away from the middle class and toward semi-literate populations, something Wesley knew quite a lot about in his time.

- It would mean selling off white elephant structures in the inner city rather than saddling the poor with their up-keep as the price of our indulging their existence.

- It would mean that the church as a whole turn toward the poor. It would mean adopting a Wesleyan view of stewardship that does not talk of fund raising for the church but of stewardship for the poor.

- It would mean that we put a stop to the diversion of funds in middle-class congregations to the building of Pharonic multi-million dollar temples and the maintenance of the upper middle-class staff so as to free resources for the relief of the poor, the announcing and enacting of good news for the poor.

- In short, it would mean repentance: a turning away from the religious imitation of worldliness in order to turn toward the reign of divine love announced and enacted by Jesus of Nazareth.

Form Without Power

When Methodists get nervous about how their church is doing they are apt to recall Wesley's own gloomy assessment of the movement toward the end of his career. The words so often cited from the essay "Thoughts Upon Methodism" (1786) run as follows:

I am not afraid that the people called Methodists should ever cease to exist either in Europe or America. But I am afraid, lest they should only exist as a dead sect, having the form of religion without the power.[20]

These words are often taken as a text (or pretext) for exposing some weakness of contemporary Methodism in order to propose some presumably Wesleyan remedy. Since we seem to be fated to hear these words quoted from time to time, it may be of some interest to see what Wesley himself had in mind.

As Wesley says, he is not afraid that Methodism will cease to exist in America or Europe. For Wesley was not concerned about loss of membership, declining Sunday School enrollment, slackening of evangelical emphasis, or a reduction in the number of converts. Methodism was an evangelistic movement in full stride. In this same essay Wesley reviews the history of the Methodist movement from its origin at Oxford, to its astonishing growth throughout England, then Wales, Ireland, and Scotland, then through the American colonies. He is well aware of the apparent "success" of the movement. The problem for Wesley is that *all that could be true and still Methodism could be a "dead sect."* Then what is the problem?

It nearly concerns us to understand how the case stands with us at present. If fear, wherever riches have increased, (exceeding few are the exceptions,) the essence of religion, the mind that was in Christ, has decreased in the same proportion.[21]

What concerns Wesley is that Methodists are becoming prosperous! And this very prosperity has the result of a loss of the "essence" of religion. To be sure Methodists had not attained in eighteenth-century England to that level of prosperity which characterizes The United Methodist Church of twentieth-century North America. But it was enough to alarm Wesley.

Since Max Weber it has become a commonplace that protestantism lays the foundation for the growth of the middle class and capitalism. But Wesley recognized the connection more than a century and a half before Weber. In this same essay he writes that "religion must necessarily produce both industry and frugality; and these cannot but produce riches."[22] But for Wesley this was so far from being a divine favor that it meant the corruption of Christian faith. If we return the just-cited passage to its immediate

153

context the point becomes even more clear:

> Therefore do I not see how it is possible, in the nature of things, for any revival of religion to continue long. For religion must necessarily produce both industry and frugality; and these cannot but produce riches. But as riches increase so will pride, anger, and love of the world in all its branches.[23]

Indeed, as Wesley notes in another sermonic essay, what is at stake here is the very self-consistency of Christianity itself:

> Does it not seem (and yet this cannot be) that Christianity, true scriptural Christianity, has a tendency, in process of time, to undermine and destroy itself? For wherever true Christianity spreads, it must cause diligence and frugality, which, in the natural course of things, must beget riches! and riches naturally beget pride, love of the world, and every temper destructive of Christianity. Now, if there be no way to prevent this, Christianity is inconsistent with itself, and of consequence cannot stand, cannot continue long among any people; since, wherever it generally prevails, it saps its own foundation.[24]

Thus for Wesley the very prosperity which we often take to be a sign of success was understood as a practical *reductio ad absurdum* of the gospel.

Of course Wesley was not content to point out the internal inconsistency of Christianity in general or of the Methodist movement in particular. He was persuaded that there was an evangelical remedy to this dilemma:

> What way . . . can we take, that our money may not sink us to the nethermost hell? There is one way, and there is no other under heaven. If those who "gain all they can," and "save all they can," will likewise "give all they can"; then, the more they gain, the more they will grow in grace, and the more treasure they will lay up in heaven.[25]

Wesley is not here talking about the making of occasional donations from our largess. He is talking about giving *all* that we have beyond what is necessary to keep body and soul together. Nor is he suggesting that we are to give to the church. We give to the *poor*. In Wesley's view, the only way to escape the satanic snare of prosperity which threatens Christendom with self-destruction and which makes Methodism liable to become "a dead sect, having the form of religion but not power" is to divest ourselves entirely of the trappings of prosperity and turn in solidarity with the poor.

What threatened the integrity of the Methodist movement was not a slow down in growth or a loss of evangelical zeal, but the growing power of a middle-class ethos which accommodated itself to the world with its emphasis on possession and prosperity and economic upward mobility. Methodism, instead of continuing in Wesley's "preferential option for the poor," was even then beginning to make another option, the preferential option for the middle class. This was Wesley's diagnosis. And it is even more applicable today. Have we not turned resolutely toward the middle-class ethos and so emptied the Methodist movement of the authentic power of the true religion?

When do we have the form without the power of religion?

- When we develop church growth strategies that target the middle class instead of the poor and marginalized, then we have the form without the power.

- When we spend more of our resources on constructing and maintaining Church buildings and property than we do on feeding the hungry, then we have the form without the power.

- When we spend more on pastor's salaries, benefits, and pensions, than we do on clothing the naked and sheltering the homeless, then we have the form without the power.

- When we turn stewardship into financial campaigns for the Church, rather than sacrifice for the poor, then we have the form but not the power.

- When we blame poverty on the sloth of the poor rather than the avarice of the prosperous and the indifference of the comfortable, then we have the form but not the power.

- When we furnish our sanctuaries and social halls in such a way as to make the prosperous comfortable rather than make the indigent welcome, then we have the form but not the power.

- When we dedicate Methodist institutions like universities and hospitals and retirement homes to the needs of the

155

affluent rather than the needs of the impoverished, then we have the form but not the power.

- When we preach a grace which saves us without changing us, then we have the form but not the power.

Above all, whenever and however we make of Methodism a preferential option for the middle class, we have the form but not the power of religion. That is what Wesley feared two hundred years ago. And it is clear that in many ways his worst fears have been realized.

Methodism was conceived as a call to scriptural holiness. Holiness means the imitation of the divine love which comes to us without worldly power and influence to dwell with us in radical solidarity and sacrificial generosity. Without this love for the least, all our Church growth strategies lead to apostasy. Without the holiness of solidarity with the poor and despised all our evangelization will only produce conversions to religious paganism. Unless we offer a radical alternative to the middle-class life style we will be but a religious reflection of the world that is perishing.

No. Methodism will not cease to exist. But unless we look beyond mere symptoms to what Wesley diagnosed as the underlying malady we will be only building larger and fancier sepulchers for a "dead sect, having the form of religion but without the power."

CHAPTER 9

The Apostolic Identity of the Church and Wesleyan Christianity

George G. Hunter III

Introduction

We have heard, *ad nauseam*, that The United Methodist Church is "declining," or has "lost its way," or is "past it."[1] Such allegations are now so commonplace that few United Methodists react defensively anymore. Virtually everyone senses, and admits, that something is deeply wrong. A once great movement is now a fairly sterile institution, not unlike the eighteenth-century Church of England within which John Wesley first fashioned an alternative movement. Twenty years ago, following the first few years of net decline, the institution's defenders announced that quantity and quality are inversely correlated. They said we were "cleaning the rolls," and "stripping the ship of excess baggage." As the denomination declined numerically, they said it would become a "better denomination." Some folks advocated "remnant theology."

All of that has changed. Too many manifestations of a quarter century of decline now hound us: a decline from over 11 million members to less than 9 million; a decline in our overseas mission personnel from 1,500 to less than 500;[2] a decline in our social and political influence; a decline in new church planting,[3] and a decline in new colleges and other "new work," with a survival mentality now replacing Methodism's earlier entrepreneurial spirit. With the greying of the denomination, we know that we will not even be able to fund the perpetuation of the past into the twenty-first century. No one except the occasional "single cause

157

advocate" now pretends that The United Methodist Church is now a "better" denomination.

In recent years, several reforming minds have offered diagnoses and prescriptions for United Methodism's pathology. So far, "the system" has ignored the issues most affecting United Methodism's future, while being driven by proliferating special interest groups and "politically correct" agendas. When the issues could not be avoided, the usual response has been denial, or an attack upon the sources of discomforting messages. Much of the conversation that has taken place has centered on comparatively secondary issues—like restructuring the bureaucracy, or the inclusion or exclusion of certain hymns in the new hymnal, or modifications in the clergy appointment system. We have not really acknowledged what may be the one vast underlying problem of The United Methodist Church—its pervasive amnesia. The vast majority of United Methodists cannot remember Methodism's distinctive understanding of the gospel, nor can they remember Methodism's distinctive understanding on three very important questions: (1) What does it mean to be *the Church*? (2) What is Methodism's essential *mission*? (3) What is the place and role of the *laity* in United Methodism's identity and mission? Of course, the latter two questions are rooted in the first, all three are ecclesiological questions.

The Identity of the Church

Whatever the strengths of its theology and tradition, Methodism has been consistently afflicted with an ambiguous doctrine of the Church—from the time of John Wesley to the present. Mr. Wesley launched Methodism as a movement within the Church of England, and he remained an Anglican his whole life. For the most part, he accepted an Anglican doctrine of the Church and maintained its sacramental emphasis. The preponderance of evidence suggests that he never intended Methodism to become a Church (at least in England, though he did facilitate Methodism becoming a Church in Scotland and in the U.S.). Consequently, Wesley apparently saw no reason to publish a comprehensive ecclesiological statement until 1785, when he was 82! Even that statement, his sermon "Of the Church"[4] engages issues that were then current and most of its truth claims are commonplaces. For instance, "church" refers more to "companies of believers" than to church buildings, and "church" may refer to a local congregation, or to the multiple congregations of a city, or of a nation, or (especially) to the universal Church. Wesley defines the universal Church as "all the persons in the universe" who are "'one body' united by 'one spirit' having one faith, one hope, one baptism; one God and Father of all, who is above all, and through all, and in them all."[5]

However, in one distinctive feature of the sermon, Wesley distances himself from the standard definition of a true church being where "the pure word of God is preached, and the sacraments duly administered." Apparently, Wesley was skittish of such an institution-serving definition which reinforced clergy-control and exaggerated the importance of mere theological opinion. Wesley believed that the quality of a church's life—seeking the mind of Christ, supporting one another in love, and living in peace, unity, and holiness—was vastly more important than theological opinion, so he "dare not exclude from the Church catholic all those congregations in which any unscriptural doctrines . . . are . . . preached. . . . Whoever they are that have 'one Spirit, one hope, one Lord, one faith, one God and Father of all,' It can easily bear with their holding wrong opinions, yea, and superstitious modes of worship."[6]

In terms of enduring ecclesiological guidelines for a denomination, Wesley's sermon "Of the Church" leaves much to be desired. Much of his understanding of the Church must be inferred from his various writings, and from what he did (e.g., deploy lay preachers), and refused to do (e.g., separate from the Church of England). Unfortunately, that vast range of data does not produce a distortion-free picture—a fact which helps justify the Church's continued employment of technical "Wesley scholars!" I am not competent to resolve the disputes in that elite company, or even to attend their meetings! But I do propose one claim regarding a Wesleyan, or Methodist, understanding of the Church: *The identity of the Church is located in its apostolic mission and ministry to people (and to whole populations) who are not yet people of faith, and this ministry and mission are primarily entrusted to the laity.* That is to say, original Methodism was essentially a *lay apostolic order* within the Church of England.

159

Some thoughtful Methodists would disagree. They would agree that original Methodism involved lay ministry, but they define the movement as essentially a renewal order—whose mission was to renew the Church of England. A canyon stands between these contrasting claims. Was Methodism's essential agenda to renew the existing Church and existing believers? Or was Methodism's essential agenda to introduce the gospel, reach lost people, and expand true Christianity in an essentially pagan population? While the "renewal perspective" may find support in Wesley's writings, it is appropriate to recover in his writings the roots for a more "apostolic perspective."

Wesley's Apostolic Vision

Wesley's understanding of Methodism's apostolic mission was based upon his reading of Primitive Christianity and also, as Franz Hildebrandt observed a generation ago, upon the realization that he faced "a pagan England . . . as we have to face paganism today, open or concealed, in the so-called Christian countries either side of the Atlantic."[7] From Wesley's extensive itineration, observation, and interviews, he understood the people of eighteenth century England. So he observed, in his essay on "The Doctrine of Original Sin," that

> The generality of English peasants are . . . brutishly ignorant . . . with regard to religion and the life to come. Ask a countryman, What is faith? What is repentance? What is holiness? What is true religion? and he is no more able to give you an intelligible answer, than if you were to ask him about the northeast passage. Is there, then, any possibility that they should practice what they know nothing of? If religion is not even in their heads, can it be in their hearts or lives? It cannot. Nor is there the least savour thereof, either in their tempers or conversation. Neither in the one, nor the other, do they rise one jot above the pitch of a Turk or a Heathen.[8]

Very early in his public career, from the pulpit of St. Mary's church in Oxford, Wesley exposed "Christian England" as a myth—in the sense that "Scriptural Christianity" was not to be substantially found in England, nor in Oxford, nor even in Oxford's leaders![9] David Bosch, therefore, rightly concludes that eighteenth-century Methodists "could see no real difference between nominal Christians and pagans and could not, by

160

implication, distinguish between 'home' and 'foreign' missions. The whole world was a mission field."[10] So, for Wesley there was precious little to "renew," the mission was much more like that which confronted the first apostles. So, how did Mr. Wesley understand that apostolic mission?

Remarkably, Wesley did not especially root Methodism's apostolic mission in The Great Commission in any of its cogent scriptural forms; he made comparatively little of Matthew 28:19-20. (William Carey was to move that text to center stage in the very late eighteenth century.)[11] Wesley did emphasize, as in concluding his sermon "Of the Church," Jesus' missiological metaphors which mandated his disciples to be the "salt of the earth," and "the light of the world," and to "let your light shine before men."[12]

Wesley's much earlier sermon on Matthew 5:13-16[13] expands upon these "salt" and "light" metaphors. While Christians should retreat from the world daily, for their souls' sake, to "converse with God . . . in secret," nevertheless "Christianity is *essentially* social religion"; to turn it into a solitary religion is to "destroy it," because it exists by "living and conversing with" non-Christian people.[14] He added that to hide, conceal, or keep private this faith is "utterly contrary to the design of its Author." Indeed, if we fail to share it, the judgment of the Lord is upon *us*.[15]

Wesley often expressed Methodism's apostolic challenge in other terms. With some hyperbole, Wesley told his lay preachers (and his class leaders), "You have nothing to do but save souls. Therefore spend and be spent in this work. . . . It is your business . . . to save as many souls as you can."[16] Mr. Wesley saw the importance of explaining what he meant by salvation, in contrast to more Gnostic, Roman Catholic, or Anabaptist meanings. In his *"Farther Appeal to Men of Reason and Religion,"* he explained that

> By salvation I mean not barely, according to the vulgar notion, deliverance from hell, or going to heaven; but a present deliverance from sin, a restoration of the soul to its primitive health, its original purity; a recovery of the divine nature; the renewal of our souls after the image of God, in righteousness and true holiness, in justice, mercy and truth.[17]

Wesley assigned the people called Methodists to do "the work of God"—which he assured us "is no cant word"; it means "the conversion of sinners from sin to holiness," and involves a movement of God through the outreach of His People that is both "widening and deepening."[18] He justified his extensive travel by horseback, and the travel vocations of many other Methodists, by explaining that "We all aim at one point, (as we did from the hour when we first engaged in the work), not at profit, any more than at ease, or pleasure, or the praise of men, but to spread true religion through London, Dublin, Edinburgh, and, as we are able, through the three kingdoms."[19] Franz Hildebrandt quoted a poem by Charles Wesley, written six years into the movement, which "comprises in a few lines . . . the whole purpose of the brothers' mission."

> When first sent forth to minister the word,
> Say, did we preach ourselves, or Christ the Lord?
> Was it our aim disciples to collect,
> To raise a party, or to found a sect?
> No, but to spread the power of Jesus' name,
> Repair the walls of our Jerusalem
> Revive the piety of ancient days,
> And fill the earth with our Redeemer's praise.[20]

In "The General Spread of the Gospel," the sermon Wesley preached in 1783 on the occasion of the opening of Wesley's Chapel in London, he strummed similar chords. He announced that "darkness [and] ignorance, with vice and misery attendant upon it, cover the face of the earth,"[21] including the so-called Christian nations. But Wesley used this public occasion to proclaim an ancient vision: "The earth shall be filled with the knowledge of the Lord, as the waters cover the sea. The loving knowledge of God, producing uniform, uninterrupted holiness and happiness, shall cover the earth; shall fill every soul"; and whole societies will be compassionate and free of violence.[22] And Wesley proclaimed this vision as a possibility to be achieved through the Christian mission! This can happen, he said, as God works in people's souls in ways consistent with how he has worked in the past—not violating, but fulfilling, people's freedom, understanding, and affections. More specifically, it can happen as it has been happening in the history of Methodism's expansion, beginning with the first "Methodist" group in Oxford, from which it has spread to many thousands and to other lands, which "is only the beginning of a far greater work." More specifically still, "the

Kingdom of God . . . will silently increase, wherever it is set up, and spread from heart to heart, from house to house, from town to town, from one kingdom to another." Indeed, the movement will so spread that "even the rich shall enter into the kingdom of God . . . [and] last of all, the wise and learned."

Wesley acknowledged that two barriers presently frustrate the apostolic vision. First, the lives of professed Christians often discredit the gospel in the perceptions of persons influenced by other religions, but the sanctification of Christians can fill them with love and credibility and thereby open the eyes of seekers. Second, Wesley recognized that many peoples and nations of the world do not yet have the opportunity to receive the gospel and experience new life because they "have no intercourse . . . with Christians of any kind," but God will raise up and send modern apostles to these populations.[23]

The Role of the Laity in Methodism

Wesley was even more a leader and organizer than a visionary, so it is not surprising that he organized Methodism, deployed the preachers, and administered the societies with "a single eye" for reaching people and advancing the movement. Henry D. Rack reminds us that a key part of John Wesley's legacy is "the concern for the pursuit of evangelism, regardless of formal church order"; that church order is "something to be improvised in response to, and in the service of, religious truth and religious mission rather than settled by dogmatic presuppositions."[24]

Wesley's most important improvisation, by far, involved the deployment of laity in Methodism's apostolic mission and ministries. Indeed, original Methodism was essentially a lay movement. Eighteenth-century Methodism was not unique in deploying lay people. Gordon Rupp demonstrates that many laity in the Church of England, quite including women, did much good in Christ's name in their communities, and they advanced such causes as penal reform, anti-slavery, and the Sunday Schools.[25] Rupp explains what was, and was not, behind that century's Anglican lay involvement.

> There was nothing doctrinaire about the laicization of religion in eighteenth-century England. It had nothing to do with modern notions about the "wholeness" of the one People of God, the

Scriptural *laos*. Nor had it . . . anti-clerical overtones. . . . It did not explore the implications of the Priesthood of Believers, as this was acclaimed at the Reformation, still less that apostolate of the laity expounded by the Second Council of the Vatican. It did not probe the mysterious questions "What is a layman? Who is a priest? . . ." It was rather the tacit acceptance of a historical situation, which had given the laity power in the Church. And this in a way which blurred earlier distinctions between the spiritual and temporal powers, and led to the lay occupation of a no-man's-land between them.[26]

Rupp's point may be stated more explicitly: As great numbers of the Church of England's clergy settled into their comfortable living—baptizing, marrying, burying, leading services and (perhaps) teaching the catechism—but doing precious little else, this left a very great deal for laity to do within a parish's total ministry. Such a reading is not unfair. The "gentrified" clergy were a scandal in their own time and some Anglican clergy even lived far away from their parishes, abdicating its work to malcompetent curates.

But Wesley had neither of those problems. He had a movement on his hands, with much need for outreach, teaching, ministry, and leadership—with virtually no ordained clergy at his disposal. The only people available were gifted lay people. Wesley did not stampede toward the lay solution, but he had experiential warrant for considering it. As an impressionable boy, he had observed for months the undeniable power of his own mother's growing Sunday evening ministry, as up to 200 people assembled in, and outside of, her Epworth kitchen. She later influenced John to conclude that Thomas Maxfield, and presumably other lay people, were called by God to preach. And he early saw the blessing of God attending the ministries and witness of many Methodist laity.

So Methodism radically "out-laicized" the other denominations, and became essentially a lay movement. Virtually all the ministry that took place in, and out from, every Methodist society was done by lay people. There were class leaders and band leaders and other kinds of small group leaders, as well as local preachers and those so-called assistants who took *de facto* charge of societies and circuits—all lay persons. Other lay people visited sick and hospitalized people; others worked with children and their families; others visited poor people, widows, and single parent families, still others engaged in conversations with undiscipled people and started new classes for seekers.

This impressive organization for lay ministries was not left to chance. Persons were selected for various ministries with care, each ministry had a "job description." People were "developed" for various roles, and were observed and "coached" in their performance. And, in Methodism's unique marriage of ministry and evangelism, everyone who ministered also evangelized. Wesley knew what the church growth movement has only recently rediscovered—that virtually the only Christians who regularly share their faith are Christians involved in some ministry, who see God working through their ministry. So, the priority objective of class leaders, visitors of the sick and the others was to "save souls." Of course, the early Methodist societies had preachers, but it would be easy to exaggerate their importance. They served "circuits" of several societies, and they itinerated every year or two; in any case, the vast majority of them were nonordained lay preachers. It is true that, in time, the preachers—through their annual conference—governed the connection, the laity were not involved in high level ecclesiastical politics, but their time and energy were thereby freed for ministries in societies and communities. Wesley, of course, served as the movement's teacher. He challenged his leaders to read, learn, and develop, and he believed they could be the agents for a great movement of the Spirit. Wesley may have overestimated the gifts and capacities of his people: Gordon Rupp comments that "Wesley's geese were too often swans in his eyes."[27] But a lay movement Methodism was, a Protestant movement that went quite beyond "priesthood of all believers" sloganeering and actually entrusted virtually all the ministry that matters to lay people. Methodism was a "lay apostolate" before we knew what to call it. So the apostolic mission of the laity is at the heart of any distinctive Methodist understanding of "Church."

The Pathology of Modern Methodism

From time to time, I become aware of how Methodism has drifted from its original identity as an apostolic people whose laity are the light of the world. In recent years, I have become aware of this as a member of my Florida Conference Board of Ordained

Ministry, while interviewing candidates for ordination as elders. The group of interviewers in which I serve once decided to begin each interview with this question: "Tell us about your appointment." The question is not as simplistic, or innocent as it appears; what people choose to talk about is revealing. In my recent book, *How To Reach Secular People*, I summarized what I learned. I invite you to discover, with me, a pathological pattern.

An associate pastor reported personal spiritual growth and a good experience with the members. Another reported good relationships with the members and "gratifying" experiences in leading worship services. Another candidate, pastoring a recently merged church, reported that implementing the merger is "consuming" him. Another reported great meaning in word and sacrament, and "satisfaction" from involvement in ministries to various age groups. Another candidate found his appointment "comfortable," and "a blessing to our family." Still another reported fulfillment in teaching scripture, and in officiating at weddings and funerals.

By now a pattern was emerging. Each candidate was focusing much more on his or her local church than upon the community the church is called to serve and reach; several candidates never referred to the community at all—though several referred to some denominational or ecumenical involvement beyond their local church. Furthermore, they were more enamored with the satisfactions they were receiving from ministry than with any outcomes, in the lives of people or in the life of the community, from their ministry.

When I probed with interviewees with follow-up questions, an associate pastor shared a job description which emphasizes "visitation to members, shut ins, and hospitals," and working with the "young married and singles" in several projects during Lent.

Someone asked, "What is the meaning of Lent?" After an adequate textbook comment about the crucifixion and resurrection of Jesus, he added "it was all for me."

I asked, "What about other people? Was it for them too?"

"Yes, of course."

"For all other people, everywhere? Not just you and your church's members?"

"Certainly."

"Is your job description consistent with that belief?" He said he assumed it was, because he inherited the job description from his predecessor!

Still another candidate, an "A" student from his Master of

Divinity degree program, was pastoring a church in a transitional neighborhood, his members were moving out, people of a different subculture were moving in. I asked if they had received any new believers last year from the community; they had not. His answers to additional questions revealed that his church is not in regular conversation with any undiscipled people in the community, that he did not know how many are out there, that no such people are on the church's prospect list, in part because the church has no prospect list!

Finally, when we asked a candidate to tell us about her appointment, she began talking about the community, and the needs and struggles that its people experience. She reported that a dozen people had joined the church as new Christians, that a handful of her members are now "ambassadors for Christ," and that much of the church has now developed "a conscience for world mission." She had acquired this agenda after becoming a Christian in another country, and as a course of study candidate, this one lone apostle was not a product of a seminary degree program.

So, from this sampling, one in nine candidates for ordination had primarily an outreach agenda for ministry. This sampling was roughly confirmed as I perused the essays on vocational ministry written by all 32 candidates. About 1 of every 8 or 9 or 10 emphasized service and/or witness to the community and/or to the world.[28]

The others were focused inwardly upon their churches, and their assumptions about ministry can be badly stated in four propositions: (1) Ministry takes place mainly in the church building, not in the world beyond. (2) Ministry's main target is Christians, not non-Christians. (3) Ministry is primarily the responsibility (or privilege) of ordained clergy persons, not of the laity. (4) The validity of ministry is indicated by the job satisfaction of the clergy person, not by changes in people's lives or by changes in the community. If these generalizations are at all accurate and representative, then at the root of United Methodism's many problems is an identity crisis, or a classic case of amnesia. A majority of our clergy do not know that we are ordained in "apostolic succession," i.e., to succeed the apostles in reaching undiscipled people. We have moved a considerable distance— from "the world is my parish" to "my parish is my world!" The "fishers of men and women" have become "keepers of the aquarium," the hired private chaplains of groups of organized

Christians. They, and their churches, have succumbed to "the chaplaincy trap."

None of these contentions is new. For a long time, some leaders and analysts within Methodism have regretted the unfortunate tradeoffs experienced when Methodism went "a whoring" after the respectability of the Presbyterians and Episcopalians and shifted its accent from lay ministry to professional ministry. But prophetic preachments and books on the theology of the laity have made little enduring difference. Furthermore, most church leaders have not known what to do—beyond theological reflection and public advocacy; it is one thing to want the priesthood of all believers to be a reality but another thing to see it realized. We have experienced a lot of "handwringing" over this dilemma. But in recent years, at least several bellwether congregations have experienced significant breakthroughs in recovering lay ministry and a lay apostolate, whose pioneering is demonstrating reproducible ways forward for many other congregations. In this essay, one such congregation is featured—Saddleback Valley Community Church, in Orange County, California.

The Example of Saddleback Valley Community Church

The Rev. Rick Warren started Saddleback Valley Community Church in 1980, as a "new breed" Southern Baptist mission to reach unchurched people. The church's first members were Rick Watten and his young growing family, and their realtor and his family. Since Warren believed that most new churches build facilities too soon and too small, the church has used rented facilities throughout its twelve-year history—though they have now acquired acreage and plan to build. In recent years, their three Sunday morning worship services have met in a high school gymnasium. They rent a suite of offices in a shopping plaza, they hold Sunday evening concerts in a rented nightclub. After twelve years of ministry, the church now averages over 5,000 people in average worship attendance. Their very active membership now stands at about 2500. They baptize over 400 new Christians per year; over 125 small groups meet weekly; over 1000 members are involved in serious, demanding, avocational ministries; and several hundred members serve each year in short-term, overseas, cross-culture mission experiences. In their twelve-year history,

Saddleback Valley Community Church has also planted 167 daughter congregations!

Saddleback Valley's obsessional approach to lay ministry is the indispensable key to their success, and the church's driving philosophy supports lay ministry and mission. Rick Warren explains that, for their church, "The people are the ministers, and the pastors are the administers." The staff make most of the necessary administrative decisions, thus freeing the laity from the consuming involvements in committee work, voting, governance, and maintenance that immobilize, divide, and exhaust most congregations, thereby freeing their time and energy for ministry and outreach in the community. The staff's key role is to "lead and feed" the laity, thereby "equipping the saints" for their ministries. The church begins where people are, and manages a "Life Development" process for helping people become serving, reproductive Christians. Rick Warren has developed a "Baseball Diamond" analogy, which he teaches to the people to guide their development. "First base" involves a commitment to *membership*, "second base" to *maturity*, "third base" to *ministry*, and "fourth base" to *mission*. Each of these milestones is facilitated through a four-hour seminar (referred to as #101, #201, #301 and #401). At the end of each seminar, a person is invited to commit his or her life around the seminar's focus.[29]

Rick Warren believes that the great challenge confronting most local church pastors is "how to turn an audience into an army," so the church's #301 seminar on ministry is crucial to Saddleback's total strategy. The chief assumption behind Saddleback Valley's approach is that you do not recruit volunteers effectively by putting square pegs into round holes—which may elicit compliance, but not performance. You do not first define a range of jobs, and then recruit people to fill each one, whether they "fit" or not. In ministry, function should follow form, so you first discover how people are "shaped," and then facilitate their placement into a ministry or role that is right for their shape. The word "SHAPE" serves as an acronym upon which Saddleback's approach to developing people is explained. In the four-hour seminar, people are helped to find ministries and roles based on their Spiritual Gifts, Heart, Abilities, Personality, and Experiences. The seminar manual explains that one's ministry should be determined by one's makeup, that when people are serving from

169

their shape they are effective and experience fulfillment.

> What God made me to *be* determines what He intends me to *do*. I will understand the *purpose* I was created for when I understand the kind of *person* I am. This is the secret of knowing God's will for my life.
>
> God is consistent in his plan for each of our lives. He would not give us inborn talents and temperaments, spiritual gifts, and all sorts of life experiences and then not use them! By reviewing and studying these factors, we can discover the ministry God has for us . . . the *unique* way God intends for us to serve him.

The seminar then proceeds to help each participant discover his or her unique SHAPE.

The seminar begins by helping people discover their "Spiritual Gifts" for ministry within and beyond the Body of Christ. Rick Warren acknowledges that the understanding of spiritual gifts is not uniform or systematic in the New Testament; the several lists of gifts vary from one another and, presumably, they are not exhaustive. Furthermore, Warrent seemed to agree with me that the Church's doctrine of spiritual gifts is not a "heavyweight" doctrine; it lacks the "explanatory power" of, say, the doctrine of the Trinity. (For example, I have never met anyone who discovered, from taking a Spiritual Gifts questionnaire, that they had the gift of "hospitality" who hadn't kind of known that already!) Nevertheless, a spiritual gifts exercise can help a Christian to clarify what his or her several gifts probably are, and consider their "gift mix," and begin ministering with this clearer self-perception, and, Rick Warren believes, we then discover our gifts with greater certainty from experiences in ministry. The seminar manual names and defines 23 different gifts[30] and gives people the opportunity to explore their possible gifts, as illustrated in the spiritual gift of Evangelism.

EVANGELISM:

> The ability to communicate the Good News of Jesus Christ to unbelievers in a positive nonthreatening way. The ability to sense opportunities to share Christ and lead people to respond with faith.
>
> ( ) I'm pretty sure I have this gift.
> ( ) I may have this gift.
> ( ) I don't think I have this one.

During the seminar, people pencil in their best self-perception in regard to each of the gifts, later they will request the perceptions of several Christian friends who know them well.

The seminar unit on "Heart" helps people to clarify their driving motivations, what they have a passion for. The seminar assumes a congruence between people's interests, passions, and motivations on the one hand, and the will of God on the other. "God had a purpose in giving you your inborn interests." (By contrast, many Churches and Christians assume that whatever God calls us to do must be contrary to our interests, that what the Third Person calls us to do is inconsistent with how the First Person created us.) The seminar manual affirms that

> . . . God has given each of us a unique emotional heart-beat that races when we encounter activities, subjects, or circumstances that interest us. We instinctively feel deeply about some things and not about others.
>
> This God-given motivation serves as an internal guidance system for our lives. It determines what your interests are, and what will bring you the most satisfaction and fulfillment. It also motivates you to pursue certain activities, subjects, and environments.

People then process and clarify their interests in the following exercise: First, they list their accomplishments—defined as things they enjoyed doing and did well, in each decade of their life to date. Then, second, they study their list of accomplishments to discover some common motivational thread(s). This enables them to identify two or three of the following possible motivators as their driving motives.

I LOVE TO:

Design/Develop—starting or making something from scratch
Pioneer—try out new concepts, even risking failure
Organize—organizing something that is already started
Operate/Maintain—something that is already organized
Serve/Help—others succeed in their responsibility
Acquire/Possess—as in shopping, obtaining, or collecting things, especially quality
Excel—to be the best, to attain the highest standard
Influence—as in shaping the beliefs, attitudes, and behaviors of others

171

Perform—to be on stage, in the limelight

Improve—taking something already started and making it better

Repair—to fix what is broken or change what is out of date

Lead/Be in charge—as in supervising, and determining what or
how things will be done

Persevere—as in persisting, and seeing things through to
completion

Follow the rules—as in operating by policies, and meeting organization's expectations

Prevail—as in fighting for the right, opposing wrong, and overcoming injustice

The unit on "Abilities" affirms that many of our skills and abilities, which we acquired genetically or in early experience, are as useful in the church's ministry as in the home or marketplace. The exercise refers participants to their earlier list of their accomplishments and directs them to "circle all verbs that denote actions performed doing each achievement." The participant then compares those verbs to a list of "26 specialized abilities"[31] which are especially useful in various aspects of church ministry—such as entertaining, recruiting, artistic, promoting, feeding, and decorating abilities, and people identify their strongest two or three.

The Unit on "Personality" encourages participants to minister in areas suited to their personalities, in ways consistent with how "God has wired your temperament." Then, building upon the well-known Myers-Briggs personality type questionnaires and other indicators of temperament, participants then identify where they are in terms of five scales.

Extroverted	3	2	1/1	2	3	Introverted
Thinker	3	2	1/1	2	3	Feeler
Routine	3	2	1/1	2	3	Variety
Self-controlled	3	2	1/1	2	3	Self-expressive
Cooperative	3	2	1/1	2	3	Competitive

The final unit helps people to understand that God has also prepared them for ministry though their life "Experiences," especially their educational, spiritual, ministry, and painful experiences. The most revolutionary of those claims is that God prepares us through the "hard knocks" and painful experiences of our lives, "that in all things God works for good in those who love him, who are called according to his purpose." Therefore, #301 class participants especially consider the possibility that God "wants you to be open to ministering to people who are going through what you have already been through." After participants record their important educational, spiritual, ministry, and painful experiences, the four-hour seminar ends with a summary of insights and Saddleback's philosophy of ministry.

People then take their materials home and prayerfully fill out a "ministry profile" indicating their best estimate of their SHAPE; they are encouraged to consider the perceptions of family members and friends as they fill it out. Then they make an appointment with a lay Ministry Guide, who directs them to the three or four job descriptions (out of more than 200 job descriptions) that best match their shape, from which they prayerfully choose one. Saddleback now has over 1,000 lay persons who have experienced this four-hour seminar, who have discovered or clarified some important things about themselves, have committed their lives to lay ministry and mission, and are now serving in some ministry for which they are "shaped." Saddleback now places several hundred new lay persons, many of them new believers, in ministry each year. The many hundreds of members now involved in community ministries and witness account for the church's growing image as a "movement" in Orange County.

Saddleback Valley Community Church is one of (at least) several churches of other Christian traditions who are demonstrating to Methodists that it is logistically possible for Methodism to do once again what Methodism once did more and better than anyone else. United Methodism does not need to remain a clergy-dominated church captured by the chaplaincy paradigm; we can become a lay apostolic movement once again. For this to happen while most of us yet live, many of our clergy and national leaders would need to experience a major paradigm shift—related to Wesley's alleged problem of seeing too many of his "geese" as "swans." That is not our problem. Too many of us see our swans as geese, and our geese as chickens or turkeys—or as mere geese who lay the golden eggs that fund the ecclesiastical machinery. Since no one sees people exactly as they are, Wesley erred on the better side. If we choose to see our people as gifted and shaped for ministry and mission, some of them will let God down, but many will become salt and light, and Methodism will become a movement again, and millions of other people will join the contagious ranks of the people called Methodists.

APPENDIX 1

"Our New Identity": A Sermon on Ephesians 2:11-21

James T. Laney

Therefore remember that at one time you Gentiles in the flesh, . . . remember that you were separated from Christ, alienated from the commonwealth of Israel, and strangers to the covenants of promise, having no hope, and without God in the world. But now in Christ Jesus, you who were far off have been brought near in the blood of Christ. For he is our peace, who has made us both one, and has broken down the dividing wall of hostility by abolishing in his flesh the law of commandments and ordinances, that he might create in himself one new man in place of the two, so making peace, and might reconcile us both to God in one body through the cross, thereby bringing the hostility to an end. And he came and preached peace to you who were far off and peace to those who were near. . . . So then you are no longer strangers and sojourners, but you are fellow citizens with the saints, and members of the household of God, built upon the foundation of the apostles and the prophets, Christ Jesus himself being the cornerstone, in whom the whole structure is joined together and grows into a holy temple in the Lord. (Eph. 2:11-21, RSV)

All over the world, people are claiming what for them is their rightful identity. Relieved of the overwhelming "either-or" of having to side with the east or west, peoples are asserting their rights to be acknowledged as nations, and as individuals, to take unto themselves their own destiny. We see it, of course, in the breaking-up of the Soviet Union, and in Eastern Europe. Sometimes, it happens with unfortunately tragic overtones, as in Yugoslavia, and always with profound repercussions, not only for themselves, but for the whole family of nations, as they claim historic names in their autonomy and their history, and refuse to be defined by the great power blocks of the past. We find it is not limited simply to parts of Europe, but is also is true in other parts of the world. In Central America, El Salvador and Nicaragua which were tormented for so long, among others, by U.S. foreign policy measures, and had to live under the shadow of the conflict of east and west. They now are all claiming their right to be who they are, that is: free! And they define themselves, nationally, ethnically, culturally, not only in terms of their own histories and their own futures, but also in relationship to the very large and powerful United States of America.

It's a whole new day for our relationships and our policies, and the architects of American foreign policies are trying, sometimes with more or less imagination, to come to terms with all these various situations. In many ways, it's a whole new era, and it is not simply for us alone to determine what the future will be. Similarly, we are all aware, and have been for several decades, about the forces for identity in this country—ethnicity, race, gender, region, culture: the claiming of the right to define oneself and not be at the mercy of the dominant other—whoever the other might be. There are great tensions that arise as a result of this. There is a refusal to be limited to traditional understandings of who people are, and that refusal and the new definitions of identity constitute the greatest opportunity in this country today, but also the greatest crisis. These are the major social issues, and gender and race are the most critical ones.

All of you are familiar with the term "PC"—"Political Correctness." "Political Correctness" is used principally by the dominant media, by what could be described as the establishment, resisting the claims of women, African-Americans, and others, to define themselves in new ways, which would involve certain implications for culture as a whole. The reason for the resistance, of course, is that none of us, grouped by gender or historical aggregations of individuals, live unto ourselves. These changes affect the entire fabric of our society. We are talking about our relationships. We are talking about what the media says and what stands in the public eye, what the establishment dictates. I don't use these terms merely in a pejorative sense, but really in a descriptive sense.

One example of how powerful this is in terms of ascribing identity to region and class, if not by way of race or gender, occurred early on in the campaign of Jimmy Carter as President of the United States. He ran as a person who was outside of the establishment, and that was his great appeal. The establishment, as well as the media and the people in the east found it very hard to accept a person from the deep South as their leader. When he got elected, it was very difficult for him to find legitimacy in the eyes of a lot of those people who withheld their support. I remember well a conversation with a prominent dean from an unnamed great university in the east.

This dean came to me and said: "Tell me about Jimmy Carter." Well, it was already a lost discussion.

He said: "He comes from Plains, Georgia?"

I said: "That's right."

He said: "And he really is a peanut farmer?"

I said: "Yes."

Well, the disdain was dripping, and that was only because of region and history, and maybe socio-economic class. Carter had to become a worldwide figure and an acknowledged humanitarian finally to win the legitimacy and the respect of such groups and people. Conferred identity can be very painful and crippling, and the liberation movements of our time are the determination of people who have lived under those definitions conferred by others.

Finally, freedom, human rights, and hope mean that I can become really who I am. But of course this carries with itself profound repercussions. Now we not only have the women's movement, but a burgeoning men's movement. We not only have multi-culturalism on campus, but reactions to multi-culturalism. And we are seeing the ugly head of racism, anti-Semitism, bigotry, and provincialism in the politics of our time, all exploiting the anxieties and uncertainties that always beset us when profound changes occur, and when relationships that have become customary are disturbed. All of this has strained the liberal fabric of our society and its assumptions that tolerance alone will suffice, that people will in fact act rationally even when their interests or perceived interests are threatened.

Like the campus, the Church has sought to be sensitive to these new identities. It, too, has been the scene of similar tensions. It is so easy for the church to reflect an untroubled identity regarding class and race and culture, to feel like others, in the words of Henry Higgins, should "be like us," to feel that mission and evangelism is really helping them to look like us. We know the inadequacy of that and its limitations, and the destructiveness that goes with it. The question is: "How do we come to terms with this new change when the Gospel seems so Western on the one hand, and so middle-class on the other?" When we look back at the history of the Church, every time we see that the Church has become captive to the dominant identity of its society, every time it has become comfortable with its role in culture, it has lost its universality. And with that loss of universality, it has lost the power to create, not merely to evangelize, but also the power to become renewed, for there to be one new person in Christ in place of two.

It is not as though the identities became nil, but they are redefined in Christ. Our fundamental humanity is understood now in terms of the scriptures, that a new power of the Holy Spirit is unleashed upon the Church. The New Testament bears witness to that very struggle for identity which is what we see now as then. Paul wrestled with the relation of his identity as a Jew and all of its great tradition and holiness to the Gentiles who were outside of it, and how to do it without betraying what he felt was the fundamental commission of Jesus Christ. And as we know, Paul got a tremendous reaction from the Church, which was then the Jewish Church. In order to achieve a breakthrough, it was Paul who finally came up with "There is no longer Jew or Greek, there is no longer slave or free, there is no longer male or female; for all of you are one in Christ Jesus" (Gal. 3:28). That was not mere rambling. Paul's letters are extraordinary in the chemistry, in the way in which he internalized the new power of Christ.

When Paul said over and over, "a new person in Christ," he continued to be proud of his Jewish heritage, as we know in Philippians. He did not let that, however, become a wall or a barrier or a ceiling to how he would relate to others who were not sharers of that same identity, tradition, glory, and power. We turn to Ephesians, chapter 2, and we see the marvelous way in which Paul puts it together. He says, "You were once strangers and sojourners," that is, you were without an established identity, (that is at the mercy of the dominant cultures, telling you who you were), you who were once sojourners and strangers have now been brought near in Christ. For he is our peace in that tension, in that struggle, in that hostility, in that alienation who has made us both one, and has broken down the dividing wall of hostility, suspicion, uneasiness, apprehension and alienation, that he might create in himself one new person in place of the two, thereby making peace and reconciling us both to God in one body.

So now, we are fellow citizens and members of the household of God, and that's the new identity—*that's the new identity*! This is what clarifies and purifies all of our other identities, all of those preceding identities that we all have. It is a basis for that creative energy and love which reach out across all the barriers of uncertainty, hostility, suspicion, and even hatred. To enable this to happen is the very principle of evangelism, bringing all into the household of God on new terms as fellow citizens. Of course, it means that, like Paul, we have to forego that reliance on any other identity in which we might take pride, or make a claim that somehow it establishes us in the presence of God over against other people. It doesn't nullify that identity, but it does cleanse it and chasten it.

We see that every time in the epochs of the Church, where there has been a great renewal, there has been a new discovery of that oneness and identity as fellow members of the Household of God. I think of the monastery movement, the monastics who voluntarily relinquished the power they held in the dominant identity and took on themselves poverty in a time of class, strict class, of chastity, not just male, but female; of obedience to a new rule, a new order of Christ. They made themselves available, without power, to those who needed to be served. Think of the Reformation of the Imperial Church which had become identified with the power of government and how Luther and his cohorts introduced that revolutionary concept of the priesthood of all believers. This new identity was not dependent upon the priest or upon an ecclesiastical order, but upon a relationship with Christ. It was Paul's understanding rediscovered, that oneness in Christ. Think of Wesley at time when the aesthetic attraction and the social power of the Church of England really served as a barrier to the great majority of the people. And now finally with a huge sense of personal loss, Wesley went outside the church and spoke as a fellow sojourner and a stranger, and offered his hand and his heart to those who had never had such an invitation. Together they found a new identity in setting up the little class meetings and forged a new life which they called holiness. It was a new

179

identity with discipline and aspiration and hope and power.

Whenever the Church has really been renewed, whenever there has been not just evangelistic rhetoric, but true mission of the Church, it has been with the discovery of this in its heart. Even the Church had to transcend itself to create a new chemistry, a new relationship in that power to cross over into the other areas of society. To be able to offer that identity and to serve the world in that way really is the creative power of God today.

I've seen it at work in a little church in a different city, in a transitional neighborhood. The church was once large, and is now very small. They no longer meet in the sanctuary because it is too expensive. Instead, they meet in the basement. They are old and young, and, well, I wouldn't say rich and poor, but of various classes, and black and white, and single parents. They are all there, not very many, but representing an extraordinary range of identities. In that little church, there is a microcosm of the Living Spirit of Jesus Christ. The dominant identity of the culture has been resolutely set aside, and here is an outpost of the Kingdom. It's almost a leaven. That leaven is powerful, and when one goes into that little congregation, you see it and feel it. There is hope in the eyes of those who didn't have hope, and a feeling of love and care and service, not only for themselves, but for their neighborhood.

In every one of our cities there are the forgotten, the lost, the afflicted, those who have been abused and are forlorn. And we live in a society where, for the most part, the Church is removed from that underclass and its terrors and its tragedy. We have here in this city a nascent project called the Atlanta Project which would call the churches out of their isolation doing many fine things and certainly ministering to each other. The motivation to move out of isolation and into the city is not to bring a superiority or some kind of condescension (or patronizing?), but to join with the young people, the children, the old people, and the forgotten, and learn what it is like to be fellow citizens of the Household of God.

We live in a time where there are all kinds of identities that are being claimed, but the one great identity is the one we can share in Christ which alone has the power to reconcile and to heal. It can open up the freshness of love and annihilate the suspicion and uncertainty that so afflict our time. It is not a panacea, but it is salvation. When the Church distinguishes between panacea and salvation and finds the oneness that we can share in Jesus Christ, when the Church finds the creativity which comes when being blessed by another being we meet for the first time in Christ, then the power of renewal and evangelism can occur. Such is the new creation which is promised for us all. Amen.

APPENDIX 2

Remembrances of
Dr. and Mrs. E. Stanley Jones

Eunice and James K. Mathews

EDITOR'S NOTE: The following remembrances by Bishop and Mrs. Mathews of her parents, Dr. and Mrs. E. Stanley Jones, were made in an informal setting following the Saturday night banquet at the symposium. These remarks have been edited for publication, but their informal style has been preserved. The complete original may be obtained on videotape from the offices of the Foundation.

Bishop Mathews:
Naturally we're glad to be here. In fact, as Bishop Ensley used to say, we're glad to be anywhere! This is our first visit to this missionary center. I'm glad I could come tonight, and Eunice with me, because tomorrow will mark for me an anniversary. It was just 54 years ago tomorrow that I sailed out of New York harbor on the Queen Mary to become a missionary to India. I know that the next day, which was my 25th birthday, I was seasick. I would not take anything in exchange for being a missionary of Jesus Christ. I believe that missionaries are evangelists; that is, evangelists who have ignored all boundaries whether of nations, or cultures, or of the mind. You think about that for a while.

About two generations ago there were four people who were always thought of more or less in the same breath. They were engaged in somewhat different activities, but they were all thought of in much the same way: Albert Schweitzer, Toyohiko Kagawa, Mahatma Gandhi, and E. Stanley Jones. We're going to talk tonight about E. Stanley Jones as you have requested. It will be a dialogue, a conversation.

183

In the middle of a British Methodist conference, an astonishing thing happens. They suddenly will stop all business and the Chair will announce a "conversation on the work of God," then launch out. Perhaps you can think of what we do here tonight as a conversation on the work of God.

Mrs. Mathews:

Grace to you and peace . . .

Bishop Mathews:

. . . from God our Father and the Lord Jesus Christ. And all of you here can say, "Amen!"

Mrs. Mathews:

I note that you almost always begin with this greeting. Why?

Bishop Mathews:

Well, because St. Paul invariably used it in his day, and if it was good enough for St. Paul, I think it is good enough for us. By the way, your Dad had a special way of beginning an address.

Mrs. Mathews:

Yes, he always bowed in head in silence and then after a few moments, he would say, "Amen."

Bishop Mathews:

The last time I saw him, about six weeks before his death, I finally asked him a question I had wanted to ask him for a long time: "What prayer did you use when you did that?" He shocked me by saying that it was not a prayer at all.

Mrs. Mathews:

That's right. He repeated his verse: "You have not chosen me, but I have chosen you and ordained you to go and bear fruit."

Bishop Mathews:

Always the evangelist, he expected things to happen when he preached, and they did. I have to confess that very often I have not expected anything to happen—and I was not disappointed. Nothing did.

Mrs. Mathews:

I know you like African greetings, too, especially from Zimbabwe.

Bishop Mathews:

Yes, at this time of the day, they would say, "Maneru."

Mrs. Mathews:

Which means, "Good evening."

Bishop Mathews:

Then they would follow it by this question, "Masquera he-re?"

Mrs. Mathews:

What is the response?

Bishop Mathews:

The question is: "Has your day gone well so far?" The answer is, "Well, *my* day has gone well so far if *your* day has gone well so far."

Mrs. Mathews:

That suggests that our welfare depends upon the welfare of our brothers and sisters.

Bishop Mathews:

Exactly. We Christians cannot really think of ourselves outside of the context of community.

Mrs. Mathews:

I wish my father could be here tonight. This audience wouldn't get all this second hand.

Bishop Mathews:

Should we not rather say that Stanley Jones *is* here tonight? And Mabel Lossing Jones, too, and Arthur Moore, who, by the way, is my spiritual grandfather. He won my brother Joe to Christ, and Joe won me. Francis Asbury is here, too—and John Wesley, and Susanna Wesley, and Georgia Harkness. The communion of the saints must mean something like that.

By the way, Eunice, you were born in India. I suppose you wanted to be near your mother.

Mrs. Mathews:

Yes, but don't feel sorry for me. Several years ago we were at a reception and met Ambassador Reischaner, who was born in Japan, and a four-star general who was born in China. All three of us were grateful for the privilege of being at home in another culture. A wonderful Muslim cook taught me Hindustani, which

185

I learned before I did English. I seemed to take in Indian manners and customs with the very air I breathed. Since I was an only child, I learned early to amuse myself. Mother taught me at home until I was ten. My playmates were boys in Mother's school. And my many pets included a mongoose, a deer, a monkey, and peacocks.

Bishop Mathews:
Tell us a little about your father's origins, please.

Mrs. Mathews:
He was born near Baltimore, on a farm in a small town called Clarksville, Maryland, on January 3, 1884. He never used his first name, which was Eli, in case you have wondered. His father was a toll keeper on the National Pike, which is Route 40. His mother and grandmother were staunch Methodists, but my father, as a young man, I understand, showed very little interest in religion. He planned to be a lawyer, and read law in an attorney's office. He learned well how to muster evidence and complete a strong case, which he later used for the Gospel.

Bishop Mathews:
All that was changed in his conversion. In fact, he speaks of two conversions: horizontal—that one didn't take. Later on, the vertical one occurred, and that did take. It was under the evangelist, Robert Bateman, who was a recovered alcoholic. He, by the way, went down with the *Titanic* some years later. But in Asbury College, Stanley Jones became a serious student. He went there partly because they would accept him, and the price was right. Then besides that, he wanted to be able to preach like Henry Clay Morrison. He conducted revivals there, and I remember hearing him tell, we both remember hearing him tell, about the evangelistic events. He went home with a farmer one night. It came time for bed; they all went upstairs. There was one bed in the house. I think it had a tick that was stuffed with corn husks or something like that. At any rate, this presented something of a dilemma. What the farmer did was ask Stanley Jones to crawl into bed first, and he was supposed to have his face toward the wall. Then the farmer crawled in, and then the wife on the outside, so that you see even St. Paul would have been satisfied that everything was decent and in order.

There was a great awakening while he was at Asbury. One time for a week there was a great upheaval, almost a Pentecost experience, on the campus. They closed all the classes and let this have free flow. It was then that he made his decision for missionary service. He was confronted with a confusion of decision: he had an invitation to go to Africa; he had an invitation from Henry Clay Morrison to teach at Asbury; and then he had a letter from the Board of Missions asking him to go to India. He put the letters out on a bed and prayed. One time he took us into the home and showed us the very bedroom. He got up from his knees and said, "It's India." He went there in 1907. It seemed to him at the time that British rule would never change.

He went to Lucknow. I think I might say at this point that Eunice's Dad was always a very convinced Methodist. This is not a very good story, but he did tell this one time about a man who was in a hotel. He went down to breakfast and the waitress put before him a luscious dish of strawberries. The man said, "Take this away and bring me prunes." And as Stanley Jones came to the conclusion of the story: "As long as there are people like that in the world, there will be people who do not appreciate Methodism."

Now, Eunice, tell us something about your mother.

Mrs. Mathews:
Mother was from Iowa, born near the bluffs of the Mississippi River. She was of Quaker and Methodist background. Her grandmother had come to Canada from Cornwall, and then had married and come down to Iowa with her husband. Mother's great love was teaching. Even before college, she taught and was principal of a small town school. In 1904, she went to India as an educational missionary, to Kandhowa, a girls' school in central India. She arrived during a dreadful famine. Her first assignment, her first week, was to go each morning with a horse and cart into the bazaar and pick up any live babies that were found on the bodies of their mothers who had died the night before, to save them. She started two teachers' training schools, one was in Jubalpuk. The second one was in Lucknow. And there she met my father, and a few years later they were married. Together they were sent to Silapur, about fifty miles northwest of Lucknow. She was given charge of three boys' schools, and he had charge of two districts.

Bishop Mathews:

I must say that I record myself as an admirer of your mother; not often do sons-in-law do that. Silapur was a very interesting town and one time, when Eunice was a little girl, a guest from this country, I think Chicago, came. She arrived about dusk, and then made a great remark, which has become a part of the family tradition. This woman said, "What a wonderful sunset for such an out-of-the-way place." Well, you know there are many out-of-the-way places made by God, who has a reckless abandon in scattering the beauties of sunsets and sunrises all around the world.

I do want to say this about her mother. She was primarily an educator, as Eunice has said. She was an effective missionary. We will say more about that a little later. She was a wise counselor, and people would almost line up to get advice from this marvelous person. Finally, she was an authentic human being. But, wait a minute! How is it that *we* are having this conversation tonight at all? We met in India. How did you happen to go back then?

Mrs. Mathews:

Well, I finished high school in India, and then college in this country. Between his traveling and my being in boarding school, my father and I were separated much of the time, and he felt that we should get better acquainted. So after college and a quick secretarial course, he took me back to India, and I spent two years traveling with him throughout the whole of India. It was a great experience, and there I met Jim. I told my father that the best gift I had ever given him was a son-in-law such as Jim. He agreed.

Bishop Mathews:

That street doesn't carry one-way traffic. I want to say that your father was the best father-in-law I could ever have had! And I want to say that your mother was the finest mother-in-law that I could ever have had! Well, your dad had the idea that one ought not simply have the young people involved arrange their marriage, or the parents arrange it, which is typical in Hinduism and tradition in India. But in south India, in the Mar Thoma Syrian Church, it was a kind of a meeting of the minds of both the young people and their parents.

Well, knowing that, when we had made up our minds on our part, I went to her dad to ask if he would agree to this. I caught him when he was having his hair cut. In India, typically, you don't go to a barber; a barber comes to you with his tools. Well, he was out on the veranda, all decked out. He claimed that when I asked him this question, the barber was poised over him with that razor, and he couldn't do anything but say, "Yes!"

He said at the time we were married, "I never want to be in the way, and I never want to be out of the way if I can be of any help." I can say that was a pretty good word to hear. And he kept his bargain.

Mrs. Mathews:

He certainly kept his part of the bargain. Before we were married, I stayed with my father at the Lucknow Ashram. He was extremely generous to anyone he felt was on the Kingdom road. One morning I overheard him talking with someone who was repenting of his evil ways as a professional jockey. I was fascinated with the story, and I listened closely. The man had been the Aga Khan's race horse jockey. Now, having repented of his evil ways, he asked my father to help him buy a horse and a tonga (that's the local taxi vehicle—a two-wheeled horse cart). He would then turn his life around. To my amazement, my father agreed and gave him the money for this. When later I expressed my disbelief in the jockey, my father gave me a good lecture on believing in the goodness of people.

Some weeks later, before Christmas, I was playing tennis at the English Club, and at tea time, I met the editor of the Lucknow English newspaper. "Miss Jones, are you related to Stanley Jones who has a horse running in the Governor's Cup on New Year's?" He said that since it was a horse originally from the Aga Khan's stables, the whole British community was betting on it. I assured him that it certainly must be some other Jones not my father, but then I suddenly realized what had happened. My father's money had indeed been used at least as a down payment on a sure winner. I could hardly wait to get back to the ashram and tell my father he owned a race horse, complete with jockey! We called it the Methodist race horse. By the way, the horse was scratched.

Bishop Mathews:

Stanley Jones established in 1930 a Christian ashram—a Christian retreat center—in Sat Tal in the foothills of the Himalayas. Then as Eunice has implied, he had another ashram in the city of Lucknow. It was to Sat Tal, even long before he had bought it and

189

made it into an ashram, that he retired for about three months in the summer. I thought you might be interested in what he did there in preparation of his addresses. He would spend those three months very, very carefully reading and then composing five addresses, down to the last pleasantry, that might go into the addresses. It was not casual at all. Then, having spent those three months, he would go down to the plains and spend nine months in traveling around to the cities of India, particularly addressing the intelligentsia.

He would hire a public hall, or it would be hired by a local committee for him, because some of the people, the outstanding Muslims and Hindus, would not come into a church, but they would crowd these halls. It was a tremendous experience, as I attended some of them, and he would give these five lectures five days of the week. Then on Sunday he would give it to the church, usually training pastors and laity in evangelism. On Sunday he would preach several times, then take the Sunday night train to his next place, and there was the same thing over again the next week. This occurred year in and year out, so that along the way he had preached in this way in every city of India with 50,000 population or over. Eunice, you used to hear some of those speeches. What was your reaction?

Mrs. Mathews:

Although, of course, I had heard him speak many times in churches, and had gone with him on the National Preaching Mission in 1937 and 1938 in the U.S.A., and knew he was an excellent speaker, I had never really experienced any of his lectures to non-Christian audiences. I remember very clearly the very first time I went to one of these. It was in south India, held in a very large hall. The hall was packed, with people standing outside the windows. After his lecture came the question time. These were, as Jim said, the intelligentsia of India. Highly educated and very erudite men would ask questions. I was appalled, for surely my father couldn't possibly answer them. I slid down in my chair, and I waited for the humiliation that I was sure was coming. But, he did answer them, and brilliantly. So it went on for the next hour. By the end of the evening, I was sitting up quite straight, and was truly amazed at how good he was. I realized that he could take care of himself, and I didn't have to worry about him. Now, Jim, how did you perceive him?

Bishop Mathews:

What kind of man was he? Well, he was open. He was friendly. He was interested in everything and everybody. He may well have struck some people as aloof, but he was good company. He was the despair of hostesses, because about 9:30 in the evening he would be off to bed.

He was a man of great good humor. I remember one night Eunice and I went into New York City to hear her Dad speak at Riverside Church. We lived nearby. We walked over there, and just as we were entering the church, who should also be entering the church but John D. Rockefeller, Jr. Well, he was entitled to be there. He had built the church. So, he invited Eunice and me to sit beside him. Over there was John D. Rockefeller, Jr., then Eunice, then I. We listened to his speech. It was on Christian unity. It came time for the offering.

Now, we have to confess to a certain interest in how much John D. Rockefeller, Jr. would put into an offering. I'm tempted not to tell you. Would you be interested? Well, he was seated where Eunice could see and I couldn't, although I was dying to do so. Then we went home, and on the way home her father showed a bit of interest in the same subject. I had noticed that Rockefeller took out of his wallet a bill and folded it in a way that disguised its identity, but Eunice saw it, and she replied to her father, "Well, he put in a hundred times as much as Jim did."

He said, "You don't mean to say he put in a hundred dollar bill?"

I said, "What makes you think he didn't put in a thousand dollar bill?"

"Well," he said, "because I didn't think that you were worth more than a dollar." This was true!

Stanley Jones was always cheerful, and he claimed that he never had a blue day. If he did, I didn't see it. He was generous, as I say, to a fault. He made more than a million dollars on royalties and gave it all away. At dinner, he couldn't abide people gathered around the table in one-on-one conversations. He wanted table-wide conversation. When we had guests, he would take me aside and say, "Now, Jim, you are the host, and you've got to see that everybody hears everything said."

191

I'll mention very quickly that one night we had three notable couples. President and Mrs. Pusey of Harvard were there; Henry Knox Sherill, the Presiding Bishop of the Episcopal Church, and Mrs. Sherill; and friends named John and Irene Goodenough (his father was a great professor at Yale, and John was a professor at MIT as well as a physicist at Lincoln laboratory). I won't say what the others said, but John Goodenough in the table conversation, when we asked him, "What's exciting in your field?" he said, "Well, we're working on something in the laboratory. We've got it pretty well perfected. So far as we know, it was no practical application at all. We call it LASER."

Well, that sort of thing kept happening. Stanley Jones was the most disciplined man I ever knew, I think. A true Wesleyan, whether applied to devotion or physical exercise or the use of time. He had his weaknesses, of course, but he surrendered them, I think, to the Lord. He had one little technique that he told us about. He said that when an unwholesome thought came into his mind, he would bat his eyes very rapidly. Try it. You can only bat your eyes when you will to do so. It would take his mind off of the unwholesome thought. Well, try that sometime, too.

He was very human. He liked baseball, and knew all of the baseball statistics. He loved his grandchildren and liked to relax with them. I'll say this: that what he appeared to be in public he was in private. Sometimes I thought he lacked humility, but he was humble enough. Back in 1928, when he was elected Bishop, he declined the office.

Mrs. Mathews:

You've recounted how he prepared his addresses. They ended up almost invariably in books, which he wrote in long hand. Most of them, I typed and edited. The first book, of course, was *The Christ of the Indian Road*, which became a best-seller. For years we searched for this manuscript, and finally in 1983, we found it in an old trunk in his doctor brother's home. In 1984, in the centennial year of his birth, and the bicentennial year of Methodism, and in his home town of Baltimore, I presented this manuscript to the General Conference for the United Methodist Archives. In token of his appreciation of things Japanese, I wrapped it in a silk scarf, which the Japanese called "Furoshiki." This makes the gift very special, and indeed that was special!

Bishop Mathews:

Yes, Eunice, I recall you made a speech that day. It was one of your finest hours, if I may say so. But, let's back up again. Let's talk a little about his work. Stanley Jones was, of course, fundamentally a preacher. At the height of his power, he was the best interpreter of the Gospel I ever heard. Without being unkind to other evangelists, they were not in the same league. It was absolutely tremendous to hear him declare the Gospel, and he didn't insult anyone's intelligence in the process. I first heard him back in 1936 at the National Preaching Mission in New York City. And I never got over it. He had a marvelous preaching voice. I suppose that was his Welsh heritage. He preached, we estimate, 60,000 sermons during his lifetime. They were always Christo-centric, and when he talked about Jesus, it was as if he knew him personally—as he did! He liked to preach on the fourth chapter of Luke, on the inaugural address of Jesus. I can hear him yet speaking about how Jesus talked about the economically disinherited, the physically disinherited, the politically and socially disinherited, the psychologically disinherited, and then a new beginning for everybody—the Jubilee Year!

Or how much he liked to preach on that tremendous text that St. Paul supplies us with at the end of the third chapter of First Corinthians! These Corinthians felt sorry for themselves, but Paul said, "Everything belongs to you, yet you belong to Christ and Christ belongs to God." By the way, that is on his grave marker. He was a towering evangelist. He preferred the designation that he was a teller of the Good News. He could start anywhere, but he would end at the feet of Jesus Christ. Of course we know the word "evangelism" doesn't appear in the New Testament, but the word "evangelist" appears there three times. That described E. Stanley Jones.

He recovered evangelism in his time. Evangelism has to be recovered recurrently throughout history. Jones made it respectable and relevant and responsible and reliable. He told the Good News and then let people decide for themselves how to respond. For him, it was God's offer of the fullness of life whether or not the offer was accepted. He saw no dichotomy between the Old Testament prophet and the New Testament evangelist. I sometimes have reflected, and Eunice has, too, that he wouldn't have been an effective organization man, the way some of the other evangelists are. He couldn't have done that. Eunice, how did he get on to preaching to the non-Christians?

Mrs. Mathews:

In our town there were two clubs—one British and one Indian. The Indians at that time, I'm sure you know, were not allowed in any British Club. And, so my father joined the Indian club. He would go over there to play tennis. He was an extremely good tennis player. Then afterwards, they would sit around and talk. Now, these were the intellectuals of the town—the judges, the lawyers, the people who were educators. One day when they were sharing conversation, the judge said to my father, "Why do you missionaries always go to the lower castes; you never come to us?"

And my father replied, "Well, I suppose because we thought you didn't want us." And the judge made a statement that changed his whole outlook. He said, "Yes, we would like you to come to us if you come the right way." That started my father thinking—what is the right way? He then made a careful study of Hinduism, Islam, and other religions. That started him off. He was invited more and more to come to address non-Christian groups.

Bishop Mathews:

Certainly one of the most well-known and effective missionaries of the twentieth century, he had been in India for eighteen years before he began to establish his reputation, and that was, of course, with the publication of *The Christ of the Indian Road*. That was a landmark book—a real watershed. Some of you, I suppose all of you, have read it. It is still insightful, still thrilling to read. He made it clear that a missionary doesn't have to represent the entire range of Western culture. A missionary does not have to defend the scriptures from Genesis to Revelation. Jones said that Christianity is Christ, and that Jesus Christ is at home on the Indian road and on every road. By the way, that book has been used as a textbook at Gregorian University in Rome in the preparation of missionaries in India. He was a great interpreter of mission.

Mrs. Mathews:

I might say a word about his style. It was always crisp and succinct. A few quotations might illustrate this:

"For me the new birth gave birth to everything."

194

"If you take the gift, you belong to the giver forever."

"Impression minus expression equals depression."

"In this world, the choice is conversion or chaos."

Bishop Mathews:

He certainly knew how to turn a phrase. I suppose he'd been quoted more by preachers than any other man in this century. For example:

"We don't break God's laws. We break ourselves on them."

"Give to everybody, don't give up on anybody."

"What Jesus commands he commends."

"Without the Holy Spirit, I'm a mess. With the Holy Spirit, I'm a message."

"I deserve nothing. I have everything."

"Charity without justice is an insult to God."

Your mother, too, was a good speaker and writer. I know that she wrote for *Harper's* and *Atlantic* and some of the other big magazines, always under a pen name, because she didn't want to lean on her husband's reputation.

Mrs. Mathews:

Mother was also a very strong and able person in her own right. While my father was travelling all over India, and finally all over the world, she stayed in Silapur, with her boys' boarding school. Mostly they were village boys from the villages nearby—from poor village homes. She was also a very practical person, supervising needed buildings. She put everything on our compound to good use. She grew most of the goods that her boys used. She bought in bulk grain or rice when the prices were down. She sold the sandalwood branches from our trees; the bamboo stalks made good income for the school. All of her boys performed manual labor each day.

Once a devastating flood put our compound and one of her schools under six feet of water. Surrounding villages were starving. When mother could reach the school, she found the soaked grain in the storage room had swollen and pushed the brick walls almost off their foundation. The grain was hot and cooked, but had not yet fermented. She sent word to the starving villagers that she had free food for them. They came by the hundreds and she probably saved hundreds of people from starvation.

Our town in Silapur was run by the Municipal Board of 21

persons. The Board asked my mother to be a member. The other 20 were equally divided between Hindus and Muslims, who always voted as a block of ten each. She voted according to her conscience, and the members knew it. So, in effect, her voice always prevailed. She held the balance of power in our little town, but she used it responsibly. She was also an educational pioneer. She introduced the practice of women teaching small boys. That was at a time when no Hindu or Muslim family considered a woman worthy or even that it was possible that they could teach a boy. Mother changed that.

Bishop Matthews:

Mabel Lossing Jones was also a missionary in her own right. For example, she knew the Koran quite well, and she could read the Bhagavad Gita in Sanskrit. She left books around her living room knowing full well that guests would pick them up. She was only too glad to have guests read them and allowed them to accept the consequences! She carried on a worldwide correspondence. Through the years she kept a thousand boys in school every year—this over a period of fifty years. She was truly a friend to the friendless.

Mrs. Mathews:

My mother supported my father's work, but in very quiet ways which she learned from her Quaker background. I remember my mother saying to a friend one time that she would rather have E. Stanley Jones for two weeks a year than any other man she knew for 52 weeks! My father's interests were wide ranging, whereas my mother's were local.

Bishop Mathews:

Yes, his interests were reflected progressively in his books. He found time to write twenty-eight of them in all—ten devotional books and eighteen about other subjects. He often repeated his ideas, that's true, but his audiences constantly changed. We receive letters nearly every week—from all over the world—from people who had been inspired by a book of his. For example: Josef Tson, a great preacher in Romania, was influenced by *Abundant Living*. We saw to it that 10,000 copies of *Abundant Living* were published in Romanian and they've been distributed there. Just last week we heard that 250,000 copies of his books are being distributed in what was the Soviet Union. This is being sponsored by the Swedish churches. Read a list of his books sometime in the order in which they are written, and you can see the kind of expansion of his mind and his interests that they reflect.

Mrs. Mathews:

He gave all of his book money away—over a million dollars in royalties.

He found time also to get to know India's leaders: Tagore, Sadhu Sunder Singh, British officials, Nehru, and of course, Mahatma Ghandi. He had correspondence with Gandhi for over twenty-one years on one theme.

Let me tell you a very quick story about a tea cloth. One time my father was visiting Mahatma Gandhi at his ashram in Serengeti. The postman brought Gandhi a letter and a package which he opened in front of my father. In the package was a tea cloth, and a letter from Nehru's wife, Kumla. In it, she said, "Mahatma, I have made a tea cloth for you. I have spun the threads, I have woven the cloth, and have embroidered it for you." It was beautiful—a real labor of love.

He remarked, "Kumla should know I cannot use a tea cloth in an ashram." He knew my mother, so he turned to my father, and he said, "Take it. Take it and give it to your wife with my love." Mother, very fortunately for me, wrote this on a piece of paper and wrapped up the cloth very carefully. After mother's death, when I was going through things, I found it, and I found the story. I took a picture of it, and the next time I went back to India, I went to see Mrs. Indira Gandhi and told her the story and showed her the picture. She said, "Oh, I was in Switzerland when my mother was making that. She was in a sanatorium there for tuberculosis. I remember that, and I have often wondered what happened to it."

And I said, "I shall bring it to you, Mrs. Gandhi, because it belongs with you, not with us." But, before I could get back to India again, she was assassinated. I did take it back, and I gave it to her son, Rajiv Gandhi. He was most grateful, and there were tears in his eyes when he felt the cloth that his grandmother had made.

Bishop Mathews:

Stanley Jones frequently cited the four points that Mahatma

197

Gandhi gave in an address to missionaries in Calcutta years ago. Gandhi said to the missionaries, "I have four suggestions to you:

First of all, live more like Jesus.

Second, practice your religion without adulterating it or toning it down.

Third, emphasize love as central, as the soul of Christianity.

And fourth, study the non-Christian religions."

We've already said something about Jones' method, but all through the years he was immersed in scripture. We have a number of Bibles that he finally put aside because he had filled all of the margins completely with his notes as he read. We have stacks of his notebooks. He would number entries from one to a thousand. At the close of each day he would write the notes of that day down. Then when he would write his books, he would say, for example, "See reference 621." He would have it ready-made for inclusion. You see, he couldn't carry many books around with him, but he made the most of what he did.

He liked to follow the inner voice. I could tell, but I won't, about his mode of writing books. Just a quick word about his theology. It always began with Christology. His theology was Christology. He emphasized also the Holy Spirit. He emphasized the Kingdom of God. It was an obsession with him—what he liked to call "a magnificent obsession." I do think that the time must come when emphasis on the Kingdom is recovered in the life of the Church. It is true that Jesus spoke of the Kingdom exactly 100 times. It must have been very important to him, and therefore ought to be important to us.

All of his books were about conversion and surrender, and about the *Way*. Jones pushed Tertullian's thought along. Not only is the soul naturally Christian, but the body—every cell in the body is naturally Christian—constructed, created to be utilized in a Christian way: just as society is created for the same thing. I think *The Way* is his most original book.

Mrs. Mathews:

On a broader scale, in the twenties and thirties, he introduced the Round Table Discussions, as part of each week's lectures or evangelistic meetings. Leaders of different faiths gathered to share what their faith had given to them. In the present day, emphasis is on interreligious dialogue. It is usually forgotten that my father was one of the pioneers in the approach as reflected in his book, *The Christ of the Round Table*. He said in his introduction, "This book wrote itself."

Bishop Mathews:

He was interested also in church unity. He gave hundreds of addresses on that subject all over the country, and indeed, all over the world. He was an ecumenical pioneer. He was ecumenical before the word had become popular. He was present at the Jerusalem Conference in 1928, at Madras in 1938, and at Oberlin at the famous Faith and Order Conference. Wherever he went, he was at it all the time and pressing the case for Christian unity.

Mrs. Matthews:

He also realized a need in India for family psychiatry, especially with a Christian basis. There was none in India at that time, so he started Nur Manzil in Lucknow, first with Swedish and Dutch psychiatrists. It has proved a much-needed success, and is now under the leadership of an excellent Indian doctor. The hospital is used by the Government of India as a model for family psychiatry.

Bishop Mathews:

Perhaps some word of evaluation of Stanley Jones' work is needed here, though I'm perhaps the last one who ought to give this. He did not hesitate to take exposed positions. Nor did he hesitate to enter into controversy, sometimes with the high and mighty. He often suffered from severe criticism and abuse. One time it was said of him that Eleanor Roosevelt and Stanley Jones ought to be hanged from the same tree—interesting company!

Sometimes people said he wasn't scholarly enough. He did not pretend to be a scholar. He read widely. He knew the works of the principal theologians of his day. He absorbed knowledge like a sponge. He was deeply schooled in the world's religions and talked with their leaders. He was accused of repeating his addresses. He used to cite John Wesley, who said one time that sometime between the fortieth and fiftieth time he preached a sermon, he got it about the way he intended. And, besides that, his audiences changed.

It was also alleged that Jones was soft on Communism. I'm sure he must be looking at this last year with considerable interest in that respect! Sometimes they accused him of vanity and pride, but he did try to lay this matter at the feet of Jesus Christ. He was often imitated. Many of his books, it seems to me, were ahead of their time. I'm astonished to see how freshly they read even today; in fact, Abingdon Press is coming out with new editions of many of his works in the "Abingdon Classics" series. And he was faithful to the end.

Mrs. Mathews:

In some books he was Christ-centered. He expressed this through earnest and effective evangelism. He was holistic, he applied evangelism to life and society, and he was Kingdom-focused. He had something to say to a highly secularized, pluralistic world. Is there a place for evangelists today? Yes.

Bishop Mathews:

Well, you have to continue the story, I think, for yourselves. It is an interesting story. Both of Eunice's parents are now deceased. Stanley Jones died in India in 1973. He left instructions that his body should be cremated, half of his ashes buried at Sat Tal and half in the Bishop's Lot in Baltimore. I feel sure, and I'm sure you feel sure, that the One who has promised us the resurrection of the dead will be able to handle that kind of situation!

Mrs. Mathews:

We, too, have plots there, but we're in no great hurry to occupy them. Incidentally, last August, the State of Iowa inaugurated my mother into their Women's Hall of Fame, hanging her picture in the Des Moines gallery with other women so honored. That was the State of Iowa, not Church Women United.

Bishop Mathews:

His last book, as some of you know, was called *The Divine Yes*. He took his cue from the first chapter of Second Corinthians: "And now at long last, the divine yes has sounded, for all the promises of God have their yes in him." How he liked to preach on that subject! I remember having heard the late Paul Reese at a memorial service. He spoke about the "divine yes," as it was dealt with by Stanley Jones. He said it was a Christ-centered "yes"; it was a conclusive "yes"; it was a costly "yes"; it was a comprehensive "yes." It included everything, and it was a contagious "yes," for when he spoke of it, other people wanted to say "yes" to the God who had said "yes" to them all. But, Eunice, tell a little about that divine "yes."

Mrs. Matthews:

I'll try to make this very brief. After my father's stroke in 1970, he was very handicapped by not being able to see anything small such as print. He was determined to put into manuscript form the fruits of his faith. Since he couldn't see, he spoke into a cassette tape recorder. His voice was almost unintelligible. However a friend painstakingly transcribed the material, but the frequent hospital interruptions made continuity of thought very difficult. He returned to India in 1971. The use of Indian stenographers with an imperfect command of English made the manuscript even more disorganized and jumbled. Much deciphering was needed.

After my father's death, the manuscript was brought back to me. It seemed impossible that it could ever be published. We struggled with it for months, and nearly gave up. What my father had wanted to say was scattered throughout the manuscript, but with no form or order. It seemed a hopeless task, and we put it aside. Then, almost a year later, my husband had an idea: cut up the manuscript paragraph by paragraph and see where the ideas would fall. We did that. We found most of the material fell into twelve questions which demanded an affirmative answer of "yes," the divine "yes." The manuscript had miraculously fallen—or were we led?—into an orderly progression of thought. It was incredible, but there were some paragraphs which didn't quite fit into these twelve categories. By their content, we could see where and when they were written. They formed a diary—a diary of affliction, if you will—and it ended with the resurrection note. It was indeed spiritually his last will and testament.

Bishop Mathews:

Stanley Jones and Mabel Lossing Jones left everything to India. It's been our privilege to be the trustees of those funds. We have tried to deal with them responsibly. You might be interested that the corpus of the money they left is held by the General Board of Global Ministries, but we are the trustees. We send the interest to India, not for immediate expenditure, but to become principle of a permanent fund. The interest on that sum, which increases each year, has now become the largest single fund our church has in India. Priority is given to scholarships. This year 175 young people are having their college and university training paid from this scholarship fund, and 400 young people in primary and secondary schools receive scholarships as well.

We also carry on other work. We've raised a good deal of money through the years for the Nur Mangel Psychiatric Center in Lucknow, and for a little school for evangelism up at Sat Tal that goes on for two months each year. They had, at the last round, twelve students. Last week, Eunice and I raised enough money to guarantee its continuation for the next three years. And I am pleased to tell you, Bishop Hunt, that we have found a way of making a provisional gift of $300,000, which will finally come to this Foundation, earmarked for an E. Stanley Jones Chair of Evangelism in Third World countries.

May I add just this further word about her remarkable mother. She died at the age of 100. She told Eunice one day when she was 95, "Eunice, I've kept careful records all my life." She could account for every penny she ever earned from the age of 14, and she could account for every penny she ever spent. Then she added, "I'm going to stop keeping books. I think I can now trust myself not to be extravagant."

Can you imagine this? She never in her life saw a television program—she preferred to read. When she was in her late 90's, she thought she was going blind, so in over a course of two weeks, she read all the works of Shakespeare. She said, "If I have to be blind, I might as well have something to think about."

She was that kind of a woman. And she was married to the kind of man we have been speaking of tonight. Theirs was a Kingdom marriage. It did not mean that they sat across the table at breakfast every day for 60 years. But, they both lived for higher ends.

I want to say this in closing: I had a chance to observe Stanley Jones and Mrs. Jones very closely over a period of 35 years. They were authentic!

CONTRIBUTORS

William J. Abraham is McCreless Associate Professor of Evangelism and Philosophy, Perkins School of Theology, Southern Methodist University, Dallas, Texas.

Kenneth L. Carder is Bishop of the Nashville Area, The United Methodist Church.

H. Mvume Dandala is Senior Minister, Central Methodist Mission, Johannesburg, South Africa, and formerly head of the Department of Evangelism of The Methodist Church of Southern Africa.

Dennis C. Dutton is Bishop of The Methodist Church of Malaysia.

George G. Hunter III is Dean of the School of World Mission and Evangelism, Asbury Theological Seminary, Wilmore, Kentucky.

James T. Laney, formerly President of Emory University, Atlanta, Georgia, is now the U.S. Ambassador to the Republic of South Korea.

Theodore W. Jennings, Jr. is Professor of Systematic Theology, Chicago Theological Seminary, Chicago, Illinois.

James C. Logan is E. Stanley Jones Professor of Evangelism, Wesley Theological Seminary, Washington, D.C.

G. Howard Mellor is Director of Evangelism, Home Mission Division, The Methodist Church [Great Britain], Cliff College, Sheffield, England.

Eunice Mathews is the daughter of the late Dr. and Mrs. E. Stanley Jones.

James K. Mathews is a retired Bishop of The United Methodist Church.

Ben Witherington III is Professor of New Testament and Methodist Studies, Ashland Theological Seminary, Ashland, Ohio.

ABBREVIATIONS

Journal = *The Journal of the Rev. John Wesley, A.M.*, edited by Nehemiah Curnock, 8 volumes (London: Epworth Press, 1909–1916).

Letters = *The Letters of the Rev. John Wesley, A.M.*, edited by John Telford, 8 volumes (London: Epworth Press, 1931).

NT Notes = *Explanatory Notes Upon the New Testament* (London: Bowyer, 1755; new edition in 2 volumes, London: Wesleyan Methodist Book Room, n.d.; reprinted Grand Rapids: Baker Book House, 1981).

Works = *The Works of John Wesley*, begun as "The Oxford Edition of the Works of John Wesley" (Oxford: Clarendon Press, 1975–1983), continued as "The Bicentennial Edition of the Works of John Wesley" (Nashville: Abingdon Press, 1984–); 14 of 35 volumes published to date.

Works (J) = *The Works of the Rev. John Wesley, M.A.*, edited by Thomas Jackson, 3rd edition, 14 volumes (London: Wesleyan Methodist Book Room, 1872; reprinted Grand Rapids: Baker Book House, 1979).

NOTES

Introduction

1. William J. Abraham, *The Logic of Evangelism* (Grand Rapids: William B. Eerdmans Publishing Company, 1989), 1.

2. David Barrett, *World Christian Encyclopedia* (Nairobi: Oxford University Press, 1987), 42–45.

Chapter 1

1. Francis Asbury, *The Journal and Letters of Francis Asbury*, ed. Elmer T. Clark, 2 vols. (Nashville: Abingdon Press, 1958), 2:787.

2. "Preface to the Sermons," *Works* 1:104.

3. "The Scripture Way of Salvation," *Works* 2:153f.

4. *Minutes of the [British] Methodist Conferences, from the First, held in London, by the Late Rev. John Wesley, A.M., in the Year 1744*, 5 vols. (London: John Mason, 1862–64), 1:9.

5. *Minutes of the Several Conversations between the Rev. Thomas Coke, LL.D., the Rev. Francis Asbury and Others, at Conference begun in Baltimore, in the State of Maryland, the 27th of December, in the year 1784* (Philadelphia: Charles Crist, 1785), 4.

6. *Minutes of Several Conversations, between the Rev. John Wesley, M.A., and the preachers in connection with him* (London: Printed for G. Whitfield, 1797), 1. This volume provides some insights into adjustments which British Methodism had to make after Wesley's death. The title page of the original carries a publication date printing mistake: it states the year as 1779! Obviously the correct date is 1797.

7. See Robert Paine, *Life and Times of Wm. M'Kendree*, 2 vols. (Nashville: Methodist Book Concern, 1874), 1:374f.

8. *Grace Upon Grace* (Nashville: Graded Press, 1990). For a very informative treatment of the biblical imperative, see also Mortimer Arias and Alan Johnson, *The Great Commission: Biblical Models for Evangelism* (Nashville: Abingdon Press, 1992).

9. *NT Notes*, Mark 16:15.

10. *Works* 7:646–47 (No. 464).

11. *NT Notes*, Matthew 5:13-15.

12. John Hick, "The Non-Absoluteness of Christianity," in John Hick and Paul F. Knitter, eds., *The Myth of Christian Uniqueness* (Maryknoll, NY: Orbis Books, 1989), 31.

13. "The Law Established through Faith, II," *Works* 2:37–38.

14. For a full expository and critical treatment of Wesley's Christology, see John Deschner, *Wesley's Christology* (Dallas: Southern Methodist University Press, 1985, "reprint of 1960 edition with a new foreword by the author").

15. "The Original, Nature, Property, and Use of the Law," *Works* 2:15–19.

16. "Upon Our Lord's Sermon on the Mount, V," *Works* 1:550–71.

17. *Letters* 3:370.

18. Quoted in Preserved Smith, *The Enlightenments, 1687–1776, (New* York: Collier Books, 1962), 401.

19. *Letters* 2:486–87.

20. "Justification by Faith," *Works* 1:194. The italics are Wesley's.

21. "Justification by Faith," *Works* 1:187. The italics are Wesley's.

22. Oscar Cullmann, *Christ and Time* (Philadelphia: The Westminster Press, 1966).

23. Ibid.

24. See Wesley's series of thirteen sermons on "Upon Our Lord's Sermon on the Mount," *Works* 1:466–698.

25. "The Righteousness of Faith," *Works* 1:208.

26. *Works* 7:545–46 (No. 374).

27. Albert Outler, *Evangelism in the Wesleyan Spirit* (Nashville: Tidings), 1971.

28. See Robert Chiles, *Theological Transition in American Methodism: 1790–1935* (Nashville: Abingdon Press, 1965; reprinted Lanham, MD: University Press of America, 1983).

29. Alfred Krass, *Evangelizing Modern Neo-Pagan North America* (Scottsdale, PA: Herald Press, 1982).

30. Gordon Rupp, *Principalities and Powers* (London: Epworth Press, 1952).

Chapter 2

1. See Thomas A. Langford, *Practical Divinity: Theology in the Wesleyan Tradition* (Nashville: Abingdon Press, 1983).

2. It is easy to overlook this. Consider the following comment by Edward W. Poitras. "Religious traditions show great veneration for their founders. The Protestant family of Christian groups is no exception, for almost all of them have early founders or leaders whose life and thought are influential, even normative for their communities' lives. The Methodists follow this pattern, but are even more dependent than most Protestants upon their founder in that they have no set of traditionally authorized creedal affirmations, so find themselves driven to analyze the career and writings of John Wesley for some kind of authoritative standard to guide their development." That Poitras himself is wary of this generalization is borne out by the qualifications which follow immediately. "There have been Methodist statements of faith, to be sure, such as the doctrinal summaries recorded in the Early Methodist Annual Conference Minutes and later affirmations from the North American and other Methodist communities, but the early ones were sketchy and most of them have never been accepted with the authority to such definitions as the Westminster Confession, Lutheran confessions and catechisms, or the Anglican Articles." See his "An Authentic Wesleyanism for Today," *Sinhak Gwa Saige, Theology and the World* 17 (1988): 97. Poitras' essay is a fine summary of "authentic Wesleyanism," but as a potential

substitute for the actual doctrinal standards adopted by the Methodist tradition in North America it is on the wrong track. The second paragraph is incompatible with the fundamental claim of the first paragraph. As he points out in the second paragraph Protestant groups do have creedal affirmations. United Methodism is no exception, and there is nothing sketchy about them. What makes Methodism different is that it has also used Wesley's *Sermons* and *Notes on the New Testament* as doctrinal standards. Important as the life of Wesley is for United Methodism, it does not count as a doctrinal standard in any shape or form.

3. See William J. Abraham, *The Logic of Evangelism* (Grand Rapids: William B. Eerdmans Publishing Company, 1989).

4. "False doctrine corrupts the life of the church at its source, and that is why doctrinal sin is more serious than moral. Those who rob the church of the gospel deserve the ultimate penalty, whereas those who fail in morality have the gospel there to help them." See Dietrich Bonhoeffer, *The Cost of Discipleship* (London: SCM Press, 1959), 264, note 1.

5. For an excellent discussion of the place of doctrine and theology in The United Methodist Church, see Thomas A. Langford, ed., *Doctrine and Theology in The United Methodist Church* (Nashville: Kingswood Books, 1991).

6. One of the reasons why United Methodism is such an interesting ecclesial body is that it does not quite fit the conventional categories we use to designate the alternatives on the issue of canon.

7. Full treatment of this issue would require much more treatment than I can afford here.

8. How this is to be mapped out is a tangled historical issue which we cannot go into here.

9. For interesting commentary on the relation between Methodism and the Enlightenment see Albert C. Outler, "Pietism and the Enlightenment," in Louis Dupré and Don E. Saliers, eds., *Christian Spirituality, Post-Reformation and Modern* (New York: Crossroad, 1990), 240–56.

10. The most stimulating treatment of this is still Robert E. Chiles, *Theological Transition in American Methodism: 1790–1935* (Nashville: Abindgon Press, 1965; reprinted Lanham, MD: University Press of America, 1983).

11. This is the language used in the First Restrictive Rule of the Constitution. See *The Book of Disciple of The United Methodist Church* (Nashville: The United Methodist Publishing House, 1988), 25. For details of the debate see the relevant essays by Richard Heitzenrater and Thomas C. Oden in Langford, *Doctrine and Theology*.

12. *The Book of Discipline, 1992*, 77–78 (¶68).

13. By far the most penetrating discussion of pluralism has been provided by Jerry L. Walls in *The Problem of Pluralism* (Wilmore, KY: Bristol Books, 1988). Walls makes a compelling case that this is an incoherent notion.

14. For an important essay on this topic see Ted. A. Campbell, "The 'Wesleyan Quadrilateral': The Story of a Modern Methodist Myth," in Langford, *Doctrine and Theology*, 154–61.

15. Some of these problems are nicely laid out by Leroy Howe in "United Methodism in Search of Theology," in Langford, *Doctrine and Theology*, 56–57.

16. *The Book of Discipline, 1992*, 84 (¶68).

17. For an insightful discussion of this issue see Albert C. Outler, "'Biblical Primitivism' in Early American Methodism," in Thomas C. Oden and Leicester R. Longden, eds., *The Wesleyan Theological Heritage* (Grand Rapids: Zondervan, 1991), 145–58.

Chapter 3

1. Cf. for instance the very helpful study of A. Skevington Wood, *The Burning Heart. John Wesley: Evangelist* (Grand Rapids: William B. Eerdmans Publishing Company, 1967), or G. G. Hunter, "John Wesley as Church Growth Strategist," *Wesleyan Theological Journal* 21 (Spring/Fall, 1988): 24–33.

2. *Works* 11:15.

3. Richard Brantley, *Locke, Wesley, and the Method of English Romanticism* (Gainesville, FL: University of Florida Press, 1984), 23. Two other quite helpful studies on this subject are Clifford Hindley, "The Philosophy of Enthusiasm: A Study in the Origins of 'Experimental Theology'," *London Quarterly and Holborn Review* 182 (1957): 99–109, 199–210, and especially Mitsuo Shimizu, "Epistemology in the Thought of John Wesley" (unpublished doctoral thesis, Drew University, 1980).

4. *Works* 11:56.

5. Cf. "The Great Privilege of those that are Born of God," *Works* 1:432–33, for the analogy with the unborn child. As Outler says (note 7), this was one of Wesley's favorite metaphors. Here Wesley draws on ideas found in a variety of sources ranging from Descartes and Malebranche to the Cambridge Platonists and John Morris.

6. Cf. the helpful article by Frederick Dreyer, "Faith and Experience in the Thought of John Wesley," *American Historical Review* 88/1 (Fall 1983): 12–30 and also Rex D. Matthews "'With the Eyes of Faith': Spiritual Experience and the Knowledge of God in the Theology of John Wesley," 14ff. (Matthews' essay, which is a condensation of some of his doctoral materials, is not in print). On the degree of indebtedness to Browne, cf. J. C. Hindley, "The Philosophy of Enthusiasm: A Study of the Origins of 'Experimental Religion'," London Quarterly and Holborn Review 182 (1957): 99–109, 199–210.

7. It is true that in some of his earlier sermons (e.g., "The Spirit of Bondage and Adoption") Wesley seems to speak of a person quite outside of the grace of God (the so-called natural human being), but in later sermons and essays he clarifies or corrects this idea to make clear none are totally without God's grace. This was essential to Wesley in order that God might hold all morally responsible for their actions.

8. Matthews, "'With the Eyes of Faith,'" 16–17.

9. Cf. for instance, D. A. D. Thorsen, *The Wesleyan Quadrilateral. Scripture, Tradition, Reason and Experience as a Model of Evangelical Theology* (Grand Rapids: Zondervan, 1990); W. M. Arnett, "John Wesley—Man of One Book"

(unpublished Ph.D. dissertation, Drew University, 1954); J. R. Joy, "Wesley: Man of a Thousand Books and a Book," *Religion in Life* 8 (Winter, 1939): 71–84; T. Kallstad, *John Wesley and the Bible* (Diss. University of Uppsala, 1974). Also, H. E. Lacy, "Authority in John Wesley," in Thomas A. Langford, ed., *Doctrine and Theology in The United Methodist Church* (Nashville: Kingswood Books, 1991), 75–88. Perhaps the most important work one can list is a recent Ph.D. thesis from Perkins School of Theology on "John Wesley's Conception of Scripture" by Scott Jones, a revised version of which is forthcoming in the Kingswood Books series.

10. The full text of Wesley's letter may be found in *Works* 11:467ff.

11. Works 11:504.

12. *Journal* 6:117.

13. *NT Notes*, Preface, ¶12.

14. *NT Notes*, Preface, ¶10.

15. As Arnett in both the works of his cited above has shown. One may particularly wish to consult the beginning of the sermon, "On Charity" *(Works* 3:292–307), which has as its text 1 Corinthians 13:1-3. Here he states that since Scripture is from God we know it therefore to be "true and right concerning all things."

16. Cf. Articles 6–7 of the 39 Articles. Wesley's affirmation of this view was not merely pro forma, for when he amended the 39 Articles for the American Methodists, while omitting some other parts, he includes these articles in the *Sunday Service*.

17. *NT Notes*, 2 Timothy 3:16.

18. Colin Williams is probably wrong to accuse Wesley of a mechanical dictation view in general. Cf. his *John Wesley's Theology Today* (Nashville: Abingdon Press, 1960). It is true that he seems to think that sometimes inspiration amounts to dictation when the human author is overwhelmed by the revelation of a vision or a dream, but at other times inspiration seems to simply mean for Wesley a guidance by the Holy Spirit that leads the human author, who uses his or her own thoughts and language to speak the truth.

19. *NT Notes*, 1 Corinthians 14:32. In this last statement he is however speaking about prophecy in general, not that which is in Scripture in particular. What he says in 1 Corinthians 7:25, however, suggests his judgment about prophecy in Scripture is the same.

20. *NT Notes*, Matthew 1:1.

21. Cf. L. Shelton, "John Wesley's Approach to Scripture in Historical Perspective," *Wesleyan Theological Journal* 16 (1987): 23–50.

22. This is found in Wesley's work entitled *A Survey of the Wisdom of God in Creation: or a Compendium of Natural Philosophy*, 2 vols. (New York: Bangs and Mason, 1823), 2:139. I owe this reference to Scott Jones.

23. As J. T. Clemons has pointed out in the paper "Insights into Eighteenth-Century English Exegesis: John Wesley's Critical Use of Scripture," which to my knowledge is still unpublished.

24. Cf. "The Character of a Methodist," *Works* (J) 8:340; and Thorsen, *The*

Wesleyan Quadrilateral, 131.

25. Albert Outler, Introduction, in *Works* 1:57–59, excerpts.

26. Arnett, "John Wesley—Man of One Book," 89–96.

27. "On Corrupting the Word of God," *Works* 4:247.

28. This is true even in regard to Wesley's treatment of the Old Testament as J. N. Oswalt has shown in "Wesley's Use of the Old Testament in His Doctrinal Teachings," *Wesleyan Theological Journal* 12 (1977): 39–51.

29. *NT Notes*, Romans 12:6.

30. Scott Jones in his discussion of the wholeness of Scripture makes the interesting point that Wesley is strikingly different from both Jeremy Taylor and John Locke at this point, especially J. Locke, *A Paraphrase and Notes on the Epistles of St. Paul to the Galatians, I and II Corinthians, Romans, Ephesians*, ed. A. W. Wainwright, 2 vols. (Oxford: Clarendon Press, 1987), Preface, 1:113. The basic reason for the rejection seems to be that it was considered to be an idea that allowed one to interpret the Bible according to a pre-determined and possible sectarian schema of doctrine or thought.

31. "The Signs of the Times," *Works* 2:526.

32. *Letters* 2:206. This letter to Thomas Church, dated Feb. 1745, is not included in Baker's edition of the letters.

33. *Works* (J) 10:482.

34. J. T. Clemons, "John Wesley—Biblical Literalist?" *Religion in Life* 46 (1977): 332–42, is quite right that the answer to the question of whether Wesley was a Biblical literalist is both yes and no. His summary is helpful: to say that Wesley was a biblical literalist is correct only if we understand (1) that his literalism was not based on a word, phrase, or verse apart from its context; (2) that the literal meaning of a word might vary from one passage to another, even within the same epistle; (3) that the literal meaning, having been ascertained through diligent study of the language, history, and church tradition, was to be used in coming to the spiritual meaning, before proceeding to its moral application; and (4) that the "analogy of faith," that is what the church understood by certain basic doctrine, was an essential control for a literal interpretation. I would disagree with Clemons on what *analogia fidei* actually amounted to in Wesley's view.

35. An example of this sort of eisegesis can be found in "The Great Privilege of those that are Born of God," *Works* 1:436, where Wesley says "Thus David was unquestionably born of God or ever he was anointed king of Israel." It is, however, rather rare.

36. Cf. *NT Notes*, 2 Peter 2:19.

37. "Christian Perfection," *Works* 2:108.

38. Cf. *NT Notes*, 2 Timothy 3:15-17.

39. W. H. Mullen, "John Wesley's Method of Biblical Interpretation," *Religion in Life* 47 (Spring, 1978): 99–108.

40. "The Law Established through Faith, I," *Works* 2:25.

41. Cf. "The 'Wesleyan Quadrilateral'—The Story of a Modern Methodist

Myth," in Thomas A. Langford, ed., *Doctrine and Theology in The United Methodist Church* (Nashville: Kingswood Books, 1991), 154–61.

42. Cf. W. R. Cannon, *The Theology of John Wesley, with Special Reference to the Doctrine of Justification* (Lanham: The University Press of America, 1984; reprint of 1946 edition).

43. "The Witness of Our Own Spirit," *Works* 1:302–3.

44. *Works* 25:615. This letter was, in the Telford edition of the *Letters*, assumed to have been written to James Hervey, but the actual letter to Hervey has been found and is published in *Works* 25:609–10. Baker conjectures the letter cited in our essay was written to Clayton.

45. *Letters* 5:313.

46. "Preface to the Sermons," *Works* 1:107. The phrase "to the law and the testimony" was just another Wesleyan synonym for Scripture.

47. *Works* (J) 10:142.

48. It must also be stressed however that Wesley did not endorse those who were guilty of bibliolatry, refusing to read or consult any source but the Bible. "This is rank enthusiasm. If you need no other book but the Bible, you are got above St. Paul. He wanted others too. 'Bring the books,' says he, 'but especially the parchments!' . . . 'But I have no taste for reading.' Contract a taste for it by use, or return to your trade." This is taken from "Minutes of Several Conversations, Q. 32," *Works* (J) 8:315.

49. This is found in a tract entitled "The Advantage of the Members of the Church of England, Over Those of the Church of Rome," in *Works* 10:33–35.

50. *Works* (J) 10:133.

51. Outler, "The Wesleyan Quadrilateral," 79.

52. What Wesley thought of those who sought to "correct" the Bible may be seen from an entry in his *Journal*: "It would be excusable if these menders of the Bible would offer their hypotheses modestly. But one cannot excuse them when they not only obtrude their novel scheme with the utmost confidence, but even ridicule that Scriptural one which always was, and is now, held by men of the greatest learning and piety in the world." *Journal* 5:523.

53. *A Plain Account of Christian Perfection* (London: Epworth Press, 1968), 58.

54. *Works* 18:248.

55. "The Case of Reason Impartially Considered," *Works* 2:592.

56. "The Case of Reason," *Works* 2:592

57. Matthews, "'With the Eyes of Faith'," 14. Matthews explains that for Wesley apprehension is the bare conceiving of a thing in the mind; judgment is determining that what one has conceived either agrees or disagrees with previous conceptions, and discourse is the movement of the human mind from one judgment to another.

58. "The Case of Reason," *Works* 2:593.

59. "The Case of Reason," *Works* 2:595.

60. "The Case of Reason," *Works* 2:598.

61. The full title is *The Doctrine of Original Sin: According to Scripture,*

Reason, and Experience.

62. *Letters* 3:157.

63. *Letters* 2:325.

64. Oswalt, "Wesley's Use of the Old Testament," 41.

65. The statement in the *The Book of Discipline, 1992*, 76 (¶68), that "Wesley believed that the living core of the Christian faith was revealed in Scripture, illumined by tradition, vivified in personal experience, and confirmed by reason" is nicely put but a bit askew. Wesley more likely would have said that it was confirmed in experience and clarified or made understandable by reason.

66. "Preface to the Sermons," *Works* 1:105–6.

67. This means that Wesley was quite happy to read and learn from many other sources of different sorts of knowledge, especially on one of his favorite subjects, such as natural philosophy. In addition he was constantly reading all sorts of non-Biblical religious literature as well and sifting it, using Scripture as a sort of Occam's razor. There is no trace in Wesley of a fundamentalist mindset about the growing work of science or the other disciplines of human knowledge. Nor is it likely that Wesley would ever have engaged in some of the modern fundamentalist battles over issues that Wesley would not have perceived as the subject matter of Scripture. He did not treat the Bible as either a scientific text book or as a source book that answers all matters of everyday life. Rather, Wesley believed God gave human beings the gift of reason to investigate and sort out matters not pertaining to our salvation.

68. Cf. Albert Outler, *Evangelism in the Wesleyan Spirit* (Nashville: Tidings, 1971).

69. G. C. Cell, *The Rediscovery of Wesley* (New York: Henry Holt and Co., 1936; reprinted Lanham, MD: The University Press of America, 1984), 297.

70. *Letters* 6:297–98.

71. "The Means of Grace," *Works* 1:382.

72. *Letters* 6:298.

73. "God's Love to Fallen Man," *Works* 2:427.

74. John Deschner, *Wesley's Christology: An Interpretation* (Dallas, TX, Southern Methodist University Press, 1985), 166–67.

75. Cf. Williams, *John Wesley's Theology Today*, 75–76.

76. Cf. Albert Outler, in *Works* 1:65–66: "Between the 'early' and the 'mature' Wesley there is a great gulf fixed by the transformations of 1738 and thereafter. The developments from the 'mature' Wesley to the 'late' are not so clearly marked. They are considerable and important and this is why the 'late Wesley' deserves so much more study than he has ever had."

77. It is more than a little mysterious why the 1788 edition of the eight volumes of Wesley's sermons does not include "The Great Assize" (along with seven other sermons that are removed) in the first four volumes which were to become 'standard' as it had done previously, especially in view of Wesley's comment in his *Journal* for September 1, 1778 that he could not write a better sermon on the last judgment than the one he wrote in 1758.

78. Cf. Frank Baker, "John Wesley, Biblical Commentator," in *The Bulletin*

of the John Rylands Library, University of Manchester 71 (Spring 1989): 109–20.

79. Bengel was a continental Lutheran, Heylyn a fellow Anglican, while Guyse and Doddridge were Calvinistic Congregationalists. Various of his other sources may be called Puritan in the broad sense. Cf. D. Tripp, "I observe the Gradation!' John Wesley's Notes on the New Testament," *Quarterly Review* 10/2 (1990): 49–64. It is interesting that while in general Wesley confines himself to "traditions" from Christian antiquity or from the Church of England when he speaks about doctrine, worship, or matters of practice, yet when he writes his *NT Notes* he draws on Protestant commentators from much closer to his own time, and not just Anglican ones either.

80. *NT Notes*, Preface, ¶7.

81. Cf. A. W. Harrison, "The Greek Text of Wesley's Translation of the New Testament," *Wesleyan Historical Society*, 9 (1914), 105–13; J. S. Simon, "Mr. Wesley's Notes upon the New Testament," *Wesley Historical Society*, 9 (1914), 97–105. Cf. also T. F. Glasson, "Wesley's New Testament Reconsidered," *Epworth Review* 10/2 (May 1983): 28–34; G. C. Cell, *John Wesley's New Testament* (London: Lutterworth Press, 1938).

82. *NT Notes*, prefatory page to the comments on the Revelation.

83. This is not to say that he did not have some hesitations about some of Bengel's conclusions. In his journal for Dec. 6, 1762, he remarks about Revelation: "O how little do we know of this deep book! At least, how little do I know! I can barely conjecture, not affirm any one point concerning that part of it which is yet unfulfilled" (*Works* 3:123). Thus we must see his comments as conjectures, not dogma, but nonetheless conjectures on which he was willing to base various conclusions and about which in his later years he was willing to preach.

84. My own count from my British copy of the notes is as follows: Revelation, 119 pages of notes; Matthew, 128 pages; Acts, 121 pages. The surprise is the significantly greater space given to Revelation than for instance to Romans (only 73 pages) or the Fourth Gospel (93 pages), or even Luke's Gospel (105 pages).

85. Wesley was in fact accused of setting a date for the end of the world in some of his sermons. His response was that he was repeating Bengel's opinions, not on the end of the world but on the date of the start of the millennium. Cf. the helpful discussion in C. L. Bence, "Processive Eschatology: a Wesleyan Alternative," *Wesleyan Theological Journal* 14 (1979): 45–59. What this shows is that Wesley not only wrote on the subject of a coming millennial reign of Christ upon the earth, he was willing to repeat Bengel's views in his preaching as well.

86. "The Great Assize," *Works* 1:356.

87. "The Mystery of Iniquity," *Works* 2:465–66.

88. "The Mystery of Iniquity," *Works* 2:470.

89. "The General Spread of the Gospel," *Works* 2:492–93.

90. "The General Spread of the Gospel," *Works* 2:493.

91. "The General Spread of the Gospel," *Works* 2:499.

92. "The Signs of the Times," *Works* 2:531.

93. "The Signs of the Times," *Works* 2:526.

94. Wesley speculates on various occasions that the actual day of judgment itself may last 1,000 years since so many had to be judged from all ages of human history, e.g. in the sermon on "The Great Assize." Outler is right that Wesley was generally impressed with the testimony of various early Church Fathers to chiliasm, i.e., that there would be a millennial reign after Christ's return (*Works* 1:360, notes 27–28). In this view, Wesley was following the more proximate example of both Bengel and Mede.

95. Again we must bear in mind that Wesley was very explicit in not affirming the final salvation of everyone. To the contrary, he believed in the eternal punishment of the wicked as is made clear in the sermon on "On Eternity," *Works* 2:366–67 As W. Strawson, "Wesley's Doctrine of Last Things," *London Quarterly and Holborn Review* 154 (July 1959): 240–49, rightly reminds us: "Wesley certainly insisted that we must not go beyond scripture in describing hell. But his view of scripture is essentially literalist so that he does cautiously believe in everlasting fire . . . and in everlasting torment. If Wesley is not as gruesome as some in his teaching about hell, he is gruesome enough for most moderns. 'The punishment of sinners is two-fold—punishment of loss, and punishment of feeling. The loss includes having no friends . . . no beauty, no light except the flames of hell. . . .' Then they will fully understand the value of what they have vilely cast away." Though Wesley affirmed a doctrine of the intermediate state, he did not believe that one could change one's eternal destiny after death.

96. Outler issued this challenge in various ways in 1984 at the Fall Convocation that took place at Duke Divinity School, and later that same year it was echoed by Wainwright and others during the "Symposium on the Present and Future Shape of Methodism and Theology in the Wesleyan Tradition," the papers of which remain unpublished.

97. Joe Hale, "Wesley the Evangelist," in *John Wesley, Contemporary Perspectives* (London: Epworth Press, 1988), 212–28.

98. Cf. Leon O. Hynson, "A Wesleyan Theology of Evangelism," *Wesleyan Theological Journal* 17 (1982): 26–42 on the social component of the whole Gospel from a Wesleyan viewpoint.

Chapter 4

1. *Journal* 4:230.
2. *Works* 25:441 (October 10, 1735).
3. *NT Notes*, Acts 6:2.
4. Albert C. Outler, Introduction, in *Works* 1:14
5. Outler, in *Works* 1:14.
6. Outler, in *Works* 1:16. See *Minutes of Several Conversations Between the Rev. Mr. John Wesley and the Rev. Mr. Charles Wesley and Others* (London: J. Paramore, 1744–80), June 28, 1744.
7. See "Thoughts Upon Methodism" in *Works* 9:101. See also his letter to Mary Bishop, Nov. 27, 1770, *Letters* 5:209–10.
8. Outler, in *Works* 1:25.

9. Outler, in *Works* 1:25.

10. Cf. Wesley's letter "To the Travelling Preachers," August 4, 1769, *Letters* 5:143–5.

11. Outler, in *Works* 1:16f.

12. Outler, in *Works* 1:17.

13. Outler, in *Works* 1:17.

14. "Letter on Preaching Christ," *Works* (J) 11:491.

15. *Works* (J) 11:489.

16. *Works* (J) 11:486.

17. *Works* (J) 11:486

18. *Works* (J) 11:486f.

19. "Thoughts Concerning Gospel Ministers," *Works* (J) 11:491.

20. *Works* (J) 11:489.

21. "Minutes of Some Late Conversations between the Rev. Mr. Wesley and Others," *Works* (J) 7:284.

22. "Minutes of Several Conversations," *Works* (J) 8:314.

23. "Letter on Preaching Christ," *Works* (J) 11:492.

Chapter 5

1. "On Working Out Our Own Salvation," *Works* 3:203–4.

2. J. Wascom Pickett, *Christian Mass Movements in India* (Lucknow, India: Lucknow Publishing House, 1933).

3. Orlando E. Costas, *The Church and Its Mission: A Shattering Critique from the Third World* (Wheaton, IL: Tyndale House, 1974.)

4. Simon Maimela, *Proclaim Freedom to my People* (Braamfomteim, South Africa: Skotaville Publishers, 1987), 77.

5. Maimela, 82–83.

Chapter 6

1. J. Verkuyl, *Contemporary Missiology* (Grand Rapids: William B. Eerdmans Publishing Company, 1978). See his discussion of impure motives, 168–75.

2. "The General Spread of the Gospel," *Works* 2:286.

3. Lesslie Newbigin, *The Gospel in a Pluralist Society* (Grand Rapids: William B. Eerdmans Publishing Company, 1989), 25.

4. Newbigin, 1.

5. Newbigin, 18.

6. Ninian Smart, *The World's Religions* (Cambridge: Cambridge University Press, 1989), 9.

7. Adrian Hastings, *A History of English Christianity 1920–1990* (London: SCM Press, 1991). Chapter 5, "Ecumenical Beginnings and Missionary Continuations," shows these dilemmas in detail.

8. *From San Antonio to Lausanne: A Letter of Evangelical Concerns* (unpublished), was largely devised and received by the same people for whom convergence is a deep desire. Whether it affects the decision-making of either

body has yet to be revealed.

9. J. D. Douglas, ed., *Let the Earth Hear His Voice* (Minneapolis: Worldwide Publications, 1975).

10. Harold Netland, *Dissonant Voices: Religious Pluralism and the Question of Truth* (Grand Rapids: William B. Eerdmans Publishing Company, 1991). See particularly the description and then arguments against pluralism in chapters 6 and 7, and comments on the approach to evangelism in a pluralist society (chapter 9) looking at evangelism, dialogue, and tolerance.

11. Pietro Rossano, "Christ's Lordship and Religious Pluralism," in *Mission Trends No. 5: Faith Meets Faith*, eds. Gerald H. Anderson and Thomas F. Stransky (Grand Rapids: William B. Eerdmans Publishing Company, 1981), 27–28.

12. Karl Rahner, "Anonymous Christianity and the Missionary Task of the Church," in *Theological Investigations,* Volume 12 (New York: Seabury Press, 1974), 161–78.

13. Paul Knitter in the Preface, *The Myth of Christian Uniqueness*, ed. John H. Hick and Paul F. Knitter (Maryknoll, NY: Orbis Books, 1987), viii.

14. Paul Knitter, *No Other Name?* (Maryknoll, NY: Orbis Books, 1985), 171–72.

15. John Hick, *God Has Many Names* (Philadelphia: Westminster Press, 1982), 58.

16. John Hick, "Jesus and the World Religions," in *The Myth of God Incarnate*, ed. John Hick (London: SCM Press, 1977), contains his famous allusion that to affirm that Jesus was God "is as devoid of meaning as to say that this circle drawn with a pencil on paper is also a square," 178.

17. Let us note that some are highly critical of Knitter and Hick. Gavin D'Costa, ed. *Christian Uniqueness Reconsidered: The Myth of a Pluralistic Theology of Religions* (Maryknoll, NY: Orbis Books, 1990; and Harold Netland, *Dissonant Voices: Religious Pluralism and the Question of Truth* (Leicester: Apollos, 1991).

18. Lesslie Newbigin, *Foolishness to the Greeks: The Gospel and Western Culture* (Grand Rapids: William B. Eerdmans Publishing Company, 1986), 16.

19. See the wide variety in *The Blue Pages*, a New Age Directory, published by Prasada, Hamilton, in Western Australia.

20. There are many books published in England about the New Age. Some of them seem intent to produce a fearful response in the face of New Age. John Drane, *What is the New Age saying to the Church?* (London: Marshall Pickering, 1991), gives a thorough explanation of its background, as well as a critique of the movement. The facts quoted in this section owe their origin to his writing. See also Douglas R. Groothuis, *Unmasking the New Age* (Downers Grove, IL: InterVarsity Press, 1991). See also Elliot Miller, *A Crash Course on the New Age Movement* (Eastbourne: Monarch, 1991).

21. John Hick, "Jesus and the World Religions," in *The Myth of God Incarnate*, ed. John Hick (London: SCM Press, 1977), 180.

22. Diana Eck, in *International Review of Mission* 77 (July 1988), 384.

23. Stanley Samartha, in *International Review of Mission* 77 (July 1988), 315.

24. Lynn De Silva, *Dialogue*, vol. 4, no. 3 (September-December 1977), 77, quoted by Lynn Price, *Interfaith Encounter and Dialogue* (Frankfurt: Lange, 1991). Lynn De Silva is a pioneer of Buddhist/Christian dialogue and was writing an article focused on interracial relationships in Sri Lanka, emphasizing the significant part that people of faith have in bringing about racial harmony.

25. Colin Chapman, "The Challenge of Other Religions," in *Proclaim Christ Until He Comes* (Minneapolis: Worldwide Publications, 1990), 179–83.

26. Kenneth Cracknell, *Towards a New Relationship* (London: Epworth Press, 1986), 48.

27. Acceptable, *dektos*, does not carry a notion of salvation achieved, rather the affirmation that non-Jews are eligible to be part of the same community.

28. William Temple, *Readings in St John's Gospel* (London: Macmillan 1961), 9.

29. Hick discusses this point in *God Has Many Names*, 75.

30. Cracknell, 75–76, has a useful summary.

31. See Cracknell, 98–109, and Christopher Sugden, *Christ's Exclusive Claims and Inter-Faith Dialogue* (Bramcote, Notts: Grove Books, No. 22, 1991).

32. John Munsey Turner, *Conflict and Reconciliation: Studies in Methodist Ecumenism in England, 1740–1982* (London: Epworth Press, 1985), 147.

33. Randy L. Maddox, "Wesley as Theological Mentor: The Question of Truth or Salvation through Other Religions," the 1992 Presidential Address to the Wesleyan Theological Society (unpublished; forthcoming in *Wesleyan Theological Journal*).

34. See "The General Spread of the Gospel," *Works* 2:486.

35. See "On Faith," *Works* 3:492–501, though Wesley tended to place Islam among the heathens or pagans.

36. Maddox, 11.

37. Lynn Price, *Interfaith Encounter and Dialogue* (Frankfurt: Peter Lang, 1989). Like Maddox, she sees a development in Wesley's response to other faiths.

38. See "The Catholic Spirit," *Works* 2:79–95.

39. *Journal*, 7: 389.

40. Cracknell, 133.

41. See "Salvation by Faith," *Works* 1:40–41.

42. *The Good News Works*, ed. G. Howard Mellor (London: The Home Mission Division of the Methodist Church in Britain, 1991). Paper 10 is entitled "Sharing Christ with People of other Faiths."

43. *Faithful and Equal*, ed. Ivan Weeks (London: Division of Social Responsibility of the Methodist Church, 1989).

44. Cracknell, 29.

45. J. G. Davies, *Dialogue with the World* (London: SCM Press, 1967), 31.

46. Harvey Cox, *Many Mansions: A Christian Encounter with Other Faiths* (Boston: Beacon Press, 1988), 7–8.

47. British Council of Churches, *Relations with People of Other Faiths: Guidelines on Dialogue in Britain* (1981).

48. E. Stanley Jones, *Christ of the Round Table* (Nashville: Abingdon Press, 1928).

49. Jones, 22.

50. Jones, 56.

51. Peter Brooks, *Communicating Conviction* (London: Epworth Press, 1983), 1.

52. G. Howard Mellor, *A Theological Examination of the Non-Directive Approach to Church and Community Development, with a Special Reference to the Nature of Evangelism* (thesis submitted for the degree of Master of Arts in Theology in the Theology Department, Faculty of Arts, University of Durham, 1990).

53. George Morris and Eddie Fox, *Faith Sharing* (Nashville: Discipleship Resources, 1986), in which three categories are cited from Win Arn, ed., *The Pastor's Church Growth Handbook* (Pasadena, CA: The Institute for American Church Growth, Church Growth Press), 139–44.

54. Morris and Fox, 79.

55. Neal Fish, *The Parables of Jesus: Glimpses of a New Age* (New York: General Board of Global Ministries, The United Methodist Church, 1979), 13.

56. Eta Linnemann, *Parables of Jesus* (London: SPCK, 1966), 19. She also notes that Eichholz takes a similar view: "The person addressed . . . belongs . . . to the structure of the parable."

57. J. Alexander Findlay, *Jesus and His Parables* (London: Epworth Press, 1950).

58. Sallie McFague, *Speaking in Parables: A Study in Metaphor and Theology* (Philadelphia: Fortress Press, 1975), 78.

59. Linnemann, 30.

Chapter 7

1. For additional commentary see Charles W. Ranson, "Mexico City, 1963," *International Review of Mission* 53/210 (April 1964): 137–46.

2. Martin Goldsmith, *What About Other Faiths?* (London: Hodder and Stoughton, 1988), 120.

3. Newbigin treats this extensively in *The Gospel in a Pluralist Society* (Grand Rapids: William B. Eerdmans Publishing Company, 1989). See especially chapter 10, "The Logic of Mission," 116–27.

Chapter 8

1. Theodore W. Jennings, Jr., "John Wesley Against Aldersgate," *Quarterly Review* 8/3 (Fall 1988): 3–22. See also, "Theodore Jennings Replies," *Quarterly Review* 8/4 (Winter 1988): 100–105; and "John Wesley on the Origin of Methodism," *Methodist History* 29/2 (Winter 1991): 76–86.

2. More detailed information of Wesley's views on this matter is presented in my *Good News to the Poor: John Wesley's Evangelical Economics* (Nashville: Abingdon Press, 1990). Some of this material has also appeared in "Wesley's

Preferential Option for the Poor," *Quarterly Review*, 9/3 (Fall 1989): 10–29.

3. *Works* (J) 6:308. All citations of Wesley's writings in this essay are from the Jackson edition of *The Works of John Wesley*.

4. *A Farther Appeal to Men of Reason and Religion*, Part 3, *Works* (J) 8:239.

5. *Works* (J) 2:178 (Mar. 29, 1750).

6. *Works* (J) 1:490 (April 15, 1745).

7. *Works* (J) 3:178 (May 21, 1764).

8. "On Visiting the Sick," *Works* (J) 7:117. See also: "On Zeal," *Works* (J) 7:60.

9. *Works* (J) 7:119.

10. *Works* (J) 4:296 (Feb. 13, 1785); cf. *Works* (J) 4:358 (Feb. 8, 1787).

11. *Works* (J) 4:295 (Jan. 4, 1785).

12. *Large Minutes, Works* (J) 8:332.

13. "Sermon on the Mount, VIII," *Works* (J) 5:377.

14. "The Danger of Increasing Riches," *Works* (J) 7:362.

15. "The More Excellent Way," *Works* (J) 7:36.

16. "On Dress," *Works* (J) 7:20 (italics supplied). See also Wesley's "Advice to Methodists on Dress," *Works* (J) 11:470–71, and his *Farther Appeal to Men of Reason and Religion*, Part 2, *Works* (J) 8:190.

17. "On Dress," *Works* (J) 7:21 (emphasis added).

18. The recent appearance of Justo González, *Faith and Wealth: A History of Early Christian Ideas on the Origin, Significance, and Use of Money* (San Francisco: Harper & Row, 1990), does us the great service of demonstrating how the themes of what I call Wesley's evangelical economics are fully anticipated in the unanimous witness of the early church tradition.

19. Dean Kelley, *Why Conservative Churches Are Growing?*, rev. ed. (Macon, GA: Mercer University Press, 1986).

20. "Thoughts Upon Methodism," *Works* (J) 13:258.

21. "Thoughts Upon Methodism," *Works* (J) 13:260.

22. "Thoughts Upon Methodism," *Works* (J) 13:260.

23. "Thoughts Upon Methodism," *Works* (J) 13:260.

24. "Causes of the Inefficacy of Christianity," *Works* (J) 7:290.

25. "Thoughts Upon Methodism," *Works* (J) 13:260–61.

Chapter 9

1. So many of the other "mainline" denominations (such as the Lutherans, Presbyterians, Episcopalians, Disciples, and United Church of Christ) are showing similar trajectories as United Methodism that we now are increasingly referred to as the "old line" denominations.

2. The Methodist Church once placed more missionaries across the earth than any other Protestant denomination in North America. Today, in ratio to its membership, The United Methodist Church now places one missionary for every 20,268 members, which put the U.M.C. "next to last" in per capita missionary sending and support, ahead of only The Episcopal Church (one missionary for every 23,220 members). By comparison, the Southern Baptist Convention's

members to missionaries ratio is 1/3,835. Other comparative ratios include The Presbyterian Church, (U.S.A.): 1/6,822; United Church of Christ: 1/7,769; American Baptists: 1/8,764; Christian Church/Disciples of Christ: 1/9,969; Evangelical Lutheran Church: 1/11,275. Nine American denominations have missionary to membership ratios of *under* 1/1,000—including The Wesleyan Church, The Free Methodist Church, and The Church of the Nazarene. (All data from membership and missionary data for 1988.)

3. For years, American Methodism averaged planting one or two churches per day; we now average two or three per month. By comparison, the Southern Baptist Home Mission Board plans to plant 15,000 new congregations in the U.S.A. in the 1990s, most of them in cities, many to reach ethnic minority language populations; at this writing they are ahead of schedule. Once, when Methodism had successfully planted a United Methodist Church in virtually every county, our leaders declared the church extension era to be "over." But with the massive demographic shift to the cities, most of United Methodism's churches are where the people used to be, and we have not yet lifted up our eyes to see the urban harvest.

4. *Works* (J) 6:392–401.

5. *Works* (J) 6:396.

6. *Works* (J) 6:397.

7. Franz Hildebrandt, *Christianity According to the Wesleys* (London: Epworth Press, 1956), 50.

8. *Works* (J) 9:225.

9. *Works* (J) 5:45–48.

10. David J. Bosch, *Transforming Mission* (Maryknoll, NY: Orbis Books, 1991), 278.

11. Bosch, 340–41.

12. Bosch, 401.

13. *Works* (J) 5:294–310.

14. *Works* (J) 5:296–97. Emphasis added.

15. *Works* (J) 5:296–307.

16. *Works* (J) 8:310.

17. *Works* (J) 4:37.

18. *Works* (J) 13:329.

19. *Works* (J) 8:380–81.

20. Hildebrandt, *Christianity According to the Wesleys*, 46.

21. *Works* (J) 6:277.

22. *Works* (J) 6:279, 287.

23. *Works* (J) 6:280–86.

24. Henry D. Rack, *Reasonable Enthusiast; John Wesley and the Rise of Methodism* (Philadelphia: Trinity Press International, 1989), 552–53.

25. Gordon Rupp, *Religion in England 1688–1791* (Oxford: Oxford University Press, 1986), chapter 25.

26. Rupp, 518.

27. Rupp, 392.

28. George G. Hunter III, *How to Reach Secular People* (Nashville: Abingdon Press, 1992), 111–13.

29. For instance, the #201 Maturity seminar engages the issues of a church member's time, money, and relationships, and therefore invites people to commit to daily scripture reading and prayer, disciplined giving, and a small group to meet weekly.

30. Saddleback categorizes the list of gifts within the church's four purposes as follows: (1) Gifts that communicate God's word: Preaching ("prophesy"), evangelism, missions, apostle; (2) Gifts that educate God's people: teaching, encouragement ("exhortation"), wisdom, discernment, knowledge. (3) Gifts that demonstrate God's love: service, mercy, hospitality, pastoring ("shepherding"), giving. (4) Gifts that celebrate God's presence: music, arts and crafts, intercession, healing, miracles, praying with my spirit ("tongues"/interpretation). Three spiritual gifts are thought to support all four of the church's purposes: leadership, administration ("organization"), and faith.

31. Saddleback lists the following "26 Specialized Abilities," inviting people to check, in order, their two or three strongest: entertaining, recruiting, interviewing, researching, artistic, graphics, evaluating, planning, managing, counseling, teaching, writing, editing, promoting, repairing, feeding, recall, mechanical operating, resourcefulness, counting, classifying, public relations, welcoming, composing, landscaping, decorating.